To Albert Glatt
Founder of the Nostalgic-Istanbul-Orient Express

To Albert Blanchard
Who had the idea of this Book

© 1984 by Editions Denoël, Paris
ISBN 1-870621-99-9

The Orient-Express

a century of railway adventures

Jean des Cars
and Jean-Paul Caracalla

English Translation:

George Behrend

Grand Express Books
1 Russell Chambers
Covent Garden
London WC2

(In conjunction with Baton Transport)

BEFORE SETTING OUT.....

For some time now the *Orient Express* has become a legend. Under cover of intimate reality, numerous stories, enticing tales and alluring reports have produced a tissue of inaccuracies, counter-truths and gross mistakes. Thus you can read that in the Nineteen Twenties, M. Paul Deschanel, then President of France, fell out of the Orient Express in the middle of the night! This "anecdote" is false. Long before talk of the World's Most Famous Train, the historians knew very well that M. Deschanel had fallen out of his special Presidential Train, which was not rolling towards the Bosphorus but going to a little town in central France called Montbrison. Doubtless this destination seemed much too modest to those seeking to attach a new tale to the *Orient Express*.....

We have wished to write this book to re-establish the true story. Without pretending to be infallible but having the use of the official and unpublished archives of the International Sleeping Car Company (Wagons-Lits) together with authentic information known only to specialists, we offer you a hundred years of real life adventures. Genuine historical references, research into forgotten sources and original documents have been a constant guide. This leads us to address our very sincere thanks to:—

The Direction Generale of the Compagnie Internationale des Wagons-Lits et du Tourisme.

The Public Relations service of the C.I.W.L.T., Mesdames Marie-Thérèse Bonnet and Colette Constantin.

La Vie du Rail, Mademoiselle Daniele Brocheton.

The Venice-Simplon-Orient Express, Mr. Anthony Spalding, Mr. David Williams, Miss Sally Humphries.

Intraflug Ltd., *The Nostalgic-Istanbul-Orient Express*, Mr. Albert Glatt and his collaborators.

As well as to:—
Mesdames Monique Nagelmackers-Morvan and Monique Richard. Messrs. Paul Bianchini, Michel Doerr, Robert Guido, Y. Hamada, Gerald Maurois, Damien Mathieu, Phillipe Mordacq, Hervé Nagelmackers and A. Numata.

English Edition. The Translator of the English Edition extends his thanks for assistance to: Anthony Powell (Grand Express Books), Philip Jefford, Archevist, C.I.W.L.T., and Gary C. Buchanan, specialist luxury train writer.

Title Page: 1-gauge scale model of a Simplon Orient Express, Fulgurex sleeping cars. The locomotive is a Pacific 231 PLM 4-6-2.
1. Poster project of 1890. All the poetry of the all-steam Orient Express veering across Europe. Here the Ostend-Constantza (Romanian port) branch extols the uninterrupted North Sea — Black Sea rail link.

DRAWING-ROOM CAR.

SLEEPING-CAR.

The Audacious Monsieur Nagelmackers

The Railway is the great adventure of the XIXth century, an adventure without precedent in the history of man. Until its advent, only the crusades and the armed conquests led to such far-reaching temporary migrations of men. To move about, man was a foot-soldier, a cavalryman, or a navigator. With the train, a new era begins: that of communication; regular and quickly organized journeys will be prepared. Certainly numerous journeys will belong to the epic chapter later on, but the train is going to transform the land into a multitude of neighbourhoods; the train is going to break open the hostile zones, open up the forests, cross the steppes, pierce the mountains and stride the rivers. In front of this rolling progress, the land shrinks.

Until around 1835, time remains a vague and superfluous notion. One lives to a simple rhythm, of day and night, from cockcrow to the appearance of the familiar evening star. One watches the return of the seasons, one awaits the harvest and the grape-gathering. One is born with the plums, one dies with the cherries. One knows about Sundays and Fair Days which are the great rest days and holidays bequeathed us by the Middle Ages. With the train, one has to know the exact time. One buys a watch, one scans big clocks, one learns what a timetable is, a departure, an arrival, and soon a connection. One becomes precise, since one goes to take *the* 8.47. Precision, which imposes itself equally in the offices and the workshops, is a profound change of habits: railway engineering is a conqueror at fixed times. But even if it amazes the astounded bourgeoisie of King Louis Phillippe, even if it encourages financiers, speculators and engineers, the first battle of the rail is to conquer an obstacle less and less excusable : discomfort. The train will not have the right to enter into the history of habits/manners until it can associate long distance and comfort with ideas already obsessive, like speed. This refinement, IS the *Orient Express:* this deed IS the *Orient Express*. This adventure, unique in the world, IS the *Orient Express*.

A night in 1853. A night for travelling.... seventy kilometres (under 45 miles)! It is the distance and the time needed to join the two little American towns of Buffalo and Westfield, in young North America. Furious at the notorious discomfort of the train which made him pass a sleepless night, an exhausted, crumpled and exasperated traveller swears to himself to do something to better the conditions of railway travel. The boy is twenty-two years old, he is the third son of ten children; the entire world could render thanks to his surname which has become a household word, Pullman, Mr.

3

2. *Extract from the Illustrated London News dated 2nd October 1869 which pays homage to the sleeping cars of G.M. Pullman, without which "the journey from New York to San Fransisco without a stop by day or by night, would have been beyond human endurance". The interiors of a sleeping car and a parlour car are presented here.*
3. *Georges Nagelmackers in 1878. This Belgian engineer, seduced by the idea of the American George Mortimer Pullman, who in 1859 invented the first sleeping cars and saloons to connect the Atlantic Coast to the Pacific Coast returned to Europe with an adapted project which will be delayed because of the Franco-Prussian war of 1870-1871.*

11

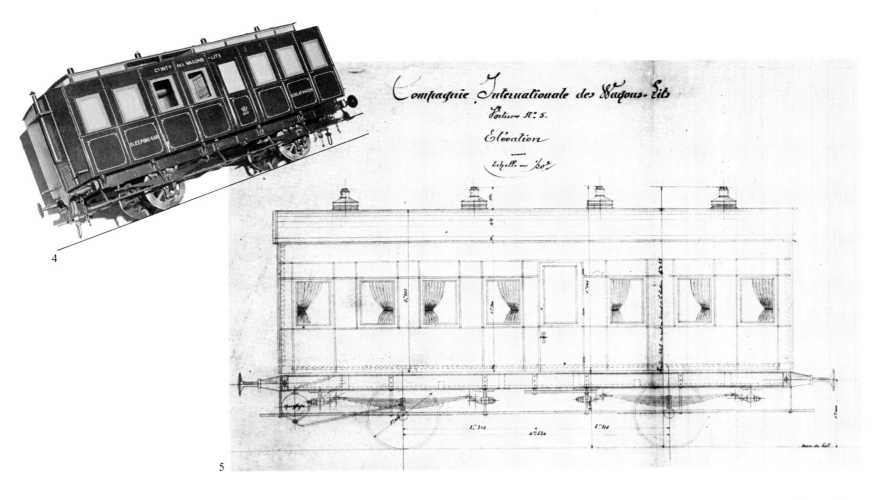

4. *Model of the first car of the Wagons-Lits Company 1872. Note at the centre, the first logo of the Company, a W and an L interlaced. The words Wagons-Lits, Sleeping-car and Schlafwagen appear on the waist line. It is already a success.*

5. *Plan in elevation of sleeping car No. 5, with two axles, built in 1873 by the Austrian works of Simmering, and turned, in 1888, into Fourgon (van) No. 1021.*

6. *Two pioneers of comfort on rails in 1873: sitting, Georges Nagelmackers who will found, in 1876, the C.I.W.L., and, standing, Colonel William D'Alton Mann, adventurer and hero of the American Civil War. The Belgian and the American will be associated to make this new form of travel triumph.*

7. *Publicity for Paris-Cologne. The direct journey, without change, is a reality.*

8. *Plans in cross section of early 4-wheel 12 berth C.I.W.L. cars. Believed to be No. 16 (Top) and Nos. 20-23 (Bottom). The latter were used in Romania (Bucharest-Jassy).*

George Mortimer Pullman. Son of a carpenter, being ingenious rather than an engineer, he arranges to rent two carriages of the Chicago, Alton and St. Louis Railroad company, one of the railway companies that blossoms on the east coast of entrepreneurial America. He modifies the decor of them to his own taste.. Mr. Pullman had many ideas. Let us recall two of them, greatly different but which respond to the same solicitate to render the journey by train agreeable; on the one hand, the use of plush to trim the cushions, the elbow rests and the anti-mocassars, on the other hand, the presence of a personage responsible to the passengers, the Porter, who is not a porter but an accompanying attendant, the legendary person in charge whom we always know under the – incorrect – term *Controlleur* of sleeping cars. The Porter is the direct ancestor of the *Conducteur* – the correct term – of sleeping cars.

The first account of the history of comfort on railways emanates from Johnathan Barnes, and he enters into history discreetly, on the night of 1st to 2nd September, 1859.

The first sleeping car ever built runs between Chicago and Bloomington (Illinois). On board Johnathan Barnes has considerable difficulty in persuading his three passengers to remove their boots, to sleep between sheets.... For Mr. Pullman, the sleeping car is not a coarse, greasy saloon. The first car of this type, entirely constructed by George Mortimer Pullman, is dazzling. Panels in walnut, mirrors of cut glass, polished copper; one can believe one is travelling on one of the luxurious Mississippi ships. With *"Pioneer"*, luxury installs itself on the rails. This car has cost twenty thousand one hundred and seventy dollars... the highest sum ever spent on railways....

Mr. Pullman is American, so he has a flair for publicity. When, one evening in April 1865, Abraham Lincoln is assassinated, America loses not only a great Statesman but also the one who had signed the Railroad Act, having permitted the construction of the *Transcontinental*, the first train joining the Atlantic Coast to the Pacific Coast. *"Pioneer"* is chosen to transport the

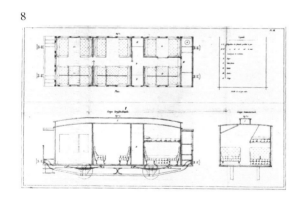

presidential remains from Washington to Kentucky. But Pullman has such grand vision that his car is "out of gauge", that is to say that at each turn of the wheel it risks collision with trains coming the other way, the platforms, the bridges, the tunnels. Pullman raises the objection:– *"Pioneer"* is ill-adjusted to the lines. Well, the lines will be adjusted to *"Pioneer!"*

No sooner said than done. Gangs attack the curves, prop up the bridges, widen the cuttings and slash the platforms. *Pioneer* can run. It is an honour to transport the deceased, to have the car admired is an investment. Going, the crowds weep for Abraham Lincoln; coming back, they praise Pullman who does not fail to arrange visits to his rolling stateroom. Thus begins the formidable career of this man of whom they will say "One per cent inventor, nine per cent businessman, and ninety per cent publicist."

Two years later, he has forty eight cars in circulation. In 1868, with his brother Albert, he launches the first dining car, *"Delmonico"*, named after a famous New York establishment. What a chance! To escape from the station buffets where a mediocre meal is scarcely served when it is necessary to depart. What progress! To savour roast beef while the Middle West passes by. Pullman's success extends from the east to the west, very quickly imitated but never equalled.

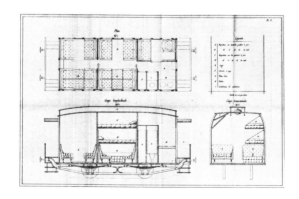

A European traveller, who arrives from Antwerp, is very struck by the inventive spirit of Pullman. And by his success. He is a Belgian mining engineer, born on 24th June, 1845, son of a wealthy family whose parents sent him to America to forget an embarrassing love affair. The young man wished, they say, to marry his cousin. To distance him, his parents profit from an opportunity: a friend of the family, the Count of Berlaymont, leaves for New York accompanied by a companion from childhood, Monsieur Maurice Aubert. It is decided: they take young Georges to open his eyes to the world.

Effectively, Georges Lambert Casimir Nagelmackers quickly forgets his sentimental grief by falling in love with luxury on rails. Even today, the name of Nagelmackers, which is also that of the oldest merchant bank in Belgium, stays unjustly unknown to the general public. Perhaps it is because it is more

In the Dining Car

"Waiter, this beef steak is completely tough!"
"In return, you have plenty of time to Bitterfeld".

"My child, what are you doing?"
"Mama, we are of course on a train, how can I otherwise empty this beer-mug?!"

"A cutlet! Quick!"
"Certainly! Mail train speed!"

(Bitterfeld is between Berlin & Leipzig)

difficult to pronounce than Pullman, and, without doubt, because it has never been used as the name of the railway firm.

However...

On 14th December 1867, the trio are embarked on the *Scotia*, a steamer of the Cunard Line. We follow all this voyage thanks to a diary, unpublished, which Berlaymont kept with a care for detail which very often makes reading it fatiguing but gives us an appreciable number of particulars on the character of young Nagelmackers.

On board the *Scotia*, Georges meets remarkable individuals, such as Mr. Cunard, who receives all sorts of complaints about the service on board. He chats with reserved bankers, and dubious adventurers without taking his eyes off the beautiful lady passengers as they go back to their cabins. At eleven in the evening of the 26th December, two cannon-shots announce arrival of the *Scotia* in Hudson Bay. Here is New York. A long itinerary will take the three men to Buffalo, Philadelphia, Baltimore, Washington, Atlanta, New Orleans, Chicago, the Rocky Mountains, Denver, Salt Lake City and San Francisco.

Curious about everything, Georges Nagelmackers visits the gold mines, hunts the buffalo, courts the pretty girls. Berlaymont notes his elegance when the young man, after each stopover in a town, goes to say goodbye to some flirtation. "Provided he does not bring trouble into the existence of this ravishing creature. Oh my God." wrote he. The engineer is revealed as tenacious, courageous, good, devoted and attractive.

This journey across North America is to last ten months. Ten months of frequent use of the railroads, and of the famous sleeping cars of Mr. George Mortimer Pullman. The Count of Berlaymont describes to us these carriages, unknown in Europe, which greatly astonished the three men:–

> They are built in a manner so as to be useful for day travel as well as night. They are devised in a sort of niche opposite each other, but always permitting passage down the middle. When one wishes to have beds, the seats of the armchairs slide in grooves and join each other: this operation completed, one places a mattress on them and one has a berth like those on steamships, but nearly twice as wide. Above, a sort of folding camp bed is found, one lowers it, tilting it on itself, one opens it, one puts a mattress on it, and a second berth is imposed above the first. All this work is achieved in less than the time I take to write about it. The car thus has eleven compartments or niches and therefore encloses twenty two beds (I speak of the largest cars). It is heated by the same system as the others and possesses, in addition to a water-closet, a wash-room where we find all we need to wash our faces when we get up.

> As we had a journey of nineteen hours to make, we took a sleeping-car. The difference in price on a journey of a hundred and fifty leagues, or to stay in the same car which only operates at night, is only one and a half dollars. One sleeps perfectly well there. The railways are not dear here. We have paid ten paper dollars per place, (37.50 francs). For the same distance in France one would pay twice as much and it would be infinitely worse.

> I have forgotten to make a remark on something which struck us vividly. It is that, there is no compartment reserved for ladies in the sleeping-car. The Americans, who push deference to ladies so far that, even in the stations, they have waiting rooms reserved for them, seem to act against their habitual prudity here. As, after all, in these cars, the niches are only shut in by simple curtains, and the smallness of the gangway makes them half open each time anyone goes through it.

Georges Nagelmackers will be very attentive to these details...

Complaints have been filed among lady-passengers scandalised by the lack of privacy. The upheaval of travel brought a revolution in morals that not everyone appreciated. Thus an English lady, assuredly not the grandmother

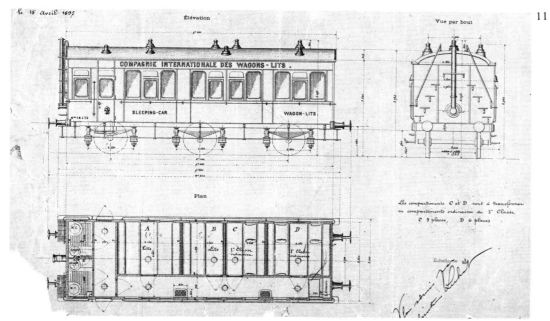

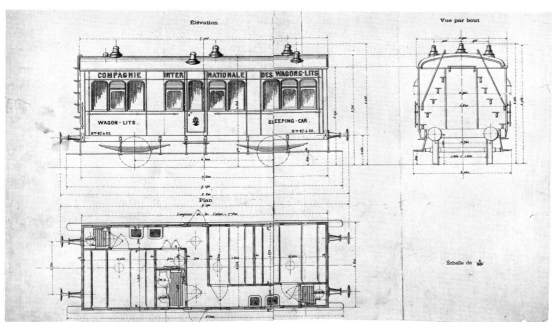

9. *Humourous designs appeared in the 8th July 1880 edition of* Ulk. *The Berlin press presents a new facet of living — the dining car.*
10. *Model of the C.I.W.L. presented at the 1878 Exhibition by the Belgian section, revealing the secrets of sleeping car No. 60, built in 1878. Left: The washroom; Centre: double compartment in day position; Right: in night position.*
11. *Plans of the same car, type K, and of the series Nos. 30, 63, 67, 71, 54, 55, drawn up on 15th April 1897.*
12. *Plan of a car with ten beds, with two axles, Nos. 47-52, 1875, built by Simmering.*

of *The Madonna of the Sleeping Cars* took offence in victorian terms. She called upon the Porter:

"The disregard for feminine privacy is offensive. It's a scandal!"

The employee, who had heard and seen others, replied:

"Madam, ninety seven percent of American women see no objection..."

The passenger, heaving, shook her umbrella but managed to control her indignation:

"That proves the Americans are ninety seven times more immoral than I thought!"

Pullman had invented the dormitory-coach. Nagelmackers will conceive the compartment, the cabin shut with a door opening onto a side corridor instead of it being central. The first success of the Belgian engineer is to adapt perfectly the American system to the mentality of the Old World. And his thought is as simple as logic: in America, the trains are comfortable. Why should they not be in Europe? And the young observer touches upon an afterthought: it is thanks to the train that the States of North America have truly become the United States. Might not the railway, thus improved, become the means to unite the States of Europe?

Back in Belgium after having accumulated notes, diagrams, figures and technical, financial and human details, the engineer follows his idea, all the while directing the ironworks of his family. For hours he remains shut in, immersed in that which will be the great adventure of his life. And, on 20th April 1870 he publishes at his expense a brochure entitled *"Project d'installation de wagons-lits sur les chemins de fer du continent"* (Project for the installation of sleeping cars on the railways of the continent). This document – of which only one copy is known – is historic because the words *wagons-lits* make their first appearance in French. Two magic words explained in thirty pages and which constitute the answer of audacious Europe to entrepreneurial America. On that day, the train emerges from its pre-history where the unfortunate users are tossed about in the bench-fitted wagons charicatured by Daumier; the bourgeoisie infatuated with Labiche could be re-assured : here is the announcement of comfort on the rails of Europe. A revolution from which we still profit.

The franco-Prussian war torpedoed M. Nagelmackers' project, even though his booklet had also been published in German. But peace returned, the obstacles remained, obstacles as much technical as political. As a matter of fact, at this time, one would not be able to speak of *the railway*. It would be more exact to speak of the European *railways*. Indeed, from one country to another, it was constantly all change: the gauge – or width of the bodies – the braking, the lighting, the heating systems, the width of the lines, the regulations. These trans-shipments, interruptions and changes made continental journeys interminable and exhausting. Beyond a few hours, the train is scarcely inviting. Now, M. Nagelmackers proposes a unified standard rolling stock, able to run in several countries. His concept is of cars which one could couple to different trains: that is, assuming that the different governments let foreign rolling stock circulate on their territories. And the mosaic of railway companies, which operate one or several lines, makes the negotiations complex. All these nationalistic factors make up a hostile thicket.

Obstinacy being the religion of pioneers, Georges Nagelmackers, who had obtained the support of his sovereign, King Leopold II of the Belgians, snatches a contract permitting him to circulate one sleeping car, which he has constructed, on the line Paris-Vienna. This is one of the most frequented axes of Europe and the Austrian Empire is a power in the fore-front of railway

13. *Designs which appeared in* La Charivari *dated 3rd February 1881, based on the same inspiration as those in the Berlin newspaper, but with the target this time being the charms of sleeping car travel (with the recommendation to pronounce it "schlepingue").*

technique. And in November, 1872, the first journey of the first *wagon-lits* of M. Nagelmackers operates without incident but with immediate success. The Viennese press echoed it: "... the fashionable world owes to the engineer Nagelmackers the American manner of travel, bettered by the function of European practices." This trial takes place on the line that will be that of the *Orient Express;* it is a premonition...

The engineer creates a Company of sleeping cars (Compagnie *de* Wagons-Lits), a company with a capital of five hundred thousand Belgian francs, and comprising a fleet of five cars of two axles (four wheels) built by Austrian workshops. At twenty-seven years of age, our hero starts to create a concept, that of modern travel. His luck holds, he wins his bet and he obtains agreements on Ostend-Cologne, Ostend-Berlin, not forgetting Paris-Berlin, a spectacular contract signed on 19th February 1873. The companies concerned "undertake to admit at least one wagon-lits in each of the agreed trains."

But financially, the enterprise remains very precarious, the only income the company possesses being a "supplement payable for each passenger". A meagre return for a heavy and unusual investment of which M. Nagelmackers must bear all the risks. Wise, or blind, the financiers withdrew. For a boy such as Georges, it is impossible to run aground so near the end.

He is thus forced to associate himself with a curious personnage, an adventurer, a true hero of the Civil War and bogus oil dealer, Colonel William d'Alton Mann. Nagelmackers brings his experience and his contracts. Mann, his money and his ideas. It is thus that the Mann Railway Sleeping Carriage Co. Limited amalgamates with the company which the Belgian in the meantime has transformed into the Compagnie *Internationale* de Wagons-Lits.

This union, chaotic and forced, permits the Belgian engineer to keep going, and, above all, to resist the assaults of Pullman, who has arrived, in his turn, to try his luck in Europe, and who has succeeded in circulating his rolling stock in England and in Italy. The war of *sleepings* is declared, and it is one of administrative, technical and financial blows.

Fifty months after his first try, Georges Nagelmackers – he is now thirty-one years old – decides to break the narrow bounds of his business and the partition of the railway networks. In his files, he possesses twenty-two signed conventions of which sixteen are regular services, the majority towards the north and the east, such as Berlin-Vienna, Vienna-Prague, and Berlin-Hamburg. Even the small Alsace Lorraine Railways have agreed to couple some sleeping cars on their network, for a duration of three years. Nagelmackers and Mann operate fifty-three cars of which two are in England to work the line Dover-London-Dover. Each of these *Wagons-Lits* carries, on average, from six to twenty passengers per night. Little by little, the use of the sleeping car expands in Europe and it is necessary to widen the horizon.

On 4th December, 1876, in the office of Maitre Van Halteren, Notary at Brussels, the Compagnie Internationale *Des* Wagons-Lits is founded. It buys the rolling stock of Colonel Mann, who returns to the United States. Among the fifteen subscribers one finds King Leopold II, grateful to his audacious subject for all his efforts to ensure that Belgium ceases to be a little country. An International Company, the only one of its kind, since it constructs and operates sleeping cars: is that not indisputable proof that the stubborn engineer is recognised as having invented the journey beyond the frontiers?

New concessions abound: Paris-Menton, Paris-Rome, Calais-Bologna, Paris-Geneva, Vienna-Orsova, Berlin-Breda. And they are not minor contracts: for Nice-Menton, M. Nagelmackers proposes a Salon-car. The comfort of a night journey is repeated in the day journey, even on secondary

The Lovable conductor: Madam rang for the chamber maid!

"Heavens! Who are you, Sir? I do not know you"
"My god, Madame, the Sleeping, they say it has suppressed distances!"

"But, Sir, you can see clearly that I am at my toilet"
"Yes, Madame, I see it clearly!"

routes or short distances. In this epic there are no little lines, there are only competitive lines. In 1882, the Company's first dining car ran, for a trial, from Marseilles to Nice. The kitchen, coal fired, is in the centre, as on American cars. A pantry, wine cellars, two saloons of twelve places each – one for ladies and non-smokers, the other for gentlemen and smokers – are linked by a corridor, where the linen and table-ware are put away. The decoration is very carefully done. Chairs and partitions in Cordoba leather, pale blue curtains, ceiling painted in Italian style. Lastly, witness of the advancing progress, two gas tanks permit lighting for twenty six hours.

Success is amplified. The last diplomatic resistances are stumped. The passengers want nothing else other than the direct journey. One gets in at departure, and one gets out only on arrival. And, soon, one sleeping car per train is found to be insufficient, and the railway companies ask M. Nagelmackers to attach two, three, or sometimes four cars to their ordinary rolling stock for one or two nights.

The bedroom, the salon, the dining room: henceforth, thanks to this marvellous engineer who knows how to live, one finds veritable apartments on rails. And the idea proceeds in his inventive mind: why not conceive a train composed uniquely of sleeping cars and dining car with some assorted vans? Why not a railway palace? Why not a train of which the whole rolling stock except the engine and tender, would belong to his company?

In the spring of 1883, the idea becomes reality, the revolutionary train exists. Officially it calls itself the *Train Express d'Orient*. We call it the *Orient Express*.

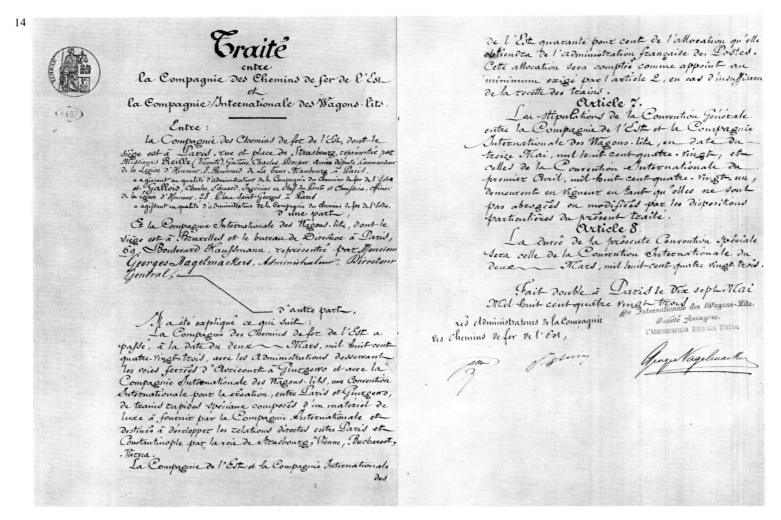

1883-1889,
The Birth of a Giant

One can question what creates the prestige that the *Orient Express* enjoys: is it the end of its journey in the town of three hundred mosques, that ancient Byzantium where Theophile Gautier was said to have found the view "so beautiful that one doubts its reality"? Is it the oriental, exotic style of the books of Pierre Loti? Or the reporting of Morand, of Kessel, or the detective stories of Agatha Christie? Is it the irresistible song that Valery Larbaud sings, of luxury trains:

> Pretez-moi, ô Orient Express, sud Brenner Bahn, pretez-moi
> Vos miraculeux bruits sourds, vos vibrantes voix de chanterelle.
> Lend me, O Orient Express, south Brenner Railway, lend me your miraculous muffled noises, your jarring sounds of a violin-string.

Is it not, rather, the end of uncomfortable and harrassing journeys, which made Madame de Staël, a century earlier say: "To travel... is one of the saddest pleasures of life"?

This *Orient Express* is also a symbol as much as a title. For the first time in Europe, one could go from one country to another without changing conveyance; for the first time a man, Georges Nagelmackers, could obtain through the railways a "de-partitioning" of the frontiers; for the first time, one could live on board a train as at home, lunch, dine, sleep in a real bed, do one's toilette, in perfect comfort.

Model of the future great European expresses, the *Orient Express* is already a positive idea of Europe; in any case it is one of the first displays of Europe being conscious of itself as a whole.

On 17th May 1883, Georges Nagelmackers, founder and managing director of the Wagons-Lits Company, appends his signature beside those of Vicompte (Viscount) Reille, and of Charles-Edouard Gallois, manager of the Est Railway Company, at the foot of an agreement specifying that "special rapid trains will be created from Avricourt to Giurgewo, composed of rolling stock destined to develop the direct connections between Paris and Constantinople by the line Strasbourg, Vienna, Bucharest and Varna". To reach there, he had to negotiate agreements with the railway administrations of the countries which the *Orient Express* would have to traverse, beside the French Est Railway at Paris:

The Imperial General Management of the Alsace-Lorraine railways at Strasbourg;

The General Management of the State railways of the grand-duchy of Baden at Karlsruhe;

14. *Agreement of 17th May 1883 between the Est Railway Company and the C.I.W.L. organizing the circulation of luxurious fast trains between Paris and Constantinople. It is the birth certificate of the Orient Express whose first trial journey took place a month later.*

15. *Interior of sleeping car in 1883. From left to right: night position for four passengers, lavatory, and day position. The upper berths are folded back and the lower berths are transformed into sofas.*

16. *Interior of the dining car of the Orient Express in 1883. Contrary to certain stories, the waiters did not wear French periwigs.*

The General Management of the State railways of the kingdom of Wurtemberg at Stuttgart;

The General Management of the State railways of the kingdom of Bavaria at Munich;

The Imperial and Royal General Management of the Austrian State Railways at Vienna;

The Management of the Austrian system of the privileged Austro-Hungarian Railway Company at Vienna;

The Management of the Hungarian system of the privileged Austro-Hungarian Railway Company at Budapest;

The General Management of the State railways of the kingdom of Romania at Bucharest.

Negotiations began at the conferences held on 28th and 29th December 1882, and on 8th and 9th February 1883, at Munich; then on 2nd March 1883, the Est Railway Company signed an agreement with all these organisations, who in their names instructed it to conclude an agreement with the Wagons-Lits Company, which was done on 17th May 1883. Under the name of *Train Express d'Orient,* the *Orient Express* as it was afterwards called, was born.

The stage of advancement of the railway systems in the Balkans did not yet permit travellers to accomplish the proposed Paris-Constantinople journey in its totality, without change. After having passed Bucharest, the train came to a halt at Giurgewo (Giurgiu today), a little Romanian port on the bank of the Danube. One crossed on board a steam ferry to the Bulgarian side at Roustchouk (Roussé). There, another train took the travellers in seven hours to Varna, on the edge of the Black Sea. One embarked on an Austrian Lloyd liner which, after fifteen hours arrived in the Golden Horn of Constantinople.

16

The trains left Paris on Tuesdays and Fridays at 7.30 in the evening. The *Orient Express* passengers arrived at Constantinople on Saturdays and Tuesdays at 7 o'clock in the morning, after a journey of 81 hours 30 minutes. Compared to the services previously in force, this train saved over 30 hours of travelling time.

The first departure of the *Orient Express* had been fixed for 5th June 1883, less than a month after the signing of the agreement with the railway administrations. Georges Nagelmackers had chosen its composition: two sleeping cars, a dining car, two luggage vans. The total weight was not to exceed 100 tonnes between Paris and Vienna, and 80 tonnes for Giurgewo.

In true theatrical style, Georges Nagelmackers, who had a flair for spectacle and publicity, had preceded this with a "première" in the form of a Paris-Vienna round trip which he had christened *Train Eclair de luxe* (Lightning Luxury Train), and had organised especially for some railway and press personalities.

At the beginning of October 1882, he set out his invitation in the form of a letter:

> You may have seen in the newspapers that our company is organizing a trial train between Paris and Vienna, called *Train Eclair de luxe (Lightning Luxury Train)*. If the spirit moves you and you do not dread a 2000 kilometre steam journey, we will be happy to see you join us. I think it will be interesting for you who travel a lot to judge for yourself the manner in which we wish to carry people more rapidly and more comfortably on the main lines of the continent. We leave Paris on Tuesday 10th October at 6 h. 40 mins. in the evening (Strasbourg station), we will be in Vienna Wednesday evening, and start back again Friday...

This lightning train was the very first great international express. It was made up of three six-wheel sleeping cars, with 14 berths each, and one car of 16 berths (No. 75) which preceded, by some twenty years, the first bogie passenger carriages of the railways of the continent, (built in Europe)[1]. This sleeping-car was not the only innovation of this train, as the dining car (no. 107) ordered from the Rathgeber company of Munich was also going to be run on the journey.

On the evening of 10th October 1882, the *Lightning Luxury Train* with its four sleeping cars, its dining car and its two vans, making up a weight of 101 tonnes, got under way at 6.31 in the evening.

After departure, the first service of dinner began with the following menu: huîtres, potage aux pâtes d'Italie, turbot sauce verte, poulet chasseur, filet de boeuf pommes château, chaud-froid de gibier, salade, crème au chocolat et desserts divers (Oysters, minestrone soup, turbot with spinach sauce, sauted chicken chasseur, filet of steak with chateau potatoes, (similar to roast potatoes), cold game in gelatine, salad, chocolate cream, assorted desserts).

The arrival in Vienna took place at 11.20 the next evening. The day of the 12th was kept for a tour of the town, then on Friday 13th at 4.40 in the afternoon the *Lightning Luxury Train* left again for Paris where it was due to arrive on the Saturday about 8 o'clock in the evening, having accomplished the outward journey in 27 h. 53 mins and the return in 28 h. 17 mins. The record for the distance was beaten, thanks to the dining car which did away with the meal-stops.

This *Lightning Luxury Train* dining car (No. 107) was a conspicuous innovation; we know that Napoleon III's Imperial Train had a dining saloon, and that, in the United States, Pullman had put them in service in his trains from 1868. Certain trials had been carried out in Russia between Odessa and Kiev in 1864, and in Great Britain on the London-Leeds sector by the Great Northern Railway, using a Pullman car in 1879.

For its part, the Wagons-Lits Company had proceeded with trials of railway refreshments in Germany on the Berlin-Frankfurt route in 1880. Two passenger coaches belonging to the Berlin-Anhalt Railway, the first transformed into a dining saloon, the second into a kitchen, providing encouraging results. The operation continued for two years in this manner.

So after this experience, the Wagons-Lits Company decided to order its first dining car from the Rathgeber works at Munich, by a contract dated 10th May 1882. The builder was only ordered to construct the whole underframe and body, the interior being decorated in the Wagons-Lits Company's works.

Rathgeber delivered the car on 1st August 1882. So only three months were available in the French works at Marly-les-Valenciennes to complete the finishing, before the departure of this first "Paris-Vienna" trip. A great feat carried out by craftsmen who worked nearly twelve hours a day without a weekly rest (Sunday shut-down did not become effective until 1906).

Let us give some technical details about this first dining car which, after its completion, was put in service between Marseilles and Nice in order to train the crew.

This car had three axles, a body of 9.320 metres mounted on an underframe of 10.130 metres. The open platforms at the ends could be closed by means of canvas curtains. They were sheltered thanks to a projection of the roof. The interior was divided into three parts, two dining saloons flanking a central kitchen. This division of the car had the advantage that smokers could be isolated. As to the decor, it was made of velvet and Cordoba leather upholstery, as were the chairs whose backs were embossed with the letters W.L. inter-twined.

The kitchen was small, 1.970 metres by 2 metres, small when an oven, two tubs for washing up, two tables, a sideboard and a coalbox were installed,

17. *Teak sleeping car No. 77, with three axles, built by Rathgeber in 1881-1882. It is the first of a series with end platform and gangway linking up two cars.*
18. *Sleeping car built in 1882 for lines in Hungary and Romania (same series as No. 77, view of opposite side to illustration 17.)*
19. *Saloon dining car built in 1883, No. 151 D, which ran in the first* Orient Express.

1 Bogie Pullman cars built USA and re-assembled, appeared in 1874 in Britain and 1875 in Italy. Translator's note.

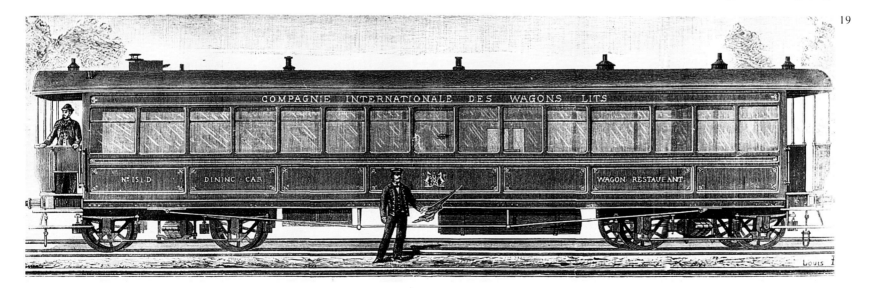

with two winecellars embedded in the floor. Other bottle racks were placed in the corridor linking the two dining saloons.

The smallness of this kitchen did not hinder the chef from preparing dishes of High gastronomic quality and their presentation on this exceptional "Paris-Vienna" run had been particularly remarkable. The lighting in this car was provided by chandeliers of 4 gas jets, for which the two cylinders of 960 litres capacity were placed under the chassis of the car, and gave an independent light of twenty-six hours.

The suspension must have been effective, since Monsieur Delaitre, an engineer of the Ouest Railway, wrote in his report: "I placed a glass of water absolutely full to the brim, and not a drop was spilt during several hours of the train moving..."

This then is the first dining car, which a year later, is going to give the *Orient Express* an independence unknown up until then on an international line.

The first journeys were made without the bogie rolling stock which the company had intended to use. This stock not being ready, the first trains were run with six-wheeled cars.

When the bogie cars were ready, Georges Nagelmackers decided to make a big hit: the glamorous celebration of putting a train of perfected rolling stock into circulation.

The official inauguration of the *Orient Express* took place with great pomp on 4th October 1883 in Paris. Journalists and writers who also participated in this journey, mingled with the personalities present from the political, diplomatic and railway circles.

It is to them that we owe the first stories of this expedition. Let Georges Boyer, special envoy of the *Figaro*, give us his impressions in the issue of his daily paper dated Saturday 20th October 1883.

> The Orient entirely by steam
> Up to now, when one had a dozen days of freedom and a taste for excursions, one left for the forest of Fontainebleu or for some Channel port, not too far away.
>
> Today, one goes to Constantinople, as I have just done, with forty very amiable travelling companions.
>
> Leaving the Gare de l'Est on 4th October at half past seven in the evening, we arrived back at six o'clock on 16th, after staying one day in Romania, and four and a half days at Constantinople.
>
> We owe this marvel to the International Sleeping Car Company.
>
> It has just put new cars into circulation, so perfect that we have run more than six thousand five hundred kilometres in less than two weeks.
>
> The *Orient Express*, that is the name of the train which we have inaugurated, is made up firstly of two service vans. One is filled with luggage which the company undertakes to deliver to one's house in its carts, and which we found in our bedrooms at Constantinople without our having to concern ourselves with it for a second. The other contains the store cupboards, the cold rooms, the shower room, staff bedrooms etc.
>
> Between these vans (fourgons): 1. two sleeping cars able to give shelter to forty travellers, equipped with excellent beds and four very comfortable toilets. 2. A dining car furnished with Gobelins tapestries in morocco-leather, Cordoba leather, and Genoa velvet, made up of a spacious dining saloon, a smoking-room-library, a boudoir for the ladies, a pantry and a kitchen where a chef of the first order works.
>
> This genius of a man – my appreciative stomach does not know how to find a more apt epithet for him – has prepared dishes of an exquisite taste, varying his menus by following the countries which we crossed, and serving us, after the dishes which one eats in an English café, Danube 'sterlets' (fish), fresh Romanian caviar, and Turkish pilaf, while the wine waiter, following his lead, pours us the most famous vintages of the Moselle, the Rhine, of Hungary and Romania.

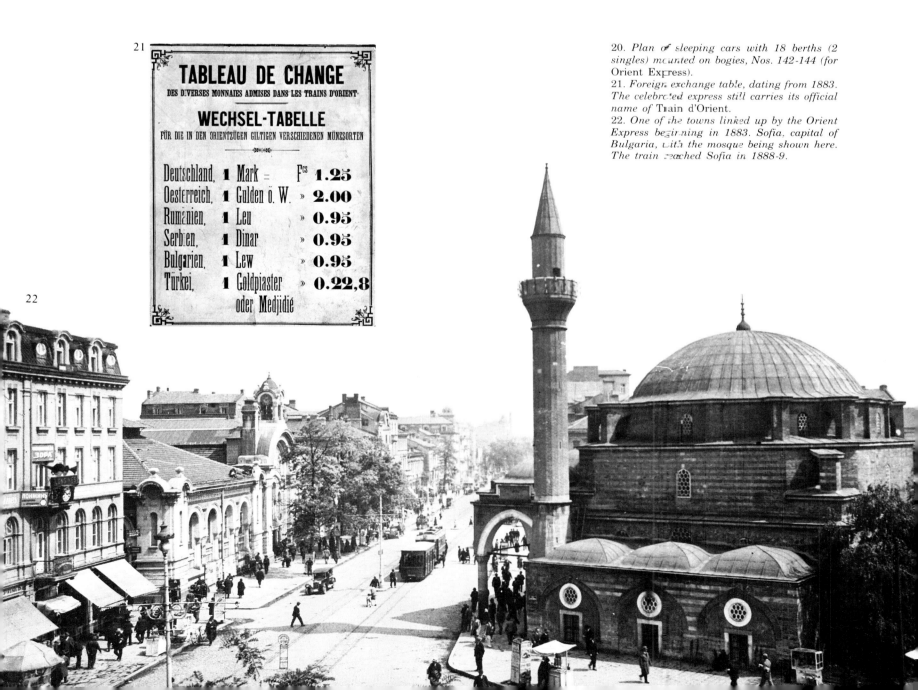

20. Plan of sleeping cars with 18 berths (2 singles) mounted on bogies, Nos. 142-144 (for Orient Express).
21. Foreign exchange table, dating from 1883. The celebrated express still carries its official name of Train d'Orient.
22. One of the towns linked up by the Orient Express beginning in 1883. Sofia, capital of Bulgaria, with the mosque being shown here. The train reached Sofia in 1888-9.

23

The whole train is lit by gas while waiting for the adoption of electricity; it is heated, and thanks to a new system, it is so admirably sprung that, even on the worst lines of Germany, one feels so little jolting that one can see to one's despatches at one's ease.

It is Georges Nagelmackers, a very young, very clever and very congenial engineer, who has endowed Europe with these sleeping-cars, so superior to any that I have seen in America and in England.

The first cars which he launched in 1873 were ten in number and cost 19,000 francs each: today, there are one hundred and eighty of them, which amount to 65,000 francs each, or a value of eleven million for the rolling stock, which runs on all the railways of Europe.

These figures prove sufficiently, I believe, the prosperity of the Wagons-Lits Company.

To inaugurate the *Orient Express,* only invited guests were welcome.

Permit me to say a word on the personnages with whom I had the honour and pleasure of travelling. These are:

M. Olin, Belgian Minister of Public Works, whose depth of ideas and the clarity with which he expresses them unite in simplicity and good grace.

MM Georges Cochery, Blavier, Eschbacher of the (French) Ministry of Posts and Telegraphs, who get off at Vienna to visit the Electricity Exhibition; if I had not been travelling entirely by steam, I would have liked to visit this exhibition...

Edmond About, who discharged intellectual fireworks, all consisting of bouquets; De Blowitz, who is exceedingly witty in French, in abusing whatever is foreign; lastly, half a dozen of my colleagues from France and abroad.

We are received by the Director General of the Wagons-Lits Company, M. Nagelmackers, who gives himself more trouble, to provide us with an abundance of his courteous attentions, than he has had to organise his marvellous services. He is admirably seconded by his Secretary-General, M. Lechat, a chamberlain supported like a prince by MM Berthier junior, Schröder and Weil. The latter has been particularly instructed to look after our life at Constantinople, and discharged his mission wonderfully...

I do not have the pretention, after Theophile Gautier, Gérard de Nerval and my collaborator Albert Millaud, to recount the Orient. I shall pass over it very quickly, like the train which carries us, casting here and there a note on the things that have struck me.

At Pesth (Budapest) one wakes up in the middle of picturesque countryside, it is the beginning of low houses, of longhorn cattle of pale colours, as though washed; it is also the beginning of boots; everyone wears them, men and women, and when one sees the tracks soaked by the rain, one no longer dreams of being astonished.

Hungary is also the country with a great liking for France; ever since we left Germany, we have only experienced more hands outstretched to shake ours, and it will be like this henceforth wherever we go.

The forest follows the plain; at its edge, we pass a man in a frock-coat, suitably booted, who takes his little morning walk with a violoncello under his arm; we are well and truly in Hungary.

All the station have pleasant verandas where a primeval vine climbs, recalling vividly the decor of the casino of the *Queen of Cyprus,* one of the last things poor Cheret painted.

But the train stops, the March of Rácókzi breaks out, spirited and rousing, and it is particularly moving as we have just arrived at Szgedin. The Tziganies know that they play for those who came to their aid at the moment of their disaster[2] and one can see their bows quivering.

The town has emerged from its ruins. It has been newly rebuilt in great luxury. The platforms have not yet been completely finished, and at the gate we notice some Hungarians driving – standing up with a gypsy swagger – carriages which bound along, drawn by two horses at a gallop.

Interesting as it may be, the landscape has been harmed. The Tziganies are hauled aboard the train, another of M. Nagelmackers, very pleasant surprises.

Successively we listen to czardas, Romanian and Turkish airs. Without stopping for nearly three hours, they play with a brio of which only those who have heard Tziganies in Hungary can get an idea. It is an enchantment and a fascination.

2   An earthquake. Translators note.

I will now return to our reception at the Pelesch castle at Sinaia. The new residence of the King of Romania takes its name from a torrent that comes down the mountain, carrying away with it enormous trees which it gnaws at, and which, deprived of their bark and branches, lie on the shore like monstrous bones of antediluvian animals.

At Giurgewo, we leave our sleeping cars to cross the beautiful blue Danube, which after all is perfectly yellow, in a little boat, and in a few minutes we arrive in Bulgaria.

As the train which M. Wiener has kindly put at our disposal, is not yet ready, we hire some carriages to visit Roustchouk.

On the square, some Bulgarian soldiers are at exercise. The Russian officer who instructs them, orders a rest: soon we hear a strange noise, all the infantrymen blow their noses into their fingers at the same time, with admirable precision.

When we return to the station, we are warned that the train could well be attacked; armed bandits, sometimes made up of a hundred men, laid waste the land. Each clutched the butt of his faithful revolver; but it was in vain that we had polished our weapons, nothing came of it.

The last stage of our journey began at Varna; when we embarked on the *Espero*, a beautiful ship of the Austro-Hungarian Lloyd line, a crowd of poor people were sleeping on deck, covered in blankets. Now and then a corner of the cloth was raised and one saw the little head of a child appear who took a puff of air and pulled himself down again immediately. All this crowd swarms pell-mell without complaining, and very happy, they seem, with their lot.

The Black Sea showed us its bad character, then it was very hot in the dining saloon, so much so that ... but night fell, its cloak hiding any weaknesses well.

At daybreak, everybody is up as no one wished to miss the entrance to the Bosphorous. I swear the first sight has nothing particularly attractive about it. All the little houses, uniformly painted in yellow or rose-grey, with their shutters closed, give us an impression as foreign as they are deprived of grandeur.

But as we advance the scene gathers strength and we are admiring it when the marble palaces appear, of Beylerby and Tcheragan, where Sultan Mourad of Dolma Bagchté is shut up.

However, that is nothing compared with what is left for us to see. Like a gigantic theatre curtain just raised, we suddenly find ourselves in front of Stamboul. The old Turkish town can be made out above the Bosphorus in a gauze of fog which envelops the mosques in a transparent mist, with their minarets which resemble enormous candles. There is Santa Sophia with its colossal dome, the mosque of Sultan Achmed, that of Sultan Selim whose minarets on fête days are encircled by a double set of lights, because Selim was the Sultan who approached closest to Vienna at the head of the Ottoman troops.

I will not write, like M. de Amincis: "And now run it down, wretch!" The spendour of the view before our eyes surpasses anything we could dream of: there are impressions which are not conveyed in a few lines, those who wish to experience them have only to make the trip like me: thanks to the *Orient Express* it is very easy today...

23. *The French writer Edmond About, born in 1828, who was one of the three literary witnesses of the first journey of the* Orient Express *in October 1883. He has left a very lively narrative* From Pontoise to Stamboul.

24. *Notepaper Heading on which the daily menu was handwritten. The menu served on 6th December 1884 after leaving Paris has been in use for fourteen months and its cuisine is already famous: Tapioca Soup, Olives and butter, Bar (fish) with hollandaise sauce, Boiled potatoes, Breton Leg of mutton, Le Mans chicken with watercress, Spinach with sugar, Fruit tart, Cheese.*

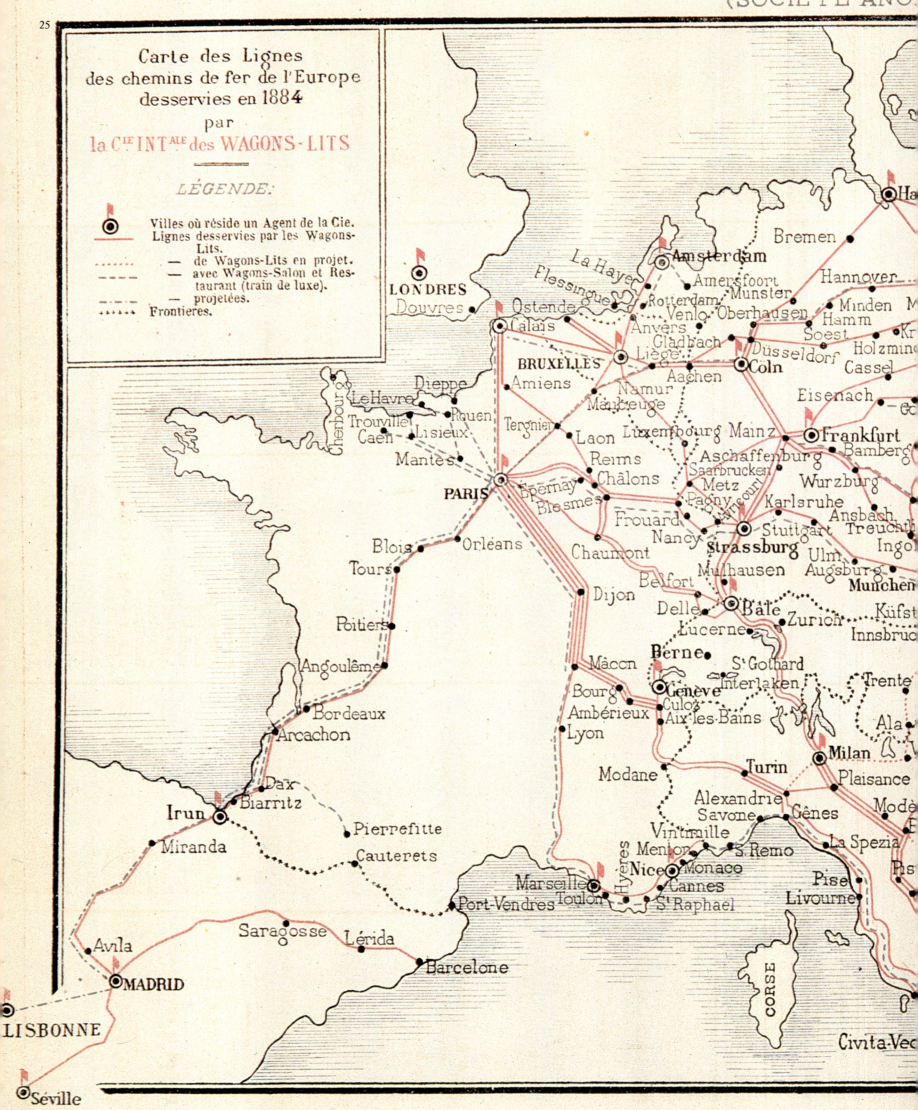

25. *Railway lines served by the C.I.W.L. in 1884 and projected lines. The* Orient Express *travellers embarked at Varna, a port of the Black Sea, to reach Constantinople by boat. Length of the crossing: 15 hours. The official name* Train Express d'Orient *will be quickly changed, due to its success and its German appellation, to* Orient Express.

26. *Notice to the public of 15th November 1886 indicating the amount of supplement which travellers reserving a berth in a C.I.W.L. car must pay. It is obligatory also for travellers to hold a "first class ticket".*

27. *Addresses in "Paris, Vienna, Bucharest, Constantinople and London for reserving berths in advance". Menu Card and price list of drinks. Note: "Hungarian wines served only on the Austro-Hungarian sector".*

28. *The inaugural journey of the* Orient Express *left Paris (Gare de Strasbourg, the future Gare de l'Est) on Thursday 4th October 1883 at seven-thirty in the evening. On board the train: ministers, diplomats and journalists, all invited. Not a woman ... Central Europe is not safe ...*

In seventy-six hours, instead of one hundred and eleven as in the past, we have accomplished the journey from Paris to Constantinople, without the slightest fatigue, in conditions of absolute comfort. On starting, the majority of those who took part in this journey did not know each other; on return, all these men of different ages and positions were bound by a lively camaraderie, and were sorry to see such pleasant contacts end...

The writer Edmond About is no less enthusiastic and confirms the comfort of this first official journey between Paris and Constantinople. In his account published by Hachette, entitled *De Pontoise à Stamboul* (From Pontoise to Istanbul) the author of *L'Homme à l'oreille coupée* (The Man with his ear cut off) relates:

The adventure which I am going to tell you about seems from its contents like the dream of a waking man. I am still dazzled and astounded by the whole thing, and the light jarring of the sleeping car will very probably throb in my spine until tomorrow.

It is exactly thirteen days since I left the banks of the Oise to go and take the "train rapide de l'Orient" *(sic)* at the Strasbourg station; and in these thirteen days, that is to say in less time than it took Madame de Sévigné to go from Paris to Grignan, I have been to Constantinople. I was conveyed, instructed and entertained there; and I have returned without fatigue, ready to start again tomorrow, if you wish, by the same car, for Madrid or Saint Petersburg. And note that we have made a twenty-four hour stop in that oriental France that calls itself Romania, attended the inauguration of a summer palace in the Carpathians, taken tea with a King and a Queen and banquetted sumptuously with the Mayor of Bucharest. They say with reason that our time is full of miracles. I have seen nothing more astonishing than this odyssey, whose dust still alters the colour of my hat...

I think it superfluous to explain why the Wagons-Lits Company is international; its end being to operate its cars on all the railways of continental Europe, and successively to borrow the traction of various companies for the same journey, it could not be exclusively French, nor German, nor Spanish, nor Italian, nor Russian.

I even say, without fear of being paradoxical that it could only be Belgian, the congenial and honoured name of Belgium being synonymous with neutrality. The assistance of a universal goodwill, so to speak, is necessary, although somewhat improbable in the sad times in which we live, to carry a passenger ill or in a hurry from Brest to Giurgewo or from Seville to the Russian frontier, without his having to submit to the vexations, tedium and delays of the customs and police. Man, living luggage whom the transport operators shook up without scruple, whom the ticket inspectors woke up without pity, whom the buffets and low pothouse keepers poisoned and fleeced without mercy, whom all the parasites and pesterers go over, one after another, will with time, nearly become a sacred animal, "an Egyptian cat". Everyone will agree to give him not only speed, but also quiet, sleep and comfort in return for his money...

I greatly like the railways, all the more since I have known the stage-coaches, and each year I use up a nice lot of kilometres. But like all Frenchmen, I have often cursed at the enclosure of passengers in these eight-seat compartments where one is only comfortable when limited to four, and cursed at the insufficient time at stops, which is a profound misunderstanding of the infirmities of human nature. Sometimes I have cast an envious eye at one of these cars of mountebanks...

But if I have often been jealous of the well-being of the American traveller, devil take me if I expect to find well-being in the sleeping cars. These long greenish cars, lit by scarce windows that look as though they cannot be readily opened, sometimes attract our attention in the stations, on the arrival of long distance trains. They are drowned in dust, and in the twilight one can scarcely distinguish between the profile of an Englishman, who gets out yawning, and the face of the valet in cap trimmed with gold.[3]

At least, that is the impression I have kept of the old sleeping car rolling stock[4], of the passengers and of the service. I have scarcely seen anything else like them except mobile hospitals or steamer cabins on dry land... I can only feel a sincere compassion for their passengers and I rejoice to be well enough to avoid the benefits of such shut-in hospitality.

So for me the evening of 4th October (1883) was a revelation; it opened a world to me that I had not caught a glimpse of, even in dreams. By a trick of fate, or perhaps by an ingenious arrangement of M. Nagelmackers, the train which we were going

3. He refers to the sleeping car conductor.
4. This rolling stock was not yet ten years old when Edmond About wrote this story.

WAGON-LIT. — Vue extérieure.

ITINÉRAIRES
ET
PRINCIPALES STATIONS

Desservies par la Cie Internationale des Wagons-Lits en 1883-84

Voir pour les détails, prix, heures, etc., le *Carnet-Guide International des Wagons-Lits* (celui du service d'été ou celui du service d'hiver selon la saison), qui est donné gratuitement dans toutes les *Agences de la Compagnie*.

PAR TRAINS DE LUXE

Wagons-Lits, Wagons-Salons et Restaurant)

Express Orient
Train-Éclair, voir plus loin.)

Nice et Rome (Express)
(*Train-Éclair*, voir plus loin.)

Paris — Nice
Pendant la saison d'hiver
Voir plus loin, Paris-Vintimille).

Paris — Saint-Pétersbourg
Pendant la saison d'été
(Voir plus loin.)

Paris — Dieppe
(*Projetée.*)

Paris — Le Havre
Paris (*Saint-Lazare*).
Mantes.
Rouen.
Motteville.
Le Havre.

Paris — Trouville
(*en été*)
Paris (*Gare Saint-Lazare*).
Mantes.
Conches.
Serquigny.
Lisieux.
Trouville.

Paris — Caen
(*en été*)
Paris (*Gare Saint-Lazare*).
Mantes.
Conches.
Serquigny.
Lisieux.
Caen.

Frankfurt-a/Mein — Basel
Frankfurt-a/-Mein.
Mainz.
Ludwigshafen.
Strassburg.
Mülhausen.
Basel.

PAR TRAINS EXPRESS
(*Wagons-Lits*)

Londres — Paris — Constantinople
(*Express d'Orient*)
Londres.
Calais.
Châlons-s/M.
Paris.
Châlons-s/M.
Avricourt.
Strasbourg.
Oos.
Carlsruhe.
Stuttgart.
Munich.
Vienne (West-Bahnhof).
 Id. (Staats-Bahnhof).
Buda-Pesth.
Bukarest.
Ciurgewo.
Roustschouk.
Varna.
Constantinople.

Calais — Bruxelles — Cologne — Vienne
Calais (*gare maritime*).
Lille.
Bruxelles (*Nord*).
Cologne.
Mayence.
Aschaffenburg.
Wurzburg.
Nuremberg.
Passau.
Vienne.

Calais — Bologne — Brindisi
(*Malle des Indes*)
Calais.
Saint-Denis.
Bercy. } Par
Mâcon. } Wagons-
Culoz. } Lits.
Modane.
Turin.
Bologne.
Ancône.
Foggia.
Brindisi.

Paris — Bordeaux — Irun — Madrid — Séville
Paris (*Gare d'Orléans*).
Etampes.
Orléans.
Blois.
Tours.
Poitiers.
Angoulême.
Libourne.
Bordeaux.
Lamothe (*Gare Saint-Jean*).
Bayonne.
Biarritz.
Irun (*heure de Madrid*).
Saint-Sébastien.
Miranda   buffet.
Avila.   buffet.
Madrid.   arr.
Alcazar de San-Juan (buffet).
Vadollano.
Menjibar.
Cordoue (buffet).
Séville.

Calais — Paris — Genève
Calais (*gare maritime*).
Boulogne.
Amiens.
Paris (*gare Lyon*).
Mâcon.
Culoz.
Bellegarde.
Genève.

Paris — Bâle
(*Voie Montreux-Vieux*)
Paris.
Troyes.
Belfort.
Bâle.
Montreux-Vieux.
(douane Suisse).

Paris — Rome
(*Par le St-Gothard, voir Calais à Rome*)

Paris — Bruxelles — Amsterdam
Paris.
Creil.
Tergnier.
Busigny.
Maubeuge.
Quévy.
Mons.
Bruxelles.
Schaerbeek.
Anvers.
Rotterdam.
Amsterdam.

D'Eydtkuhnen à St-Pétersbourg
(*en projet*)

Paris — Eydtkuhnen — Saint-Pétersbourg
Paris (*Gare du Nord*).
Tergnier.
Maubeuge.
Liége.
Verviers.
Herbesthal.
Aix-la-Chapelle.
Cologne (*Central-Bahnhof*).
Dusseldorf.
Hanovre.
Berlin (*Friedrich*).
Berlin (*Schl. Banh.*).
Cüstrin.
Kreuz.
Schneidemühl.
Bromberg.
Dirschau.
Marienburg.
Elbing.
Braunsberg.
Königsberg.
Insterburg.
Gumbinnen.
Eydtkuhnen.

Paris — Cologne
Paris (*Gare du Nord*).
Tergnier.
Busigny.
Erquelines.
Charleroi.
Namur.
Liége.
Verviers.
Herbesthal.
Aix-la-Chapelle.
Duren.
Cologne (*Central-Bahnhof*)

Paris — Francfort-s/Mein.
Paris (*Gare de l'Est*).
Frouard.
Pagny.
Metz.
Forbach.
Saarbruck.
Creuznach.
Bingerbruck.
Mayence.
Francfort-s.-Mein.
(*Westbahnhof*).

L'EXPRESS-EUROPÉEN

Calais — Rome
par la voie du St-Gothard).

Calais.
Amiens.
Tergnier.
Laon.
Belfort.
Delle.
Montreux-Vieux.
(douane Suisse)
Bâle.
Lucerne (correspondance de Berne).
Rothkreuz (correspondance de Zurich).
Goeschenen (déj.).
Bellinzona (correspondance pour Gênes).
Lugano.
Chiasso (douane italienne).
Milan.
Plaisance.
Bologne.
Florence.
Rome.

Paris à Rome
(par Modane).

Paris (Gare de Lyon).
Dijon.
Mâcon.
Bourg.
Amberieux.
Culoz.
Aix-les-Bains.
Modane.
Turin.
Gênes.
Pise.
Rome.

Paris à Vintimille
(par Marseille).

Paris (Gare de Lyon).
Dijon.
Mâcon.
Lyon.
Avignon.
Marseille.
Toulon (pour Hyères.)
Saint-Raphaël.
Cannes.
Nice.
Monaco.
Menton.
Vintimille.

Paris — Toulouse
(en été)

Paris (Gare d'Orléans).
Orléans (buffet).
Châteauroux.
Limoges (buffet).
Saint-Yrieix.
Brive (buffet).
Toulouse.

Paris à Saint-Malo
(en été)

Paris (Gare de Montparnasse)
Le Mans.
Rennes.
Saint-Malo.

Paris — Avricourt — Munich — Vienne

Paris (Gare de l'Est).
Châlons-sur-Marne.
Nancy.
Avricourt.
Strasbourg (déjeuner).
Carlsruhe.
Stuttgart (dîner).
Augsbourg.
Munich (souper).
Salzbourg.
Vienne (Kaiserin-Elisabeth)

Ostende — Cologne

Ostende.
Gand.
Bruxelles N.
Liége.
Verviers.
Herbesthal.
Aix-la-Chapelle.
Cologne (CentralBahnhof).

Ostende — Bâle

Ostende (Quai).
Bruxelles (Nord).
Namur.
Bettingen (douane allem.).
Luxembourg.
Metz.
Strasbourg.
Bâle.

Hamburg — Berlin

Hamburg (Berliner Bahnhof)
Bergedorf.
Büchen.
Hagenow.
Ludwigslust.
Wittenberge.
Neustadt a D.
Spandau.
Berlin (Hambg. Bahnhof).

Hamburg — Wien

Hamburg.
Magdeburg.
Halle.
Leipzig.
Dresden (Neustadt).
Id.   (Altstadt).
Tetschen.
Lissa.
Wien.

Cöln — Wien

(voir Calais-Vienne)

Cöln — Munchen

Cöln (Central-Bahnho,).
Mainz.
Aschaffenburg.
Würzburg.
Ingolstadt.
Munchen.

Cöln — Berlin

Cöln (Central-Bahnhof).
Düsseldorf.
Oberhausen.
Dortmund.
Hamm.
Minden.
Hannover.
Stendal.
Spandau.
Charlottenburg.
Berlin (Friedrichstrasse).

Frankfurt a. M. — Basel

Frankfurt.
Mainz.
Ludwigshafen.
Strassburg.
Mülhausen.
Basel.

Wien — Berlin

Wien.
Lissa.
Tetschen (Grenze).
Dresden (Alstadt).
Berlin.

Wien — Orsova

Wien.
Budapest.
Orsova.

München — Hof — Berlin

München (Centralbahnh.).
Ingolstadt.
Nurnberg.
Bamberg.
Hof.
Reichenbach.
Leipzig (Bayr.Bahnh..
          (Berl.   »).
Bitterfeld.
Wittenberg.
Jüterbog.
Berlin (Anhalter Bahnhof).

München — Berlin
(par Wiesau)

München.
Landshut.
Regensbrug.
Wiesau.
Juterbog.
Berlin.

Aachen — Berlin

Aachen T. (Bergisch-Mærk Bahn.).
M. Gladbach.
Neuss.
Düsseldorf.
Elberfeld.
Hagen.
Arnsberg.
Scherfede.
Holzminden.
Kreiensen.
Boerssum.
Magdeburg.
Potsdam.
Berlin (Potsdamer Bahnhof).

Berlin — Halle — Bebra - Frankfurt a. M.

Berlin (Anhalter Bahnhof).
Halle.
Corbetha.
Weissenfels.
Weimar.
Erfurt.
Gotha.
Eisenach.
Bebra.
Fulda.
Elm.
Hanau.
Frankfurt a. M. (Westbahnhof.)

Les trains express de jour quittant Berlin et Frankfort contiennent une voiture-restaurant. Les voyageurs trouveront à des prix très modiques toute espèce de consommations. Un dîner est servi entre Weimar et Eisenach au prix de Mark 2.50.

Berlin — Nordhausen Frankfurt a. M.

Berlin (Friedrichstrasse).
Charlottenburg.
Potsdam.
Magdeburg.
Güsten.
Sangerhausen.
Nordhausen.
Cassel.
Giessen.
Frankfurt a. M. (Anh.).

Berlin — Breslau

Berlin.
Friedrichstrasse.
Schlesisch. Bahnh.
Frankfurt a. O.
Guben.
Sommerfeld.
Sorau.
Hansdorf.
Kohlfurt.
Liegnitz.
Neumarkt.
Mochbern.
Breslau.

Berlin — Eydtkuhnen

Berlin.
Friedrichstrasse.
Schlesch. Bahnhof.
Cüstrin.
Kreuz.
Schneidemühl.
Bromberg.
Dirschau.
Marienburg.
Elbing.
Braunsberg.
Kœnigsberg.
Insterburg.
Gumbinnen.
Eydtkuhnen (Ostbahnhof).

Berlin — Warschau

Berlin (Friedrichstrasse).
Warschau.

Warschau — Trzebinia

Warschau.
Petrokow.
Czenstochau.
Trzebinia.

Bukarest — Roman — Paskani

Bukarest.
Ploesci.
Buzeu.
Focsani.
Marasesti.
Roman.
Paskani (pour Jassy).

EXPRESS D'ORIENT

Train éclair

composé de wagons-lits, wagons-salons et restaurant.

Déjeuner à 4 francs

(VINS NON COMPRIS)

Œufs ou poisson. — Viande chaude. — Legumes. — Viande froide. — Dessert.

Dîner à 6 francs

(VINS NON COMPRIS)

Potage. — Hors-d'œuvre. — Poisson. — 2 plats de viande. — Legumes. — Entrements. — Desserts.

Déjeuners et diners à la carte

Service direct sans arrêt aux stations intermédiaires.

Visites des douanes dans les voitures.

Nombre de places limité

Les supplements à payer pour l'usage du train d'Orient sont fixes à 20 p. c. du montant du billet de chemin de fer de 1er classe.

L'Express d'Orient prend des voyageurs de et pour les stations ou le train s'arrête.

Pour reserver les places à l'avance s'adresser :
A Paris, à l'Agence des Wagons-Lits, 2, rue Scribe. — A Vienne, à l'Agence des Wagons-Lits, 15, Karntherring. — A Bucharest, à l'Agence des Wagons-Lits, Szollosy 40 calea Victoriei. — A Constantinople, provisoirement au Lloyd Austro Hongrois. — A Londres, à l'Agence des Wagons-Lits, 122, Pall-Mall, et aux chefs de gare des stations intermédiaires du parcours.

NICE et ROME EXPRESS
TRAIN-ÉCLAIR DE LUXE

Nice à Rome (express)

Londres, samedi	dép.	10 » m.
Calais, samedi	»	2 36 s.
Paris (g. du Nord)	arr.	7 45 s.
Paris (g. de Lyon)	dép.	9 30 »
Dijon, dimanche	»	2 32 m.
Mâcon	»	4 33 »
Lyon-Perrache	»	5 53 »
Marseille	»	11 39 »
Toulon	»	12 53 s.
Cannes	»	3 14 »
Nice	»	3 57 »
Monte-Carlo	»	4 37 »
Menton	»	4 57 »
Vintimille	arr.	5 12 »
— (h. de Rome)	dép.	6 20 »
Gênes	»	10 30 »
Pise, lundi	»	3 12 m.
Rome, lundi	arr.	10 45 »

ROME et NICE EXPRESS
TRAIN-ÉCLAIR DE LUXE

Rome à Nice (express)

Rome, lundi	dép.	8 15 s.
Pise, mardi	»	3 40 m.
Gênes	»	8 25 »
Vintimille	arr.	12 37 s.
— (h. de Paris)	dép.	12 25 »
Menton	»	12 42 »
Monte-Carlo	»	12 57 »
Nice	»	1 37 »
Cannes	»	2 14 »
Toulon	»	4 37 »
Marseille	»	6 08 »
Lyon-Perrache	»	11 50 »
Mâcon	»	1 04 m.
Dijon	»	3 03 »
Paris (g. de Lyon)	arr.	8 » »
Paris (g. du Nord)	dép.	9 40 »
Calais	arr.	3 06 »
Londres	»	7 30 s.

to board was drawn up parallel to an old sleeping car, a type that had done its time. On one side the hospital-car, the prison-car, the old car green and dusty; on the other, three moving houses, seventeen and a half metres long, steam-heated, brilliantly lit by gas, amply ventilated and at least as comfortable as a rich apartment in Paris. The forty guests of the company, their parents, friends and the curious who surrounded us at the Gare de l'Est could not believe their eyes...

It is not immaterial to note that the company took pains to introduce us from day to day to the national dishes and the illustrious vintages of the countries which we were crossing...

What was not very well arranged the first evening was the service, either because the cook had not yet the elbow room in his cupboard of surprises that served as his kitchen, or the servants were a little disconcerted by the affluence and opulence of the new cars, or perhaps quite simply because the guests felt too happy at table and tarried longer than was reasonable to form acquaintanceships, glass in hand. It was not far from midnight when we took the road to our bedrooms. Although some groups had found the means of standing in the open air on the little platforms that separate the great cars...

The sheets, which are changed every day in a refinement unknown in the richest houses, gave off a fine smell of washing, and my two companions, MM Grimprel and Missak Effendi are exemplary sleepers...

Becoming used to this propriety, we are already exacting, and the two washrooms which open onto the ends of each sleeping car no longer suffice us, we need at least four. They are luxuriously installed... but, either for washing or other needs of life, they could not harbour more than one passenger at a time. We were thus obliged in the morning to wait for each other, and sometimes for too long. It is our only desire among the delights of this "moving hedonism" and I well believe it would be materially impossible to improve on what had been done. Moreover, consider the ordinary passengers in an express train who would render a thousand thanks to God if they had one of these lavatories for a hundred people. But we have two of them for twenty...

We discover yet another thing that we found moving: the dining car where they do such good cooking has a small construction fault, the axle overheats; there is no danger in living with it, besides the passenger could quickly communicate with the driver...

Where, then are we? I don't know. Somewhere between Pesth and Temeswar (Budapest & Timisoara). The train stops and we are saluted by Tzigany music. To tell the truth, these brilliant artistes are Tziganies only in name. If their character is Hungarian, their clothes would not make a sensation in the square of La Ferté-sous-Jouarre. But bohemians or not, they have the devil in their bodies and they play with a marvellous brio not only national melodies but also the music of Rouget de l'Isle in honour of the French guests. But the engine whistles, good-bye music! No! The orchestra has jumped into our luggage van, it has soon passed into the dining salon; the floor is cleared of tables and chairs, and here are our young men who dance with the amiable Viennese ladies a waltz of all the devils. This little fête only ends at Szegedin...

It is not only music which enhances the *Orient Express* between two stations, it is also sometimes the gastronomy. Sybarites of various countries which we cross do not refrain, I am told, from taking the train for two or three hours just to recollect the delights of French cooking and to taste M. Nagelmackers' excellent wines...

We often run for four or five hours without meeting another train...

It was agreed on departure that we would stop twenty-four hours at Bucharest, to wait for the ordinary train, which left Paris on Friday evening, and connects like ours with the boat at Varna. But thinking that the town of Bucharest is too new, too civilised, and too like Paris or Brussels to hold travellers as hurried as us throughout the day, the hospitable company organized a country party, four hours from the capital. Four hours in an express train is about the distance from Paris to Dieppe. Do you see here the townsman, who, to allay Sunday boredom, takes a cup of tea at the Gare St Lazare, bathes on the beach in front of M Bias's casino, lunches at the Hotel Royal, listens to concerts on terrace, and comes back to Paris around ten o'clock to sup at an English café? There is the plan for our day on 7th October, drawn up by the inventive spirit of M. Nagelmackers.[5]

---

29. *Itineraries and principal stations served by the cars of the C.I.W.L. Publicity and information is organised. The revue* L'Express européen *(European express) publishes, from the winter of 1883-1884, the itineraries of the luxury trains, permanent and seasonal. Due to its speed and its punctuality, the* Express d'Orient *is also called the* Train-Eclair *(Lightning Train), in particular from Paris to Vienna.*
Comfort and speed are distinctly improved by the bogies, mobile trucks on which the wheels are fixed.
30. *Sleeping-car No. 145 of the series 145-147 built in 1884 at Savigliano (Italy).*
31. *Sleeping-car No. 190 built in 1886 at Nivelles (Belgium).*
32. *Dining-car No. 193 built in 1886 with clerestorey, the leather interior of which is decorated up to the ceiling. (see illustrations 36 to 39).*

5. Arrive at Bucharest at 5 o'clock in the morning. Breakfast in the station buffet – Visit to King Charles in his new residence at Sinaia.

30

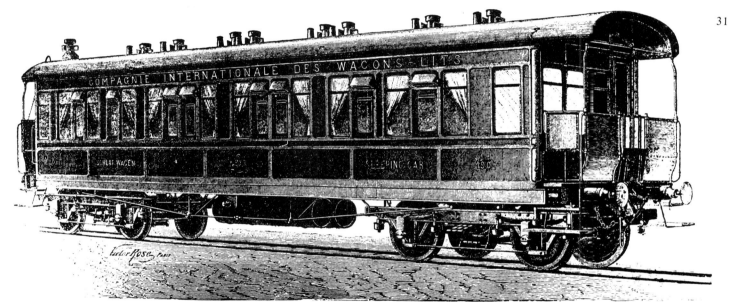

31

32

33. *Constantinople Station.*
34. *Two cylinder simple expansion locomotive, used for hauling the Orient Express in 1883 in France, (on the Est Railway). Built at Epernay in 1870.*
35. *Recommended hotels. Publicity appearing on 29th March 1884. The clientele of the luxury trains know where to stay when they disembarked from the palaces on rails.*

6. 'King of the Mountains' was a well known novel about a Greek bandit who was actually very courteous. Note by GB.

I fell asleep with pleasure. I dreamt that the train which left Paris twenty four hours after us had been attached to ours; the signal to start was given and one hour and several minutes later we arrived at the Romanian frontier, and as dream and reality are the same on this miraculous journey, it turned out that I had dreamt correctly, as at six-forty five, we had put our feet on the ground at Giurgewo. We have only the Danube to cross, to enter Bulgaria by Roustchouk...

In Europe, we started with the sedan chair which we have placed on wheels and little by little we have created the stage coach and the railway carriage. In America, the point of departure is just the opposite, America has taken its house, reduced it to proportions strictly necessary to make it run on railways, and put it on wheels.

I have never felt the accuracy of this observation so well as at Giurgewo, on leaving our mobile hotel and the well trained servants who have followed us as far as there. Man is a domestic animal, he wishes to be at home... even when travelling. Well! I was at home no more, especially when I put my feet on the ground right in the middle of the country, in front of the shabby and dilapidated Danube boat, and at the moment when twenty street porters seized our baggage to carry it onto the ferry, I felt vague and unsteady on my feet. After all, though the old wooden landing stage, badly cut and much used, was not exactly easy to walk on, the little morning steamer which took us to Routschouk in less than half an hour, was quite welcoming. The Captain's face was plump and pleasant, the barman on board tirelessly poured little cups of excellent Turkish coffee, and M. Nagelmackers' valet uncorked twenty bottles acquired for the occasion from the Wagons-Lits cellars...

Our landing was a little delayed by the call of one of those great Austrian boats which look like Noah's Arks, and which will continue to compete with the railways between lower Hungary and the mouth of the Danube for some time to come...

I will say nothing about Roustchouk station, except that this terminal establishment would seem mediocre in a village of the Landes. Arriving at eight o'clock (in the morning), we could only get into the carriages at half past nine; so with two or three companions I took one of the big horse-cabs, open and falling apart, whose horses were as dishevelled as steeds of some ballad, and whose coachmen, dressed like the companions of the 'king of the mountains',[6] offered us the service, shouting unknown words at us. So I have seen Routschouck, that is to say an amalgamation of dried mortar more or less lined up along improbable streets where the broom and shovel would make a sensation, if ever they had whim to wander there like us...

Now and then some hovels showed us the semblance of a village... cows wandered without herdsmen across the plain, and sat down on the line which no fence protected. Our engine arouses them with whistle blasts: it is also provided for the purpose with a large cow-catcher constructed of strong iron bars and as strongly linked together, to sweep a cow off...

Moreover the security of the countryside is almost nil. Two stations had been pillaged in the last fortnight, a stationmaster wounded, the receipts taken, and the goods depots set up by some private firms along the line, plundered. These malefactors' tactics consisted of invading the station after the passage of the last train, and there were just two trains in twenty four hours.

We lunch at the station of Scheytandjik ("little devil" in Turkish) where we were served partridges. We run alongside extraordinary ponds, one of which alone was seventeen kilometres long and thus we arrive at the sad hovel of Varna. We saw just enough of it not to be tempted to look any further at it. For us the essential thing is to learn that we could embark, which does not happen every day... Five or six big barques vigorously handled by some Greeks, load us with our baggage and carry us on the heaving sea to the Lloyd liner *L'Espero* (the Espero), where the best cabins have been kept for us...

We land at the gate of Top-Hané, which is the imperial gun-factory. Ten well-appointed landaus, their coachmen trimmed with braid, await us with interpreters on the box: our luggage follows on the backs of 'Hammals', or Turkish street porters, who are the most honest people in the world. And there we are, galloping Indian file on the wayward stone sets and in the sticky mud of Galata, passing butcheries, cafés and pothouses of which the smell alone would provide M. Zola with a dozen chapters...

The guests were housed at the Luxembourg Hotel also called the Grand Hotel, in the main street of Pera...

Avricourt, Nancy, Bar-Le-Duc, Chalons, Paris, the rest of the journey is not more than a nice outing. We somewhat scorch the rails, as we had a two-hour delay which we have made up since Vienna, so well that our odyssey ends at six o'clock in the evening, watch in hand...

A nice outing indeed, taking more than eighty-one hours to go and nearly seventy-seven to come back. The timetable will slowly get better from year to year until the moment when the direct line is open. But for that one must still wait six years.

36

37

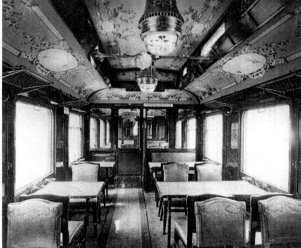

38

39

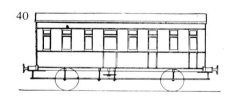

40

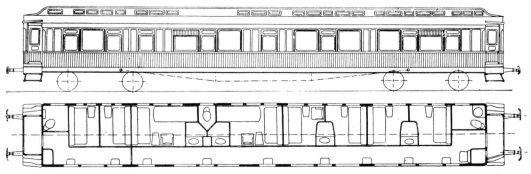

1889-1906
The First Belle Epoque

On June 1st 1889, for the first time, the *Orient Express* ran from the Seine to the Bosphorus without any change because the line between Belgrade and Nis was linked to that between Philippopolis and Constantinople via Pirot and Sophia.

Thus the old dream of George Nagelmackers was realised. This direct routing gave a time saving of 14 hours, and the length of the journey reduced to 1991 miles. A total journey time of 67 hours 46 minutes from Paris to Constantinople, with the following timetable:

STATIONS		TIMETABLE	TIME OF JOURNEY FROM PARIS	DAYS OF RUNNING
Paris	D	6 h 25 e		Paris to Vienna, daily
Munich	A	11 h 55 m	16 h 49 m	Paris to Constantinople Sundays and Wednesdays
Vienna		8 h 13 e	24 h 56 m	
Budapest		2 h 10 m		
Belgrade		9 h 09 m		Paris to Bucharest Mondays to Fridays
Nis		3 h 10 e		Arrive at Constantinople Wednesdays and Saturdays
Sofia		9 h 03 e		
Constantinople	A	4 h 00 m	67 h 46 m	Arrive at Bucharest Wednesdays and Sundays
Bucharest	A	11 h 00 m	51 h 06 m	

You can see in the following table the progress made by the *Orient Express* in linking Paris to Constantinople between the years 1883 and 1908:

36. Dining-car No. 999 with Italian-style decor by Poteau. Exhibited at Liége in 1905.
37, 38, 39. Three other examples of Italian-style painted ceilings which were designed for the dining-cars of 1900 to 1905.
40. Plans and elevations extracted from "Note on the rolling stock of the C.I.W.L. et des grands express européens, built from 1872 to 1909". Above: Dining-car built 1873. Below: Sleeping car built in 1909 (Note: the 1873 car was bought 2nd hand by C.I.W.L. from the Berlin-Anhalt Railway in 1883 and transformed into a diner. The sleeping car is type A, series Nos. 1884-1890.)
41. Basil Zaharoff, the celebrated gun merchant, meets the lady who will become his wife on the Orient Express. Before he can marry her, he must await the death of her husband, the Duke of Marchesa, in 1924. Rich from arms dealing, flourishing during the conflict, he was covered in honours by the allies at the end of the Great War. Here he is photographed with the beautiful Maria, a short time after their union.

1. In the "Timing" column "e" means evening, and "m" morning, as shown on the original document. At this period, the fusion of times did not exist. Berlin time was 44 mins. ahead of Paris time, Vienna 56 mins, Constantinople 1 hr. 47 mins. The dining car clock kept Paris time.

LENGTH OF JOURNEY BETWEEN PARIS AND THE TOWNS BELOW										
Stations	1883	1884	1885	1886	1889	1894	1895	1897	1900	1908
Munich	18 h 24	–	17 h 42	17 h 27	16 h 49	16 h 15	16 h 15	14 h 55	14 h 20	14 h 06
Vienna	26 h 53	–	26 h 08	25 h 53	24 h 56	24 h 05	24 h 05	22 h 47	21 h 49	21 h 35
Constantinople	–	–	–	–	67 h 46	65 h 05	–	62 h 40	60 h 53	61 h 02
Bucharest	55 h 46	–	55 h 46	51 h 36	51 h 06	50 h 10	50 h 10	45 h 50	45 h 22	44 h 25
Constantinople	81 h 41	–	81 h 41	81 h 41	–	83 h 15	82 h 15	64 h 25	64 h 27	62 h 15

LENGTH OF JOURNEY BETWEEN THE TOWNS BELOW AND PARIS										
Stations	1883	1884	1885	1886	1889	1894	1895	1897	1900	1908
Constantinople	77 h 49	76 h 49	76 h 49	–	–	80 h 39	73 h 40	72 h 20	72 h 28	72 h 15
Bucharest	51 h 54	51 h 29	51 h 24	–	51 h 10	51 h 29	51 h 40	50 h 20	50 h 28	50 h 00
Constantinople	–	–	–	–	72 h 10	66 h 29	–	65 h 23	66 h 48	67 h 01
Vienna	–	27 h 27	26 h 57	26 h 52	–	25 h 33	24 h 59	25 h 00	23 h 45	23 h 53	24 h 15
Munich	–	18 h 52	18 h 27	18 h 03	–	17 h 08	16 h 59	17 h 00	15 h 25	15 h 38	15 h 30

42. *On 5th March 1899, the Bucharest-Jassy express derailed between Barnova and Cinera. Among the entanglement of broken up carriages, the sleeping-car does not appear to have suffered from the accident. In a little monograph published in 1900, the C.I.W.L. notes, not without some pride, that the resistance of its rolling stock offers an incomparable comfort to railway travellers.*
43. *The Strasbourg Station, today the Gare de l'Est in Paris, was built from 1847 to 1852. Léonce Reynaud was the architect. The Orient Express left from there for the first time on 5th June 1883. People arrived there by double deck horse bus or by horse-cab, and already at that time Parisians were complaining of the traffic jams which made the station difficult to reach at peak hours.*
44. *First page of an album published in 1898 which carried a list of agencies of the Wagons-Lits Company. Above the firm's name, note the train with teak cars. The different illustrations present the comfort of the sleeping cars, restaurants and saloons as well as one of numerous examples of the famous Two Lions monogram.*
45. *Poster for the* Orient Express, *by Raphael de Ochoa y Madrazo about 1895, carrying the times of the Paris-Vienna and Paris-Constantinople trains as well as the address of the Company's agencies in the towns served by the* Orient Express.
46. *Poster by Choubrac for Oscar Sachs's two scene revue* Orient Express, *with music by Henri Neuzillet, played at the Trianon Music-Hall in 1896. On the left, the sleeping-car conductor in the standard chestnut uniform edged with red, turns his back on this buffoonery.*

From 1889, the *Orient Express* was the most prestigious type of luxury train, serving the greatest number of capital cities along its route in conditions of comfort hitherto unequalled. Along the backbone of Europe the *Orient Express* linked people as diverse as Sadi Carnot's French with Abdul-Hamid's Turks, passing through Ludwig II's Bavaria, Francis-Joseph's Austria-Hungary, Alexander the First's Serbia, Ferdinand's Bulgaria, and Carol the First's Romania.

As a former French Ambassador who frequently took the train recollects, the *Orient Express* has always enjoyed a rather special reputation. Spies and shady characters rubbed shoulders with fallen Princes and Diplomats bearing State secrets. Oriental merchants rich in leather and furs were so wealthy, according to Paul Claudel, that they put their diamonds in their luggage.

Extraordinary people would travel on the train, like the illustrious 'Mister five per cent' – Calouste Gulbenkian (Nicknamed from his petrol dividends) who in July 1896, while fleeing from massacres of his Armenian compatriots in Turkey carried his son and sole heir, Nubar, rolled up in a Daghestan carpet.

Basil Zaharoff, born in a miserable Anatolian suburb, had practiced many trades before becoming an arms dealer at the age of 26. This little Greek was to use his business acumen and make his fortune as a gun merchant in the wars between Greece and Turkey as well as China against Japan.

During the Great War, England made him a Knight while France made him a commander of the Legion of Honour for exceptional services – my God, how jolly war is when it assures your fortune.

In the *Orient Express,* he gambled with seducers and behaved like a gentleman in concealing Maria Pilar-Angel-Patricimo Simona del Marquiso y Berrete from her husband, the Duke of Marchesa. The Duke was a strange individual and wished to strangle his unhappy wife who he had married only two days before. Basil Zaharoff got carried away with himself and declared his passion to Maria in his cabin. "Maria de Pila, I love you" he declared. A man who had never wished to embarrass himself with a woman suddenly found himself amorous on board the *Orient Express*. The engagement between Maria de Pila and Basil Zaharoff was a long one, as the Duke, although mad, did not die until 1924. Whether they made their honeymoon journey on the *Orient Express,* no one knows. On the other hand what is known is that their conjugal happiness was short lived. Less than two years after their marriage, Madam Zaharoff killed herself mysteriously.

The *Orient Express* has had many lovers, indeed passionate ones. King Ferdinand of Bulgaria was one such lover. Modestly dressed, he would emerge from his private carriage, make the express stop, then climb on board the locomotive, donning a Parisian white overall of great quality he would place himself between the driver and the fireman. The King loved to make the locomotive whistle and became intoxicated with the speed of the express. Despite the protestations from the driver, the King set the train running faster and faster and when he came to curves where speed limits were imposed he would brake sharply, just to verify the quality of the equipment.

42

Not everyone enjoyed such speed. Passengers were jostled dangerously and staff were upset and the complaints began to reach George Nagelmackers' desk. As the Director General of the Wagons-Lits Company he decided to let it be known diplomatically that the *Orient Express* was not a toy. His Majesty paid no heed, and from his private carriage pulled the alarm handle, and stopped the great express, only to leap onto the locomotive declaring that after all Bulgaria is his territory and he is at home. The King quoted the great Romanian landowner, Prince Bibesco who claimed that the Orient Express "took four hours to cross me!" In letters to George Nagelmackers, the Secretary of his Secret Cabinet was begging him to believe in the "thankful expression (*sic*) of his august master", to excuse, no

43

doubt, His Majesty from being majestic. To close the incident, George Nagelmakers was decorated.

Another illustrious personage of the *Orient Express* was Cosima, daughter of Liszt, widow of Richard Wagner, who 'receives' in the dining car as though it were her salon. Ferdinand Bac, a great Wagnerian who travelled with her in 1910, relates in his book *La fin des temps delicieux*[1]: "The dignified manner in which she covered herself with veils, commanding respect, receiving the homage of the fans of the master of genius, was greatly diminished by the arrival of a maître d'hotel crying "Premier Service" (First dinner)".

They say that at the same time a sleeping car conductor of the German network, who became known because he demanded back a sum of money which he had advanced to a passenger from Frankfurt was called... Richard Wagner!

There is also a story that the four goods vans attached to the *Orient Express* in 1924 for nearly six months, loaded on leaving Paris, empty on return, and which intrigued the passengers who believed they contained mysterious arms traffic, only contained old-fashioned hats. Mustapha Kemal Ataturk, founder of modern Turkey had just banned the wearing of the fez. A revolution which favoured the total liquidation of old French stocks of hats and caps.

The cholera epidemic which broke out in Turkey in 1892, followed by the very hard winter of 1893, put the *Orient Express* in difficulty. Napoleon Schröder, one of Nagelmackers' deputies, wrote to him on 26th February 1893:–

> "If, in spite of this, receipts are bad, it is because the deadly period of cholera has been followed immediately by an excessive winter, in which the temperature remained in constant fashion on the majority of our lines, between 8 and 30 degrees Reaumur[2] below zero. In Austria-Hungary (I do not wish even to speak of Romania, Serbia, etc.) the snow is up to 3 feet deep.[3] Half our rolling stock was put out of service. The state of health of the staff was gravely compromised and the public no longer travelled.
>
> The rolling stock of the Orient train is inadequate: it has been exceedingly overworked during the time of the cholera and still more during this rigorous winter. Four fourgons unheatable, one train buffer-locked at Temesvar (Timisoara), another which has derailed at Ichtimann, two sleeping cars stopped at Saint Polten. All that has put us in an impossible situation from an operating point of view.
>
> If the kitchen service leaves something to be desired, there is need to take into consideration that the new cooks have started by losing around 200 francs per month: we were even menaced by a general strike. At this time the contractors were feeding more staff than passengers, and were not even obtaining from the chefs the expected indemnities. I could not seek to remedy this situation by increasing percentage takings given to these cooks, not wishing to expose myself to the other contractors demanding the same favour.[4]
>
> The waiters who have not had any salary, resign one after the other, not being able to earn their living.
>
> The irregularities in the inventories as in the service in general, tend to disappear, new personnel joining each day. I am happy to state that, in spite of all the difficulties we have had to overcome, the postal service has been correctly carried out, except for some errors of small importance. The new chefs de train have given us even more satisfaction with respect to this than the old ones, who repeatedly lost post-bags, and even a sack containing registered mail, which we have never recovered.
>
> I will have the honour to present to you in a little while, some more proposals which I judge indispensable to ensure the good running of my services.
>
> I remain, Monsieur le Director-General, entirely devotedly,[5]
>
> N. Schröder.
> Head of the Direction Générale of Brussels.

47

47. *Portrait of Georges Nagelmackers by Theo Van Rysselberghe, oil on canvas (237 × 149). The painter accomplished this great scene about 1897. With his compatriot Octave Maus, it was he who created the Group of XX in 1884, to stimulate cultural exchanges between Belgium and France.*

48. *This map of 1898-1899 indicates the lines on which the cars of the C.I.W.L. ran. Note at that time, the* Orient Express *has abandoned its old route which led it to Varna on the Black Sea for the more direct route to Constantinople. At this date only single track existed on the sections Belgrade-Nis and Philippopolis-Constantinople.*

49. *The cover of the February 1901 C.I.W.L. Timetable-Guide reproduced the posters of the principal great luxury expresses as well as the facades of the hotel establishments run by the Company. In the centre, a dining-car, symbol of comfort on rails, majestically lords it over all the rest.*

50. *In this notice to the public, the railway administrations of the countries traversed by the* Orient Express *annouce that from the 1st July 1891, the* Express d'Orient *undertakes to transport packets, express goods, and fresh provisions.*

1. The end of delightful times. Published by Hachette (in French).
2. Between −6 and −24 degrees Centigrade, approximately
3. About 1 metre.
4. At this time Wagons-Lits provided the dining cars and equipment and the chefs provided the food and engaged the staff, their uniforms provided by the company, and receiving a large percentage of the total takings, the rest going in payment for the car and its equipment. The inventories are shown in the Appendix. Note by GB.

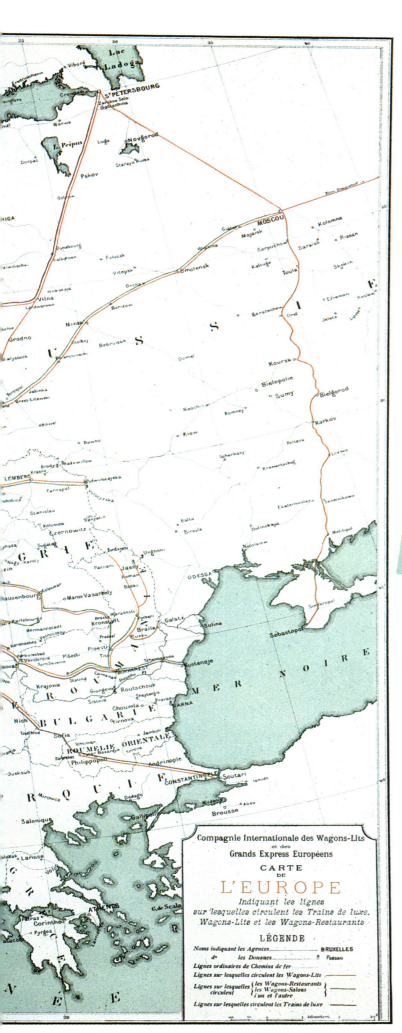

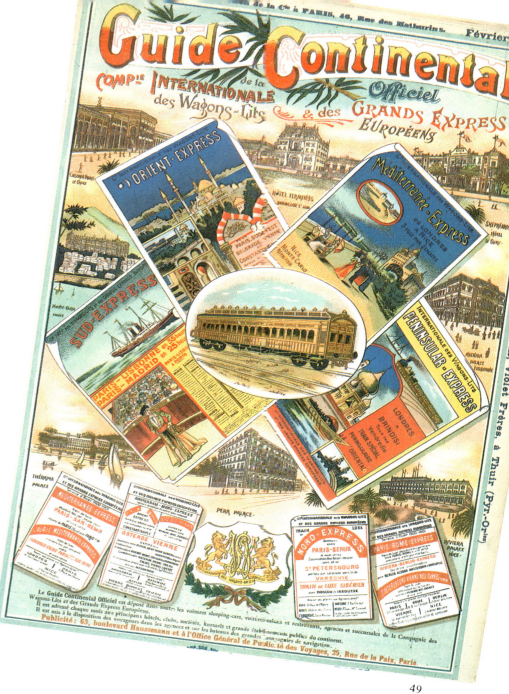

51. *Interior of a cabin of the* Orient Express *in 1900 1/50th scale model of a compartment with three beds, containing the elements of comfort necessary for a long journey. It is one of the first efforts in the democratization of a sleeping-car journey. At this time the well-off clientele for preference occupied "singles" or "doubles".*

52, 53, 54. *Marquetries which decorated the Golden Arrow type Pullman cars of the 4000-4015 series, built at Birmingham in 1926. These cars, of which some were run in the "Flèche d'Or" (Golden Arrow) and "Étoile de Nord" (North Star) services, have undergone many modifications. Some were transformed into dining-cars for Greece, and one of them (4013) into a shower car: it is regularly part of the composition of the* Nostalgic-Istanbul-Orient Express *which has been running since 1977.*

55. *Menu and wine list of the* Orient Express *in 1890, in French and German. Already it suggested the famous bottle of Listrac at . . . 3 francs! as well as Rhine, Moselle, Hungarian and Portuguese wines and all the great names of champagne. As well as the classical menu, it offered other suggestions for people with small appetites and for those following a diet.*

56. *In this 1901 notice distributed in the sleeping cars, it is stipulated (in German) that throughout the journey it is possible to have hot or cold dishes à la carte and to have a drink — Wine, Beer, Mineral water, Coffee &c., but during meal times only the menu will be served.*

57. *On 4th January 1898, the C.I.W.L. celebrates its 25th anniversary. It was in 1873 that Georges Nagelmackers had created with his associate Colonel Mann, the Mann Boudoir Sleeping Car Ltd., which operated the first sleeping cars in Europe. After the departure of Colonel Mann for the United States, Georges Nagelmackers founded the C.I.W.L. on 4th December 1876, and the statutes were deposited with Maitre Van Halteren, Notary at Brussels. These texts are those which still govern the Company today. This menu was offered by the Company to the personalities of the railway world who forgathered at Brussels for the luncheon.*

58. *For the millenium of Hungary, Theo Van Rysselberghe sketched a proposed poster glorifying Budapest, one of the most prestigious capitals served by the* Orient Express.

59. *The Belgian Chateau Royal d'Ardenne situated between Dinant and Jemelle was acquired by the C.I.W.L. and transformed into a hotel at the end of the last century. In its vast 4000 hectare park you could, for a special all-in price, enjoy full board, hunt roe-deer, hare, or shoot pheasant, fish for trout in the Lisse or the Yvoigne, or go horse-riding: the first country club was born.*

60. *Sleeping Car No. 438, built in 1894 at Breslau, — Wroclaw today — was allocated to the Ostend-Vienna service, in 1927 under the number 3105.*

61. *Sleeping Car No. 507, built in 1897 by the Compagnie Générale de Construction, at Saint Denis, near Paris; (a C.I.W.L. subsidiary). Renumbered 3131 in 1927, it originally had four-berth compartments.*

62. *The* Orient Express *at the Turkish frontier in 1897. Behind the engine one sees the fourgon which precedes the two sleeping cars. The train also included a dining car and a second fourgon (van).*

63. *An office in a Belgian C.I.W.L. Agency. On the wall can be seen the* Orient Express *poster and that of the* Trans-siberian *of the Paris Universal Exhibition of 1900. The company served Russian and Chinese meals in the dining-cars while a panorama unrolled behind the windows evoking the crossing of Siberia and the arrival in China. What this desk-bound employee is dreaming of!*

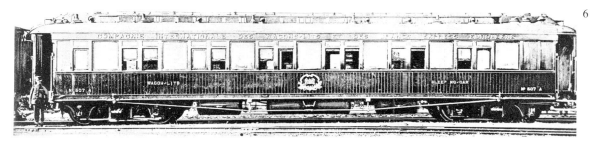

64

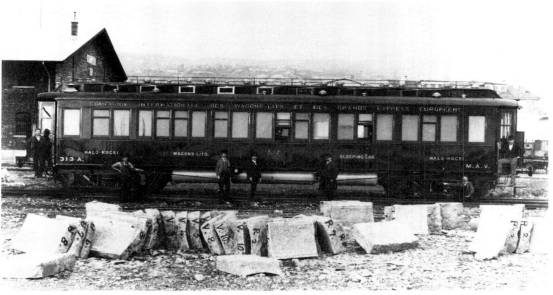

65

66

64. *Victoria Station, London, about 1900. The English who were going to the Orient, set off from there. Taking the* Ostend-Vienna *from Calais to Vienna, they joined onto the* Orient Express *in the Austrian capital.*
65. *This sleeping car No. 313 was built in 1880 in the works of Jackson Sharp at Wilmington Delaware (U.S.A.). It ran on Austro-Hungarian services. It offered 18 berths (5 double-berth 1st class cabins, 2 four-berth 2nd class cabins). The cars of this series were withdrawn in 1920.*
66. *Buffet-stop! On 6th December 1901, the* Orient Express, *which could not brake soon enough at Frankfurt station, intrudes under the sumptuously decorated ceiling and the chandeliers of the station buffet. An unexpected sight, specially made for those who, fifteen years later, will create the surrealist movement.*
67. *The Pera Palace, built to welcome the* Orient Express *passengers, was for a long time the best hotel in Istanbul. Open all the year, it was also reputed for its French cuisine. One sees, from top to bottom: the Moorish room, the Therapia Palace beside the Bosporus, the restaurant, the hotel view of the Golden Horn, and a drawing room of one of the palace suites.*

5. Until 1914 Wagons-Lits was run as a sort of dual monarchy, Germany, Austria & Central Europe being answerable to M. Schröder at Brussels, the rest including Russia to M. Nagelmackers in Paris, who of course had overall control. M. Schröder joined M. Nagelmackers at the start, (Page 25) and became Director General on his death. Hence the way he writes with little explanation, and puts "my services". Note by GB.

Epidemics, accidents, the *Orient Express* is spared nothing. The train, put in quarantine because of the cholera, hinders the passage of the diplomatic bags. Monsieur Pierron and his English colleague of the Foreign Office are blocked seventy kilometres from Constantinople. The mail must not suffer any delay. What can be done? The Turkish policemen are unmanageable, they threaten to fire at the least gesture. After some long palavers, the two diplomats, along with their luggage, are sprayed with disinfectant. The State secrets are scented!

During this period, the fear is so great that even railway tickets are only shown for inspection in a white-metal box filled with vinegar-water.

A little later, the train is attacked at Tscherkesskeuy (Cherkeskoy) in Turkey, by brigands. The passengers are prisoners and the mail confiscated. The driver has three days permission to come back with his engine, armed with the ransom of £50,000 sterling, otherwise it is death for the passengers.

Thank God! He comes back within the permitted time. The taking of hostages goes on all the time.

In February 1895 the *Orient Express* is stopped, as a violent flood has carried away a bridge. It will be a week before its passage can be made. Monsieur Pierron – him again – has the care of an urgent diplomatic mail: he requisitions porters who cross a makeshift bridge of beams and planks, carrying suitcases and mailbags on their backs. Mission accomplished, the Quai d'Orsay breathes again: at Constantinople, the ambassador is relieved.

FROM THE GREAT EXPRESSES TO THE GREAT HOTELS

The success of the *Orient Express* will bring about the creation of other luxury trains: the *Nord Express*, the *Sud Express*, the *Calais-Nice-Rome Express*, etc.

They bring about a social phenomenon: from Monte-Carlo to Vienna, from Paris to Saint Petersburg, from Lisbon to Constantinople, Crowned Heads, Austrian Archdukes, Russian Grand Dukes, British Lords, American multi-millionaires, politicians, businessmen, artists, intellectuals, all find themselves meeting each other again, side by side or crossing each other's paths on board these rolling hotels whose amenities ensure a luxury conforming to their habitual living standard.

Ahead of this evolution of habits which it has itself provoked, the C.I.W.L. interests itself about 1890 in the hotel business, so it can make the passengers of its trains welcome in the terminal cities where, very often, the most elementary comfort was lacking. In 1894 it founds the Compagnie Internationale des Grands Hôtels (International Grand Hotels Company): an experience without precedent, the first international hotel chain.

Brindisi, Ostend, Monte-Carlo, Nice, Constantinople, Lisbon, Cairo are the first establishments of the chain which will afterwards extend to China, opening on 1st May 1904 at Peking (Beijing) *The Grand Hôtel des Wagons-Lits*.

In Belgium, the royal castle of the Ardennes, between Dinant and Jemelle is transformed into a sort of Chateau-hotel. In the 4000 hectare park you could hunt the roe-deer, shoot pheasant and hare, or fish for trout in the Lesse and the Yvoigne which cross the estate. The price of a stay, all-included, is a special one. For 15 francs a day, the high life of the chateau! "Which is the perk of only a few great landowners" as the publicity of the time states. It is the first Country Club.

At Constantinople, the *Pera Palace* has been built in the centre of the Pera quarter on a rise where it dominates the Golden Horn. The view takes in all the panorama of Stamboul. It is destined to receive the travellers of the *Orient Express*. The premier palace hotel in the city, its comfort, its luxury and its service have a world renown, and when the *Anatolia Express* and the *Taurus Express* enter service, it will become the obligatory stopover point for travellers in transit to the East or West.

In summer, the *Pera Palace* offered its clients its sister establishment situated on the banks of the Bosporus, the *Therapia Palace*, which benefitted from a more clement climate during the great heat.

In the euphoria of the "Belle Epoque", while the railway operation enjoyed an increasing success, the hotel branch experienced serious difficulties. When on 10th July, 1905 the death of Georges Nagelmackers intervened, the Peking hotel had to shut its doors, the Russo-Japanese conflict having removed its clientele. Certain other establishments started to be shaky. The war of 1914 will put an end to the C.I.W.L.'s first hotel experience. With the proceeds of the sale of the hotels, it will reconstruct the fleet of sleeping and dining cars, decimated by the conflict.

SIMPLON-ORIENT-EXPRESS
TAURUS-EXPRESS

TRAIN DE WAGONS-LITS

RELIE 14 PAYS
LINKS UP 14 COUNTRIES
CONGIUNGE 14 PAESI
VERBINDET 14 LÄNDER

RELIE 3 CONTINENTS · LINKS UP 3 CONTINENTS
CONGIUNGE 3 CONTINENTI · VERBINDET 3 ERDTEILE

PARCOURT 11.630 Km
RUNS OVER 7.226 Mi
PERCORRE 11.630 Km
DURCHFÄHRT 11.630 Km

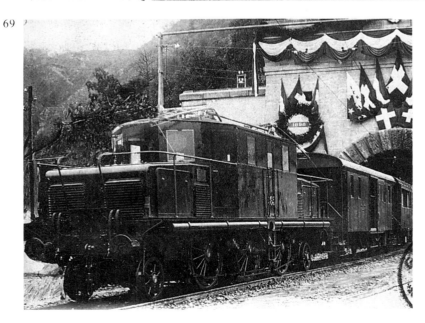

68. *The Simplon Express which at the start will run Paris-Milan, then Paris-Venice, will become in the 1930s one of the most prestigeous luxury expresses. It will extend its route as far as Constantinople, then, thanks to the connection of the Taurus Express on the Asiatic shore of the town, it will link up Aleppo, Bagdad, Beyrut and Cairo.*

69. *The inauguration of the Simplon Tunnel, on 19th May 1906. The townships of Brig (Switzerland) and Iselle (Italy) are linked up. H.M. Victor Emmanuel III, King of Italy, and Monsieur Forrer, President of the Swiss Confederation, open the line which will create a new liason between Europe and the East. This gigantic work of 19,803 metres becomes the longest railway tunnel in the world. An imposing set of figures: 2,400 working days, a million cubic metres of rock excavated, 280,000 cubic metres of masonry, 1500 tons of dynamite and, alas, 65 deaths.*

70. *A Dante-style chimera to celebrate the inauguration of the Simplon tunnel at the Milan International Exhibition in 1906. A couple come out of the tunnel on the front of a locomotive. The man wears the helmet of Mercury, Roman god of travellers.*

1906-1914

A Rival from the South: the *Simplon Express*

The Alps are an obstacle to the progress of man. German, Austrian, French, Swiss, or Italian, the Alps are studded by several of the most beautiful engineering feats, wrought to support the triumph of the railway. Arlberg, Mont Cenis, Saint Gotthard, Loetschberg are names immortalised by technical achievement. Without forgetting the tunnel which will give a spectacular impetus to the *Orient Express* – and to European traffic – the Simplon.

An old Roman way, the Simplon route is a pass at the boundaries of Canton Valais (Switzerland), and Piedmont (Italy). Reaching a height of 2,005 metres, the pass was greatly used by pilgrims in the XIIIth century and in the XVIIIth, an audacious Valaisian, – Gaspar Stockalper – became 'the King of the Simplon' by organizing a post-boy service from Milan to Geneva. In 1800, the abandoned and scarcely practicable route impressed Napoleon I as a capital passage. From 1801 to 1807, he constructed the first proper highway through the Alps. Some particularly impressive figures for the time: nearly 10,000 workmen, 60 kilometres long, 611 bridges and some burrowings in tunnel into the rock, 500 metres long. Half a century later, on both sides of the massif, the possibility of running through trains was studied. A series of mostly financial but partly technical difficulties held up the project for nearly forty years, although the necessity for a railway line daily became more apparent. Finally the Swiss and Italians set to work on the North side on 1st August 1898, and on South side on 16th August. Three teams of 1500 miners each, worked in relays under very dangerous conditions: two hundred and twenty-eight springs; cascades of hot water, raising the air temperature and that of the rocks, to 54 degrees! There was also poisonous gas, collapsing timber-work, etc. Two engineers-in-chief succumbed very near the end, weighed down by a death toll that had already cost 65 lives...

70

The junction of the galleries was achieved on 24th February 1905: the underground line of the Simplon is laid 3,600 metres under the glaciers. 19803 meters in length, it is the longest railway tunnel in the world. The figures are imposing: 2,400 working days, a million cubic metres of rock excavated, 280,000 cubic metres of masonry installed, 1520 tons of dynamite used. On 19th May 1906, sumptuous festivities associating not only the two townships of Brig (Switzerland) and Iselle (Italy), but also Geneva, Lausanne, Milan and Genoa, marked th inauguration of the line in the presence of H.M. Victor Emmanuel III, King of Italy, and Monsieur Forrer, President of the Swiss Confederation.

A date in the history of Europe and that of "her" train.

Immediately, the project of a new liaison with eastern Europe is studied. Paris, Lausanne, Milan, Venice, Trieste, Laibach (Ljubljana today), Belgrade and the Balkans: on the one hand, it will serve new towns, on the other hand, it will gain 60 kilometres over the North itinerary, by Bavaria and the middle Danube. The Italian, Swiss and French governments are agreed. But the others?

One month after its inauguration, the Simplon is the subject of an international conference drawn up at Bremen... M. Gustave Noblemaire, Director General of the P.L.M. (Paris-Lyon-Mediterranée) Company exposes the advantages of this south axis of the *Orient Express*. In vain. He runs foul of the refusal of the Austro-Hungarian government, supported by the German government. Neither Berlin, nor Vienna nor Budapest could admit a line which, under pretext of passing through the prestigious tunnel, would be, in fact an implacable rival for the North line. The *Orient Express* being the master card of European communications, must serve the powerful capitals of the central empires, not towns which are politically secondary. Let us add that the government of the Emperor of Austria, Francis Joseph and of the Kaiser, William II could not forget that they were tied by the Triplice, the defensive Triple Alliance concluded at Vienna on 20th May 1882 with Italy. The latter, whose diplomatic interests were often opposed to those of Austria, was hoping, with the Simplon, to show her influence in a direction more westward than eastward. In return, of course, Vienna and Berlin concentrated all their efforts to limit Italy to central Europe.

The timetable conference ended on the categoric veto of the Empires. Railway expansionism copied political expansionism, and in this instance ran up against it. However, a compromise was adopted in the form of a train London-Calais-Paris-Lausanne-Milan. Its name: *Simplon Express*. It functioned from the winter of 1906. Two years later, it went on as far as Venice. The service, at first weekly, became daily. The 1,106 kilometres were covered in 23 h 45 mins.

Like the *Orient Express*, the train had a right to the label "train de luxe" (luxury train): it was exclusively composed of sleeping, dining, and saloon cars and fourgons of the Wagons-Lits Company. It had to end at Venice because Trieste was a very important Austrian port, with a traffic of more than 6 million tons in 1913, seat of the powerful Austrian Lloyd company, whose ships, you will recall, carried the *Orient Express* passengers from Constantza to Constantinople.

In spite of the Austrian refusal, numerous western travellers found the terminus of the Simplon Express alluring enough: it was the period when Venice started to become the capital of honeymoon journeys. And was not Constantinople represented in Saint Mark's cathedral by several of the most fascinating treasures of Byzantium?

A brochure published in Paris in March 1914, with a pink cover, entitled "*Service Order concerning the operation of the train de Luxe 'Simplon-Express'* " and written out in French and Italian, provides for the applications of the agreement. Article 17 of the Agreement, set out in the second paragraph, orders that "the staff allocated to the service and working the whole journey must have French, Swiss or Italian nationality, in a proportion close to the kilometric sections worked in each country on the train *Simplon Express*. The staff must know sufficiently the official languages of the countries crossed". Besides the Wagons-Lits Company, owner of the rolling stock, the *Simplon Express* interests four railway systems: the Nord (Northern Railway) (Calais-Paris Nord: 298 km), the P.L.M. (Paris Gare de Lyon P.L.M. – Pontarlier: 454 km), the Swiss Federal Railways (Pontarlier – Iselle: 239 km), and the Italian State Railways (Iselle – Venice: 417 km), making a total of 1,408 kilometres.

71. *Prince Umberto, son of King Victor Emmanuel III, King of Italy for several days (9th May-13th June 1946). He will abdicate after the referendum favourable to the Republic. The Prince leaves a new sleeping car during a visit which he made to a railway exhibition in Milan.*
72. *The Simplon Express in Iselle station in 1913. Since it extends its route to Venice, it becomes the train of honeymooners. Composed only of sleeping cars, a dining car and a saloon car, the* Simplon Express *has the right to the label "Luxury Train" (Train de Luxe).*
73. *The Gare de Lyon has scarcely changed its external appearance. Its 64 metres high clock tower shows travellers the time from afar. Its restaurant (Le Train Bleu) has one of the best tables in Paris. Station for the Simplon Express, then the Simplon-Orient Express, it has become the point of departure for the high speed trains (T.G.V.) which have led the S.N.C.F. (French Railways) to carry out important improvement works.*

74

77

75

78

76

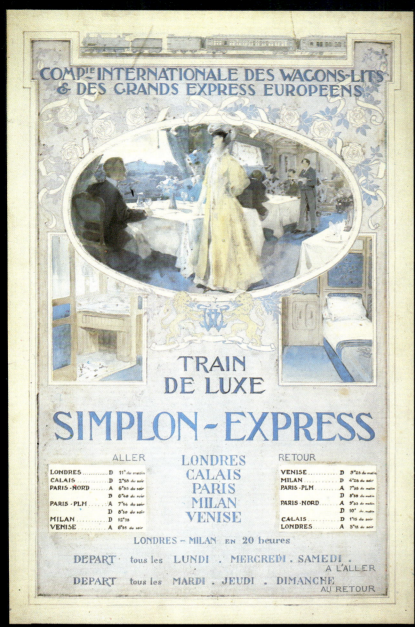

74. In the S-Type sleeping cars (R-type shown here), the washroom was situated between 2 cabins. The passengers had access to it one at a time, and shut themselves in, thanks to a bolt placed on the door of the adjoining cabin, to proceed with their ablutions there. See also illustration No. 96.
75. The Ostend-Vienna Express in 1910. S.N.C.B. Belgian Railways 4-4-0 built in Britain. The train connected with the Orient Express in Vienna station.
76. Dining car No. 2422 built in 1913 by the Compagnie Générale de Construction, St Denis, Paris. It is the same series as No. 2419 in which the Armistices of 1918 and 1940 were signed at Rethondes. The car, destroyed following its transfer to Germany, has been replaced by a car of the same series No. 2439, renumbered for the circumstances 2419.
77. The dining car No. 1651, built in 1906 by Ringhoffer at Prague, is a unique (one-off) model with four axles. Here it features in a publicity photo, showing the attentive service of the staff. The luggage controller (who travelled in the fourgon) carries the suitcase of the lady traveller, who is welcomed by the sleeping car conductor at the foot of the car, and by the dining-car chef de brigade in French breeches and white stockings, on the step.
78. Menu served on 14th November 1910 on board the Ostend-Vienna dining-car. The abundance of dishes is characteristic of the period. That did not spoil their quality as the fresh produce — e.g. the Ostend Oysters — were put at the disposal of the chef a short time before departure of the express.
79. Proposed poster project for the Simplon Express which gives this train's timetable between London and Venice. This water-colour sketch by H. Toussaint was not pursued further. It evokes, by its freshness of tone, the elegance and refinement of the service of this luxury express.
80. This British postcard, after a contemporary print depicting the beginnings of the Orient Express, hardly respects the colour of the cars.
81. The arms of the C.I.W.L. et des grands express européens (and Grand European Expresses) date from 1884. Fixed on the flanks of the cars of the Company, they stayed in the public mind as the emblem of railway comfort.

82. *The luggage labels were fixed to the trunks, suit-cases and packages which were to be placed in the C.I.W.L. fourgon. They were returned to the passengers at the destination stations.*

83. *The Company Agency at Budapest in 1914. One sees, on the public side, behind the big mahogany counter, the cupboards for tickets. On the service side, the staff in uniform are placed under the surveillance of the secretary, head of the office.*

84. *Another version of the arms of the C.I.W.L. on the binding cover of a work containing a history of the Company and sent in 1884 to the Prussian Minister of Works.*

85. *Master Menu destined for the restaurants in the chain of establishments of the Compagnie Internationale des Grands Hotels which were, in general, situated in the terminal cities of the great luxury expresses.*

86. 1 & 2. *Controleurs. These controllers were at principal terminal and intermediate stations to assist the train staff with any last minute defect repairs by the Petit Entretien — small repairs staff, like say a broken windowpane. They also countersigned the conductor's papers in sleeping cars running singly in ordinary trains so that the conductor was satisfied all was well. The conductor could not leave his car once having taken over from the cleaners who assisted with the luggage.*

3, 3bis, 4, 4bis. *Aides Serveurs. Dining car attendants.*

5, 6. *Maitres d'Hotel. Tail coats disappeared after World War I, the head dining car conductor being entitled Chef de Brigade.*

7-8. *Baggagistes-nettoyeurs. The cleaners referred to in 1 & 2 above. Each empty car was consigned to one of them at the terminal point by the sleeper conductor. They took it empty to the carriage shed and were responsible for the cleaning, alone or assisted, during the day, and returned to the starting station in the evening, where they took passengers' hand baggage into the cars from the porters or loaded it through the windows. Railway porters normally did not do this, except in Britain on the Night Ferry.*

"If the railway administrations authorise the transport of dogs by the Simplon Express, the Wagons-Lits Company will have the right to collect in its favour a supplement of 20 per cent in addition to the transport charges due to the railway administrations". Put another way, dogs like humans must pay a sleeping car supplement. Train de luxe, dogs de luxe! Lastly, paragraph 19 (article 5 of the agreement) regulates the postal service: "After agreement between the Postal administrations and the Wagons-Lits Company, the train *Simplon Express* can, in conditions to be determined in advance in each case, transport letter postbags, but excluding parcel post, provided that this transport can be carried out without doing anything to harm the normal service of the train, without increasing the number of cars, and without overloading the train, which must not attach any special postal car".

During this time the *Orient Express* continued its service in the north. In 1909, new rolling stock was allocated to it with a softer suspension and the dining car windows were "made larger to allow passengers to enjoy the countryside better." In addition to the dining salon, these cars always included a salon with a dozen armchairs. The sleeping cars' comfort was still more perfect. The windows were provided with ventilators (louvres) of movable blades of glass (turned against the direction of the engine to keep out the smoke), and the incandescent gas lamps were fitted with a night-lamp, where formerly it was necessary to mask the lamp with a curtain, which was dangerous. Lastly – and this was big progress, the upper berth could be lifted up higher and thus disappear when the compartment was occupied by one passenger alone. In 1913, with a daily service Paris-Budapest, Belgrade-

86

Sofia and Constantinople, and thrice-weekly between Budapest-Bucharest and Constanza, the *Orient Express*, maintains its predominance over its embryo rival. The first route takes sixty-three hours, the second, seventy-six. Europe of *Trains de Luxe*, a book which Abel Hermant published in 1908, masks her political tensions under a relative heedlessness. The grandees jokingly say "We are only really at home in the Calais-Nice or the Paris-Vienna..."

J.-K. Huysmans extols the sleeping car with its rich, warm decoration, and observing the work of the conductor, wrote: "The man gets out the bundles, undoes the belts, holds the ropes, leans on the springs, extracts from goodness knows where, bolsters for dollies, pillows for dwarfs". In his *Voyageuses*, Paul Bourget evokes the cosmopolitan society who are accustomed to commodious journeys and punctual communications. Albert Flament entitles a limited edition book *Palaces et sleepings* while Valery Larbaud gives, with *Barnabooth*, proof of a passion for the pleasure of life in a train and the celestial air one breathes there. In his *Journal* he notes: "Serbia and Bulgaria crossed only once in the *Orient Express*, of which I recall only vast, sad fields of roses... and mountains of great harshness" The scenery the writer prefers is the decoration of the sleeping cars. To dream better, he asks the *Orient Express* to lend him its miraculous muffled noises".

And, incredible though it may seem today, thanks to this magic train, one could travel from London to Constantinople without a passport... a visiting card would do... the *Orient Express* is truly an act of European union...

But soon, in spite of this last courtesy of the Belle Epoque, the storm thunders and finally broke at Sarajevo...

11, 12, 11bis, 12bis, 11ter, 12ter. *Serveurs-receveurs*. Head waiters. The white jackets soiled easily owing to smuts from the engines, and also the car kitchen chimney. So dining car staff had blue uniforms as well. The great coat was much the same for all staff to wear in winter when on the station platforms. Staff usually changed into uniform in the section offices in the stations.

13-14. *Brigadiers-Postiers*. In charge of the fourgon which contained many small packages — vital spare parts for machinery in backward Balkan countries, as well as the mails. All had to be signed for, and got ready for discharge at points en route, with receipts prepared etc. The fourgons usually contained a couple of berths, the other used by the Chef de Brigade.

9, 10. *Chefs de Brigade*. On Trains de Luxe the Chef de Brigade was in charge of both the diner staff under the Maitre d'Hotel, and all the sleeping car conductors. For night stops a guard system was arranged, only one conductor normally being awake — the one whose car contained the berths of passengers joining at that point, usually. After world war I, one conductor would be appointed head conductor of a train of sleeping cars entitled Chef de train. Chefs de Brigade pre 1914 were really Train Managers. Their special concern was royalty, incognito or otherwise.

15, 16. *Conducteurs*. The sleeping car conductors, the most romantic of the jobs, but very hard work, and necessitated speaking at least 3 languages. Very often based abroad to balance workings of various nationalities.

87. *Four examples of flowers in marquetry of the English decorator Morison. They ornamented Lx type sleeping cars (Luxe) built by the Metropolitan Cammel Carriage & Wagon Co. Ltd., at Birmingham (Great Britain) in 1929, series 3466 to 3495.*

Deuxième année № 276 — 10 centimes le numéro — Samedi, 7/20 Juin 1914

L'ECHO DE BULGARIE
JOURNAL QUOTIDIEN

Abonnements:
Bulgarie: Trois mois 6 fr.; Six mois 12 fr.; Un an 24 fr.
Etranger: „ 9 fr.; „ „ 18 fr.; „ „ 36 fr.
On s'abonne au journal et dans tous les bureaux de Poste.
Mandats et chèques doivent être adressés à l'Administrateur.

Bureaux du Journal:
50, Boulevard Dondoukoff, Sofia.
Téléphone 129. — Adresse télégraphique Echo-Sofia
Administrateur: **Sp. Mirtcheff.**

Annonces:
Deuxième page 2 fr. la ligne; quatrième page 1 fr. la ligne
Autres annonces prix à forfait
Toutes les lettres et manuscrits doivent être adressés au Secrétaire de la Rédaction.

Une audace inconcevable.

Les ennemis de la Bulgarie ont déployé une tactique abominable dans les circonstances les plus critiques, afin de la perdre moralement après avoir tenté vainement de l'écraser matériellement. Le peuple bulgare, à entendre ses détracteurs, était un peuple de brutes entouré de voisins chevaleresques et humains. La vérité est tout autre; le rapport de la Commission Carnegie a déjà jeté un rayon de lumière sur ce tissu de calomnies et les faits montrent tous les jours de quel côté sont la modération et la civilisation. Nous avons vu un journal parisien se faire tout récemment l'accusateur virulent du peuple bulgare en faveur de la Serbie; presqu'en même temps le rédacteur d'un journal serbe était condamné à un mois de prison pour des attaques odieuses dirigées contre le roi de Bulgarie. Voici un nouveau fait qui illustre l'état d'esprit qui règne chez nos voisins du nord-ouest.

Sa Majesté le Roi Ferdinand rentrait en Bulgarie et traversait la Serbie dans l'Orient-Express. Le conducteur serbe du train, ayant appris la présence du souverain pénétra dans le wagon royal afin, disait-il, de s'assurer de l'identité du Roi et poussa l'audace jusqu'à arrêter le train entre les stations de Pirot et de Soukhovo pour mieux satisfaire sa curiosité. Le train ne repartit que lorsque cet extraordinaire employé eût été rappelé à son devoir par les personnes de l'entourage du Roi. Le Président du Conseil des Ministres, avisé de l'incident, a porté ce fait à la connaissance du ministre de Serbie à Sofia qui lui a aussitôt exprimé ses plus vifs regrets.

On nous assure que cet employé extrêmement distingué, a choisi, comme sport préféré, le délicat plaisir de molester les Bulgares forcés de traverser la Serbie. Si cela se passait dans l'administration bulgare, on entendrait un beau tapage dans la presse européenne! Comme c'est un Serbe, parions qu'on n'en dira rien!

Actif
Encaisse métallique
Portefeuille sur l'étranger
Portefeuille
Comptes-courants spéciaux
Emprunts à long terme
Avances au Trésor

Passif

Ces deux tableaux ... d'abord que les ... férentes branches ont reg... mentés. Seules les som... feuille sur l'étranger o... minution sensible en ... plique par les nombr... effectués à l'étranger ... l'Etat que par les pa... la faible exportation q... mobilisation. Les compt... ciaux se sont développ... rapide et ont atteint le ... 78 millions en 1912. L... a fait baisser qu'à 64 ... sif a suivi le même co... pement. Le maximum ... billets de banque est e... dernier compte-rendu ... pendant parallèlement ... métallique augmentait ... si de 31 millions en ... presque de 79 millions ... une valeur de 188 mil... de banque, en circulat...

Les dépôts à terme ... une diminution dans l... ont atteint un maximu... en 1913 avec une aug... millions sur l'année p...

Les obligations hypo... pour l'emprunt de 30 ... 1909 à 4 ½ %, dimin... ment en raison des am... guliers. En 1913 la det... 28,810,000 fr. Nous a... plus loin les bénéfices ... qui ont une tendance m... sans cesse. Elles ont ... dans le cours de l'ann...

Un fait réconfortant ... tion régulière des Capi... de la Banque. Ces rés... noms différents ont au... de réductions des bén... lions en 1911 à plus

ns
1914-1919

The *Orient Express*, War Victim

28th June 1914. The shooting at Sarajevo, in Bosnia-Herzegovina of the archduke-heir to Austria-Hungary, Francis Ferdinand, by the Serbian student Princip, sets the world alight.

One month later, the emperor Francis-Joseph declares war on Serbia. Perhaps the crime at Sarajevo is the immediate cause of the first world conflict, but for some fifteen years the rivalry between the imperialisms and nationalisms in the Balkans acted like a poison in European relations. Sarajevo is the detonator of the powder-magazine traversed by the *Orient Express*.

The politico-diplomatic climate had never ceased to deteriorate due to incidents of attempted crimes, and of touchiness in notes of protestation. In the Balkans, whatever the pretext, tension was breaking in hostility, and in a revealing manner, the forgotten archives of the train bear witness to it. Thus the *Echo de Bulgarie,* a French daily newspaper published in Sofia, reported on the front page of its 20 June 1914 edition, that is just eight days before Sarajevo, an affair under the title of *An inconceivable audacity*:

> H.M. King Ferdinand was returning to Bulgaria and was crossing Serbia in the *Orient Express*. The Serbian railway guard, having learnt of the presence of the sovereign, penetrated into the royal car so that, he said, he might make sure of the identity of the King, and pushed his audacity to the length of stopping the train between Pirot and Soukhovo stations so as to satisfy his curiosity better. The train did not re-start until this extraordinary employee had been recalled to his duty by the members of the King's entourage. Advised of the incident, the President of the Council of Ministers brought this fact to the notice of the Serbian Minister at Sofia who immediately expressed his regrets to him. We are told that this extremely distinguished employee had chosen as his favourite sport, the delicate pleasure of annoying Bulgarians forced to cross Serbia. If that had happened within the Bulgarian administration, one would expect a big uproar in the European press. As this is a Serb, we can bet that nothing will be said!

Naturally the affair made a big noise. The Secretary-General of the Wagons-Lits Company, who happened to be on a visit of inspection, wrote a memorandum – unpublished – in the train between Sofia and Belgrade, the result of an enquiry as circumstantial as it was prompt. His writing is large and trembling, arising from the movement of the express. Interrogated, the chef de brigade Aunesser gave his version of the incident:

> I had already been warned at Vienna that His Majesty the king of Bulgaria would board my train at Budapest, but the king did not get on until Heubana, although at Budapest everybody knew that His Majesty would be catching the train.

89

88. The *Echo de Bulgarie* appeared in French at Sofia. This number had appeared eight days before the Sarajevo drama. The article tells of the Orient Express incident, when King Ferdinand of Bulgaria, having boarded the train with his suite, was crossing Serbia. The Serbian railway guard, impelled by excessive zeal, to confirm the King's identity, stopped the train between Pirot and Soukhovo to satisfy his curiosity.

89. This notice which warned travellers to curb their tongues was placed in the dining car during the First World War. It was posted in all public places by order of the French Minister of War. The psyche of espionage was very acute during this conflict.

SHUT UP! BE ON YOUR GUARD! The enemies' ears listen to you.

> **EXTRACT of ORDER**
>
> of the MINISTER of PUBLIC WORKS, TRANSPORT and FOOD
>
> dated 25th January 1917
>
> **DECREE:** .....
>
> **The consumption of eatables in Restaurants, Buffets, Dining-Cars and all refreshment establishments open to the Public is subject to the following regulation:**
>
> ART 1. — It is forbidden to serve at the same meal to the same person more than two dishes, of which one only may be meat.
>
> Outside these two dishes, a diner may be served a soup or an hors d'oeuvres (the hors d'oeuvres being limited to 4 varieties), a cheese course or a dessert (fruits, jam, marmalade, patisserie).
>
> Vegetables cooked or raw count as one course when these are eaten separately, that is to say when they are not served as trimmings.
>
> In order to reduce the consumption of flour, milk and sugar, the side-dishes are suppressed.
>
> Made at Paris, 25th January 1917.
>
> Signed: **HERRIOT**

90

(The chef de brigade continued:) Everything went normally as far as Pirot. There, a policeman came to me, asking if the King of Bulgaria was on the train. I answered him that I was not aware of the quality of the travellers who occupied the berths but that, according to the lists which had been given to me by my conductor, it was to be supposed that the King was not travelling.

Meanwhile, after the train had re-started, the Serbian railway guard came to question me, demanding of me yes or no, whether the King was in the train. Afterwards he went to each car, opening all the compartment doors except those in which His Majesty and his suite were to be found, which were locked on the inside. I remarked to him that there were, in fact, in one or two compartments, some passengers who did not wish to be disturbed, but who were in order with the railways, since they had paid for four first-class tickets and five supplements. Having asked the Serbian guard why he was so keen to know who occupied these compartments, he told me that he had received a telegram saying that His Majesty was in the train, and wished to make sure of it. To have some peace, I then said to him that in fact, the King occupied the compartment 7-8 and his servants had the numbers 5-6. Nevertheless, the Serbian guard persisted in wishing to open the compartment doors and, without success, made use of the *clef carrée*[1] which he had in his possession. The first servant of the King, who had gone out into the corridor at this moment, pushed back the guard. At this instant I intervened, begging him to come with me and explain himself in the fourgon (van). He was very overexcited and even threatened me that he would stop the train and make me get off, adding that on my return to Serbia, I, as well as the conductor of the car, would be hearing from him. He took my name and, as the train arrived at Tzaribrod, the altercation came to an end. I reported to the King all that had happened, and the King said to me that I had done my duty.

The secretary general pursued his enquiry the next day at Belgrade. M. Doroco, head of Movements of the Serbian State Railways, had to admit "he had an excess of zeal and above all, a lack of tact". A press despatch stated "the government had ordered a most stern enquiry, whose results will be published as soon as they are known". On 23rd June, we learn that the guard had been sent into compulsory retirement and the Bulgarian government declared itself satisfied with this action. In return "the news published in some newspapers that King Ferdinand had been insulted while passing through Pirot, is pure invention, the more so as during the journey the presence of King Ferdinand in the train was completely concealed from the public".

Five weeks later, the same day of the Austrian declaration of war on Serbia, the *Orient Express* coming from Constantinople, made up of two sleeping cars, a dining car and two fourgons (vans), is halted at Nis. The next day another train is halted at Sofia. The staff are sent to Germany and Austria. International railway circulation is suspended. Only some internal services continue (Sofia-Varna, Salonica-Nis).

A notice dated this same 28th July 1914 in Paris, bluntly announces: "Because of the present political crisis, we have had to limit the *Orient Express* and the *Ostend-Vienna Express* to the sector Vienna-Budapest". The Munich-Vienna, Munich-Trieste and Stuttgart-Trieste services are suppressed.

The *Orient Express* is replaced by the *Balkan Zug* (Balkan Train) which links Berlin to Sofia and Constantinople on 16th January 1916 with requisitioned rolling stock and running under the title of *Mittel Europaische Schlafwagengesellschaft* (Central European Sleeping Car Company), abridged as Mitropa. This company placed under sequestration the rolling stock of Wagons-Lits to be found in Germany. In total 64 dining cars and 35 sleeping cars were appropriated from their legal owners.

After Europe has torn itself apart for four years, peace is achieved at last.

---

1. See Glossary Page 155, and Illustration No. 190. Translator's note.

International railway communications could be restored, witnessing the end of hostilities.

On 13th February 1919, Circular No. 17029 of the Wagons-Lits Company's Sales Department announces that "the luxury train *Orient Express* is re-instated from Paris to Vienna, Budapest and Bucharest twice a week". This re-establishment is one of the consequences of the Peace Conference held in Paris from 18th January. But the circumspect route shows the desire to carefully avoid German territory: Paris (Est)-Chaumont-Vesoul-Belfort-Delle-Basle-Zurich-Buchs-Linz-Vienna-Budapest-Bucharest. Actually this train does not yet have the right to the appellation *Orient Express*. Its official name is *Train de Luxe militaire*. Its four sleeping cars, its dining car and its three vans – one of which carries the post – are only available "to military or civil passengers armed with an authorisation from the French War Minister, who, alone, issues the sale of berths." Although the price of meals is fixed throughout the journey in francs at 2.50F (breakfast) and 10F (luncheon or dinner without wine) for officers and grandee civilians, "troops forming the armed guard of this train will exceptionally be served with meals at 1F (Breakfast) and 4F (Lunch or dinner)."

One traveller, neither military, nor diplomatic, nor a politician, came on board on the evening of 12th April. He is M. Bourgiet and belongs to the Management of the Grand Hotels Company (the Wagons-Lits subsidiary). In his unpublished journey note-book, he gives his impressions of his trip, precursor of Paul Morand, who brilliantly describes the new Europe:—

> Thanks to the kindness of the 4ième bureau and to friendly relations with the Ministry of Foreign Affairs, and although my case is outside all the conditions generally foreseen, I could personally, easily enough insinuate myself into a comfortable sleeping car whose destination is Bucharest. My cabin companion, Lieutenant X, a young American Army Officer is going as a diplomatic courier to Romania. He is a cheerful companion, much more interested in love and a few good little affairs than in the surveillance of his suit cases. It seems that this mentality is common to all the officers of the young United States (...) Those with the right of access to the train, numbering about sixty, in general are French, Polish, Czech, Yugoslav and Romanian officers, some diplomats returning to their posts, five or six politicians, four individuals of no well-determined profession, and eight ladies, one of them a nurse.

90. *In this order of 25th January 1917, signed by Edouard Herriot, French Minister of Public Works, Transport and Food, it is specified that dining car passengers must undergo food restrictions due to the state of war.*

91. *Table giving in 15 languages the company title of the C.I.W.L. One can see that, in 1872, Georges Nagelmackers founded the Compagnie de Wagons-Lits, then after his association with Colonel Mann, "Mann Boudoir Sleeping Car". On 4th December 1876, the articles of the new company named Compagnie Internationale des Wagons-lits were deposited at Brussels: in 1884 "et des Grands Express Européens" was added to underline the importance of the great luxury trains. Lastly in 1967, the diversification of the services offered by the Company in the Hotel, Restaurant, and Tourism fields had acquired so much importance that the Board of Directors decided to remove "et des Grands Express Européens" and to replace it by "et du tourisme" (Not painted on the cars). The luxury trains of the C.I.W.L. had ceased to exist. (See note page 130).*

Leaving Paris at 19.20, the train reached Basle at 8.40 next morning. For the first time since its creation thirty years earlier, the *Orient Express* runs on Swiss territory. Our traveller, recalling the Helvetic neutrality during the war, emphasizes that:

> The passage of a military train of the belligerent armies on its territory constituted, in some way, a violation of that neutrality... consequently it was necessary to give the Swiss Government visible satisfaction, and thus it was arranged that the officers travelling in the *Orient Express* would be dressed in civilian clothes, and that the soldiers forming the police and escort service of the train would be strictly confined to the fourgons, and stay there throughout the crossing of the Swiss Confederation. Two Swiss officers and an armed picket were to take possession of the train from the French frontier to the Austrian frontier, to ensure the strict execution of these orders. The first journeys were carried out without incident and without any difficulty, then, little by little, the restrictions were relaxed. In reality it was inconvenient to impose the very costly purchase of civilian clothes on officers going on field service. Accordingly it was later decided that military personnel of all grades could take the *Orient Express* in uniform, like the soldiers, on condition that they did not show themselves during the crossing of Switzerland. But this tolerance soon opened the way to new transgressions. It was quickly seen that the best course was non-interference and turning a blind eye. After all was not France victorious, and in this case free to impose its will? Accordingly the only essential condition imposed was that at the Austrian frontier station of Buchs, travellers in uniform would stay in their compartments, blinds drawn, and only civilians had the right to stand by the windows, or indeed to get down onto the platform close beside the access doors of the cars.

Our witness states, with regret, that an Austrian hospital train provoked scarcely any interest in Buchs station:

> By contrast, the Orient Express was surrounded, examined and scrutinised with extreme curiosity. Having set off with an officer hiding behind a blind, there were those looking for a 'conversation' with him, by speech or by gestures. Flowers and cigars were even offered to men of the escort through the half-open doors of the fourgons. For thanks they kissed the visitors, who, giggling and blushing with pleasure, excused themselves in German for not being able to do better. In my French eyes, my feelings were that this mentality is odious to us, and concluded that either the women were quite simply immoral, or that the defeat of their country made them lose all feeling of prudence, shame and decency![2]

Next day at Vienna, profiting from the long halt – from ten o'clock to midday – at Vienna West Station, our traveller surveys the capital and remarks sadly:

> Those who knew Vienna before the war and saw it again in this spring of 1919 are astounded by the different aspect of the town and its inhabitants. Dreary streets, deserted squares, cafés, brasseries and restaurants three-quarters shut and almost empty of patrons. A very few carriages drawn by skeletal horses. All the inhabitants have a starved look and are miserably dressed. One feels, without doubt, that these people, one of the happiest, noisiest and most rousing in pre-war Europe, are literally dying of hunger.

The train restarts. The traveller observes his companions. He has time enough: Constantinople is still far away... Each wants to convey some signs of kindness, when passing each other in the corridor or going to take their seats in the diner. In Cabin 1/2 a Romanian diplomatic courier is accompanied by his wife.

---

2. M. Bourguet is being diplomatic. He probably knows Buchs town is 100% Swiss! Note by G.B.

> A delightful, extremely pretty person who pleases herself by making a remark to those of us who pretend not to have been noticed by her yet... Since one cannot make a long journey without slurs, the well-informed folk maintain that for reasons of personal convenience, the occupants of Cabin 5 have made arrangements with those in Cabin 6 for a discreet exchange of places. However, as the fifth cabin occupants are two gentlemen and the sixth cabin contains two ladies, it is easy to see that these jovial fellows have no need... to feel bored on the journey!!! This conjecture is furthermore the subject of all the conversations at breakfast when the beaming features of the ladies are noticeable despite the rings under their eyes, noticeable too is the conquering air of the young Romanian captain, and the rather ragged appearance of M. Mourot, born in Bordeaux, Counsellor at the Overseas Trade Ministry, who is evidently a little bad-tempered: he is 58!

Less agreeable incidents took place. A German " the said Von Papen, a name of illustrious repute" is arrested. He carries fase papers and the Romanian police make him get off the train. Then, the wife of a Transsylvanian colonel declares in a peremptory tone, with a thick accent, during luncheon, which she thinks disappointing:

"It is only in *Baris* at *Brunier's* that one can get a good *veesch!*"[3]

A Romanian nurse, who has done field service on the French front, gets up, brandishing a trench helmet. And staring at the colonel's wife in the face, says to her:

"I thought I only had the boche's head-gear. There! now I have the pig's head!"[4]

On the verge of a fainting fit, the colonel's wife rejoins in a dying voice:

"You dirty ———————"...

Obviously, on the "luxurious, military and diplomatic" *Orient Express*, peace has not yet been signed.

The colonel, furious, strikes the table a terrible blow with his fist, and in perfect French, says to his wife in the most icy tone in the world:

"My dear, would you force me to regret, once again and in the presence of these gentlemen, a youthful mistake so dearly paid for?"

Our traveller, M. Bourget and his neighbours, who were now travelling along beside the Danube very slowly, notably because of the bad quality of the coal, only recovered a sincere smile when, despite the regulations, they welcomed a young girl aboard who carried with her a chicken in a basket "where it laid an egg during the journey, a very meritorious action on its part"...

A new Europe improves on this mundane tone, in this first spring of peace. A Europe bruised, weak, decimated and remodelled, whose survivors are going to surrender to all the joys of existence, with frenzy. A rousing revenge, systematic, explosive, to forget and, one hopes, to ward off the fatality of wars.

It was a time of international conferences. Around the green baize table the negotiations continued. So a new era began, that of the train of revenge and romanticism, the train of the Crazy Years...

En voiture! Montez s'il vous plait! All aboard the *Simplon-Orient Express*...

---

3. Refers to Prunier's famous fish speciality restaurant, also in London.
4. "Boche" was the World War I French rude word for German, like "Kraut" used by the Americans in World War II, and "Hun" by the British in both. Translator's notes.

A. DESCELLIERS ARC.¹⁰ D.P.L.G.

AGENCE PRINCIPALE DE PARIS

A. DESCELLIERS ARC.¹⁰ D.P.L.G.

1920-1939

The Crazy Years of the *Simplon-Orient Express*

The *Simplon-Orient Express*, younger brother of the *Orient Express*, had a difficult childhood. If politics had hindered its development, it was politics which revived it later, after the storm of 1914-1918.

With Germany conquered, the Austro-Hungarian Empire was split up to give birth to new states which forged new alliances among themselves.

In 1919, the obstacles had disappeared which had caused the postponement of Gustave Nobelmaire's proposal to extend the journey of the *Simplon Express* beyond Venice. The opening of the Peace Conference at Versailles had put the creation of the *Simplon-Orient Express* on the agenda.

The end of the conflict saw Italy in the Allied camp; the new Yugoslavian State now had a common frontier with Italy; Romania sought a more direct connection with the friendly western countries. Great Britain like France realised all the interest that setting up a great international train could have on the political plane, by linking up the capitals of central Europe and the Near East, without passing through the Germanic countries (Germany and Austria).

Actually, it would suffice to use the existing Swiss, Italian, Austrian and Hungarian lines that terminated at Belgrade, link-point with the *Orient Express*. The new line would follow the long valleys of the Po and the Save, and thus save some sixty kilometres on the *Orient Express* route.

A commission of political and technical representatives of the allied nations met from 18th to 26th March 1919 at the Ministry of Public Works in Paris for the creation of this new great international express, whose echoes we find in the minutes of a meeting between M. André Noblemaire, General Manager (France) of the Wagons-Lits Company[1] and his assistants, at the Paris regional headquarters of the Wagons-Lits:

> ... the question has come about very swiftly, not only because of the sympathy which the project of French initiative, has met with in all the interested countries, but also because of events in Hungary which has cut the train militaire Paris-Vienna-Budapest-Bucharest on its Hungarian sector[2].
>
> So it has been decided to make a start from 15th April in the form indicated in the inter-governmental convention, which was signed after the conference of 26th March.
>
> ... A luxury train will be put in service as soon as possible, named *Simplon-Orient Express,* between London, Calais (or Boulogne), Paris and the Orient, following the itinerary: Vallorbe – Lausanne – Simplon – Milan – Venice – Trieste – Laibach

92. *The principal C.I.W.L. agency in Paris at 14 bd. des Capucines, whose layout was the creation of the architect A. Desceilier. It was he who also created the beautiful Boardroom of the Direction General of the Company in the bd. Haussmann in Paris. A striking detail: it was in this same bd. des Capucines building that the first (Paris) public cinema projection took place, during which Louis Lumière presented* The Arrival of a train in La Ciotat station, *first film of a moving train.*

1. André Noblemaire became Director-General of the Wagons-Lits in 1923. Note by GB.
2. After the proclamation of a Republic on 16th November, the Hungarian President facilitated the arrival of the communists in power. The amputation of territory imposed by the Allies on 20th March 1919 caused the people to turn to Soviet Russia to help defend the historic frontiers. After 133 days of disorder and riots, the Romanian army attacked and dispersed the "red legions". On 6th August, the counter-revolutionaries appointed Archduke Joseph as Regent.

(Ljubljana) – Steinbrück – Zagreb – Vincovce (Vinkovci), where it will divide: one part to Bucharest – Constantza – Odessa, the other part Belgrade – Constantinople – Athens. The division point will be brought back to Belgrade as soon as a more direct junction between Serbia and Romania is built. At Milan, the *Simplon-Orient Express* will connect with a *train rapide* (express train) following the itinerary: Gannat – Lyon – Chambery – Mont Cenis – Turin – Milan. The *Simplon-Orient Express* and the *Bordeaux-Milan* will run throughout the year, daily, following timings to be determined with a view to obtaining as quick connections as possible. The *Simplon-Orient Express* will exclusively be made up of cars of our company. The *Bordeaux-Milan* will have an international portion composed of our company's cars and one first class cariage.

The sales department of the Company published a circular destined for its sales offices on 10th April announcing the creation of the new train, which included the following timetable of the principal stations served by this train comprising sleeping cars and a dining car:

94

ALLER					RETOUR				
		Londres		8 h 50			Bucarest	D	14 h 30
		Boulogne		14 h 30			Verciorova	HO A	0 h 30
		Paris-Nord		19 h 30				HEC D	0 h 30
		Paris-P.L.M.		21 h			Zegedin	A	8 h 30
		Dijon		1 h	Belgrade	9 h 30		D	9 h 30
		Frasne		4 h	Vincovce	14 h 30	Vincovce	A	14 h 35
		Vallorbe	A	5 h 15			BIFURCATION		
			D	5 h 47			Vincovce	D	15 h 15
		Lausanne	A	6 h 35			Agram	A	22 h
			D	6 h 45			(Zagreb)	D	22 h 10
		Vevey		7 h 02			Longatico		3 h 16
		Montreux		7 h 12			TRANSBORDEMENT		
		Martigny (en été)		7 h 57			Trieste	A	6 h 30
		Sion	A	8 h				D	8 h
			D	8 h 20			Venise		12 h
		Brigue	A	9 h 20					12 h 15
Bordeaux	7 h 30		D	9 h 50			Padoue		12 h 55
Gannat	A 17 h 30	Iselle	A	10 h 13			Vérone		14 h 15
	D 17 h 40		D	10 h 50			Milan		17 h
St-Germain-		Domodossola	HEC	11 h 10					
des-Fossés	18 h 15		HI	12 h 20	CORRESPONDANCE AVEC S.O.E.				
Lyon	A 21 h 55	Pallanza		12 h 52			Milan		17 h 25
	D 22 h 20	Baveno		12 h 58			Arona		18 h 35
Modane	HF 5 h	Stresa		13 h 05					18 h 40
	HEC 7 h 30	Arona	A	13 h 25			Stresa		19 h 05
Turin	A 10 h 15		D	13 h 30			Baveno		19 h 12
	D 11 h	Milan		14 h 40			Pallanza		19 h 20
Milan	14 h						Domodossola	HEC	19 h 55
CORRESPONDANCE AVEC S.O.E.								HI	19 h 05
		Milan		15 h 05			Iselle		19 h 42
		Vérone		17 h 30					20 h 18
		Padoue		19 h			Brigue	HI	20 h 50
		Venise	A	19 h 40				HEC	20 h 20
			D	19 h 55			Martigny		22 h 20
		Trieste	A	23 h 30			Montreux		23 h 16
		TRANSBORDEMENT							23 h 18
			D	0 h 15			Vevey		23 h 26
		Longatico	HI A	3 h					23 h 28
			HEC D	2 h 45			Lausanne		23 h 49
		Agram	A	7 h 51	Milan	18 h			23 h 57
		(Zagreb)	D	8 h	Turin	21 h	Vallorbe		0 h 57
		Vincovce	A	13 h 15		21 h 25			2 h 15
		BIFURCATION			Modane	HEC 24 h	Frasne		3 h
Belgrade	A 18 h 15	Zegedin	A	19 h		HF 0 h 30			3 h 40
			D	20 h	Lyon	6 h	Dijon		5 h 50
		Verciorova	A	4 h		6 h 30			5 h 56
			D	6 h 30	St-Germain-		Paris-P.L.M.		10 h 35
		Bucarest	A	16 h 30	des-Fossés		Paris-Nord		12 h
					Gannat	10 h 25			
						10 h 35	Boulogne		16 h
					Bordeaux	20 h 55	Londres		20 h

HEC : heure d'Europe centrale. - HF : heure française. - HI : heure italienne. - HO : heure orientale. - HE : heure d'Europe occidentale. - A : arrivée. - D : départ

93, 94. *First Class steel Sleeping car No. 2644, built by the Leeds Forge Company Limited at Leeds, (Yorkshire, Great Britain) in 1922, which could carry 16 passengers. 23, 452 metres long (overall) and weighing 54, 365 tonnes, the cars of this series were painted midnight blue, lined out in gold — yellow. Assigned to the Calais — Mediterranée Express service the public christened this express the* Train Bleu. (Blue Train).
Right, view of the car, corridor side. Left, view of the car, compartment side.
95. *"Double" compartment in day position of car No. 2644, one of the first steel cars built in 1922 at Leeds, in Great Britain. The partition marquetries are by the decorator Morison.*
96. *The washroom of car No. 2644 was placed between two cabins. The passengers wishing to wash, occupied it one by one, a system of bolts to the neighbouring door, allowing them to lock themselves in in total security. The bolt on one side was linked to that on the other.*

Bearing in mind the European railway situation just after the war, and the dilapidation of the lines in the Balkan peninsular, this train could go no further than Trieste. Beyond, in Yugoslavia where the *Simplon-Orient Express* should have 1,200 kilometres, numerous portions of line needed to be repaired, bridges strengthened, stations and signalling systems put in order again.

The new luxury train was placed under conventional rules, having its own autonomy. Its operation was assigned to the Wagons-Lits Company, its management to the P.L.M. Company. Its make-up was the following:

From Paris:
1 Fourgon Paris-Trieste
1 Dining car Paris-Trieste
2 Sleeping cars Paris-Trieste
1 Sleeping car Paris-Venice
1 Sleeping car Paris-Milan
1 Fourgon Paris-Trieste

From Milan:
1 Fourgon Paris-Trieste
1 Dining car Paris-Trieste
2 Sleeping cars Paris-Trieste
1 Sleeping car Paris-Venice
1 Sleeping car Bordeaux-Trieste
1 Fourgon Paris-Trieste

From Bordeaux; the Wagons-Lits Company's cars attached to the Bordeaux-Milan train comprised one dining car (Bordeaux-Lyon) and one sleeping car (Bordeaux-Trieste).

The Wagons-Lits Company's sleeping car fleet had been so greatly weakened by the war, that at the beginning of its operation, its reputation as a great luxury express was harmed by an absence of the splendour synonymous with such a train.

The head of its operation made a list of criticisms in a confidential report on the 10th October 1919 which are summarised thus: general fatigue of the

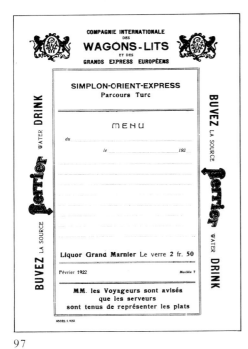

97

98

rolling stock, frequent withdrawal of cars during the journey, too prolonged a rotation of the direct Paris-Bucharest cars. Add to this the sloth of carrying out the renewal works of the line in Yugoslavia and Romania, and the difficulties in passing from theory to practical realisation of the *Simplon-Orient Express*, during its first years, can be imagined.

However, from the end of 1919, one part of the *Simplon-Orient Express* reached Bucharest (the Paris-Bucharest cars were detached from the main train at Vinkovci), and the other part Zagreb and Belgrade. In 1920 it reached Sofia and Constantinople, detaching a rake at Nis for Salonica and Athens. Really it is only from this date that it at last justified its prestigious name.

In a troubled Europe, for good or ill the new train links up the allied countries' capitals which represented the political will of the victors of the Great War. Conforming to these governments' wishes, the Wagons-Lits Company struggled to continue a service which commercially, was barely viable... It was to these governments that it turned, to ask them to make up the deficit which it could not sustain.

These first years of the Simplon-Orient Express are difficult. The countries crossed are disturbed. So Italian strikes force it to divert by way of Vienna; often Bucharest cannot be reached.

In 1922 the Bordeaux-Milan branch, called the "45th Parallel line" is suppressed because it is impossible to make it pay.

In 1920 the *Simplon-Orient Express* journey between Paris and Constantinople took ninety-six hours, then seventy-six hours in 1926 and finally fifty-seven hours in 1930. Reductions of the same order were recorded on the Paris-Athens and Paris-Bucharest sectors.

The *Simplon-Orient Express*, created to establish a connection by way of southern Europe between London, Paris and Constantinople, finished up, with all its branch lines, by presenting an appearance of a complex network encompassing numerous countries, including those which at the beginning of the century, did everything possible to oppose its birth.

97. Simplon-Orient Express-*type Menu card in 1922. The price of luncheon and dinner was fixed at 15 francs, breakfast at 3 francs. Passengers were advised that the staff were obliged to offer second helpings.*
98. *The Simplon-Orient Express on the Villeneuve Saint Georges curve near Paris, in 1923. The two fourgons (vans) can be seen at the head of the train. (P.L.M. engine).*
99. *Thanks to its great expresses, the C.I.W.L. could ensure the rapid transport of small packages. They were forwarded by direct fourgons to the towns served by the* Simplon-Orient Express.

In the spring of 1920, recognizing that Austria must participate once more in international traffic, the Austrian Federal Railways administration restored the contractual rights to the Wagons-Lits Company which had been granted previously to it. During the hostilities, at the time of the Mitteleuropa of Frederick Naumann, this contractual situation had been denounced after forty years of existence, as the objective of the germanic powers was to bring all international traffic into their sphere of influence, thanks to the presence of the newly-formed Mitropa. The outcome of the war stranded this smart scheme. The new states, Czechoslovakia, Yugoslavia, Poland, Estonia, Latvia, & Lithuania concluded contracts of long duration with the Wagons-Lits Company. In Austria, the contract broken under pressure of Germany, was enforced again, and on its side Hungary renewed theirs with the Company, for forty years. To save its entity, Mitropa had to renounce its international character and was not more than an enterprise whose field of activity was limited to Germany.[3]

As a result of energetic interventions, some of the vehicles (about thirty sleeping cars) which it had annexed during the war were returned to Wagons-Lits Company. At the beginning of 1922, Mitropa still possessed an important number of the Company's cars, which it operated on its own account. It was necessary to await the judgement by arbitration of the mixed Germano-Belgian Tribunal in July 1922, before the Company recovered twenty-five of the sixty-four dining cars which it was entitled to reclaim.

The contract which the Company had signed with the Austrian Railways administration was in force until 1932 but could be broken by notice, at the end of the years 1923 and 1925. To avert the contract's precarious character, which made good operations difficult, the Company strove to obtain an extension, to guard against an expected cancellation. It was ready to make great sacrifices. The endeavours set out by the Wagons-Lits Company were supported by the French Government, who had repeatedly pointed out to the Austrian Government the interest that it had in linking these negotiations to a trade treaty, the French Government stating precisely that it was incomprehensible that Austria, under the circumstances, wished to favour the Mitropa, an instrument of war whose hostile intentions had been expressed during the conflict.

On the English side, Sir Davidson Dalziel[4] discussed this question with the Austrian Minister of Finance and it seemed likely that important economic and political reasons finally were going to settle the affair, in spite of the Austrian objection that she could not consent to a monopoly contract with the Wagons-Lits Company, bearing in mind the important railway connections which she maintained with Germany.

In spite of the secretive means to which Mitropa had recourse in creating a Swiss company in Geneva, Transcontinent, whose object was to organise, control and even finance transport enterprises in diverse countries, this ingenious combination could not delude the railways of the Allies. Thus its ambitions were checked, and its intentions thwarted.

As a result of the preliminary conference held in London in 1924, the Wagons-Lits Company on 20th May 1925 concluded a contract in which it consented to the Austrian Railways operating in collaboration with the Mitropa, the Vienna-Berlin and Vienna-Nuremberg (via Passau) sleeping car services. It renounced in addition the debt of 16 million francs[5] owed to it by the Mitropa in accordance with the St Germain agreement relating to the

3. Despite this, Mitropa started a Berlin-Hook of Holland (-Harwich-London) luxury train, using the ex-Kaiser's royal Hofzug cars, competing with C.I.W.L.'s Nord Express, Berlin-Ostend (-Dover-London) via the rival Southern Rly. in England.
4. President of the C.I.W.L., and Chairman of the Pullman Car Co. Ltd., London. One reason why Pullman cars began running on 11th November 1920 in the London-Harwich Great Eastern Railway's boat trains.
5. Mitropa had no means of paying this debt and Wagons-Lits expected to force it into bankruptcy and absorb it. Instead one morning C.I.W.L. woke to find 40% of Mitropa's capital now belonged to Transcontinent, free of German inflation, and financed by the Canadian Pacific – and Great Eastern Rlys., especially to save the Berlin-London Express! Notes by GB.

100

100. *In Syria, then under French Mandate - the Homs-Tripoli line is undergoing repairs. General Gouraud, assisted by the Governor and manager of the States of Damascus, Greater Lebanon and the Alouite territory, gets ready to bolt down the last rail of the new line. Note the carpets, thrown between the rails to make the task more comfortable. The Asiatic family of the Simplon-Orient Express grows.*

101. *In all latitudes the gastronomic reputation of the train is defended. Are we in London or in Paris? We are on board the Anatolia Express inaugurated on 1st August 1927 with this menu drawn up in French and Arabic.*

102. *A beguiling stage of the Simplon-Orient Express: Aleppo (Halab today) and its imposing fortress.*

101

102

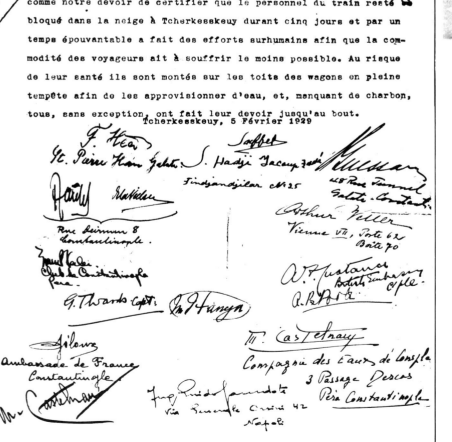

103. *The most celebrated incident that befell the* Orient Express: *in 1929 the train was held up for five days by an icy snowstorm near Tcherkesskeuy station, 80km. from Istanbul. The event, which made a sensation, inspired Agatha Christie and was the starting point of her famous book* Murder on the Orient Express. *The single track considerably delayed the arrival of help.*

104. *An extraordinary document: despite this unprecedented delay and their overwhelming distress, on arrival at Instanbul the passengers wished to express their satisfaction and recognition to the staff who had done the impossible. A certificate worthy of the Simplon-Orient Express story: there was not a single complaint!*

withdrawal of proceedings in action before the mixed Germano-Belgian Tribunal and the Belgian Office of Verification and Compensation. The episode and similar concessions which bore witness to the Wagons-Lits Company's lofty spirit of conciliation, did nothing to alter the expansion and vitality of the Company, and, beyond the difficulties – sequels of the Great War, it was going to multiply its money and extend the quality of its services.

After these difficult beginnings, the *Simplon-Orient Express* had been remarkable for its regularity during twenty years. Neither the length of the journey, nor the complication of its timetables had checked its irresistable ascent to fame. It needed natural disasters to hinder it from regularly completing its faultless journeys.

The train that left Paris on 31st January, 1929 became blocked by snow near Tcherkesskeuy in eastern Thrace, 130 kilometres from Istanbul. The cold reached $-25°$. Help was slow to come, and the staff of the sleeping cars and the dining car struggled to ensure the survival of the passengers, in spite of the storm; the train seemed to sink into the snow, which froze and made enormous blocks of ice.

Was it single track which obstructed the rescuers? The fact remains that the snow-plough needed four days to reach the train. It was not until the 12th February that the S.O.E. reached Constantinople after a journey of 12 days! A record in the annals and a record delay: five days!

The grateful passengers addressed a note to the Direction Generale of the Wagons-Lits Company which they drew up on 5th February at Tcherkesskeuy, whose text is followed by the signatures of the stranded passengers of the *Simplon-Orient Express*.

> We travellers of the *Simplon (Orient) Express* No. 3, consider it our duty to certify that the staff of the train blocked in the snow at Tcherkesskeuy during five days and in appalling weather, made superhuman efforts in order that the comfort of passengers should suffer as little as possible. At the risk of their health, they climbed on the roofs of the cars in full storm conditions, in order to refill the water tanks, and lacking coal, everyone did their duty to the end. Tcherkesskeuy, 5th February 1929.

The incident created a great stirr in Turkey. The journal *Akcham* of 11th February 1929 headlined on the front page *The careless negligence of the Oriental Railways Company:*

> As we announced yesterday, the long wait in the snows of the *Orient Express* passengers, blocked at Kabakdja is ended. It was none too soon. And on this some reflections come to mind. If we recall that to come to Turkey, the train has crossed the highest pinnacles of the Alps on the frontier between Italy and Yugoslavia, the Balkans and the Rhodope mountains, the region of Nis in Macedonia where the snow in places reaches a height of ten metres, and lastly the Bulgarian plain, and that, everywhere, it could pass without incident to come and be stranded in eastern Thrace where the snow does not exceed 5 metres, we cannot be prevented from stating that the organisation of the Oriental Railways here at home is inferior to that in the little neighbour States.

And the journalist, whose national pride is visibly wounded, goes on:

> We have interviewed several of the involuntary heroes of the odyssey of the *Conventional*.[6] They are unanamious in branding the concessionary company[7] for its total lack of interest in having any concern for them though it is, however, morally responsible for their fate!

---

6. Name given to the S.O.E. whose responsibility was that of C.I.W.L. and the P.L.M. under a convention.
7. The C.O. – Oriental Railways Company had the concession for the line from the Turkish Government.

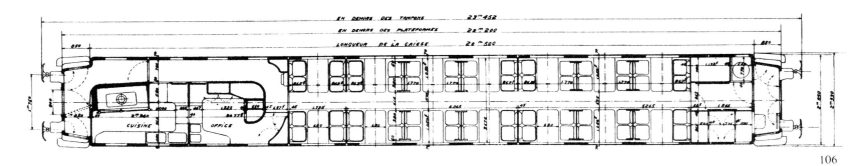

106

107

105

108

105. *Pantry of the dining cars in illustration 106, comprising double sink unit, the working surfaces and the hatch communicating with the kitchen, above the coal-box of the latter.*
106. *Plan of the dining cars of series 3341-3360 built in 1928 by Enterprises Industrielles Charentaise (E.I.C.) at Aytré-La Rochelle (France) which could welcome 56 persons. On the left the pantry (office) and kitchen (cuisine) as well as the boiler and the wine-cellar.*
107. *Exterior views of dining cars of series 3341-3360: the corridor side of access to the dining saloon and the kitchen-pantry side.*
108. *Dining saloon of the same series. The seats are bench type — for two people — upholstered individually in leather embossed with the initials W.L. The decorative marquetry panels came from Great Britain.*

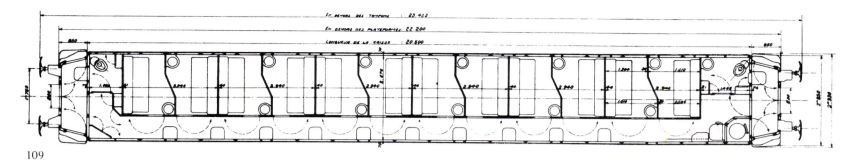

109

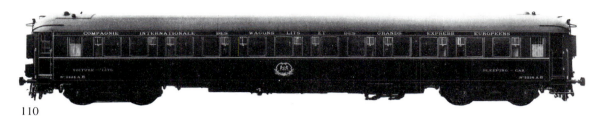

110

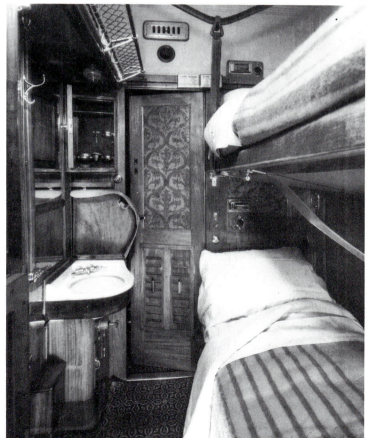

111

109. *Plan of Z-type sleeping cars of the series 3311-3340 with 12 non-intercommunicating compartments of 2 beds, or 24 berths separated 2 by 2 by a partition designed with an angle (Z). Each compartment could be used as a single.*

110. *Exterior Views of a Z-type sleeping car of the series 3311-3340, corridor side and cabin side. Also built by E.I.C. in 1927, some ran in the various Orient Expresses until 1962.*

111. *Interior of a Z-type sleeping car cabin in night position. In addition to the 4-language notice on the Alarm Signal handle (hidden by the strap), an extra notice in Balkan languages is placed next to it, for working the Orient Express.*

112. End view of an S1-type sleeping car of 1930, of the series 3456-3465, built at the Simmering Works near Vienna (Austria) which shows the corridor bellows and stepplate which allows passage from one car to another. Below, the coupling elements; assorted air brake hoses to fit different countries' coaches, and vacuum brake hose for use in Austria.

113. A bogie (PP type) destined for S1-type sleeping cars built in Austria.

114. The S1-type sleeping car originally had 16 berths, then 24 berths. The double cabins were separated by a washroom for the use of the passengers of each cabin. This arrangment was characteristic of the S type cars. No. 3456 ended its career in Egypt in the Star of Egypt Express *Cairo-Luxor-Aswan-El Shallal*.

> "Without the friendliness and care of the management and staff of the Alpollou refinery," one of the survivors told us "we should all be dead from hunger and cold. The company had even refused to allow us to use the telegraph to communicate with our friends in Constantinople".

And the journalist specified that:

> ...the clearing works were not undertaken consecutively, which made it necessary to wait three days for the first rescue crews to be sent, and during that particular time the snow accumulated on the cars and turned itself into massive blocks of ice.

Welcomed as heroes at Constantinople, our travellers have kept their memories of this adventure which are enriched with details, difficult to verify from the yarns told over the years. We have contented ourselves with irrefutable documents to write this story.

On 21st November of the same year another episode, as dramatic, took place, of which the *Simplon-Orient Express* was the victim of a crime. A dynamite charge exploded on the line between Pirot and Tsaribrod on the Bulgar-Yugoslav frontier. The locomotive was blown to bits. The culprit was a mentally deranged person who had a horror of trains!

In 1931, other incidents due to natural disasters delayed the *Simplon-Orient Express*: on 17th February the train could not go beyond Sofia, the floods of the Anda blocking its passage. On 8th March the Athens portion was stopped at Skopje by an earthquake. On 28th of the same month, the snow was so thick near Inoi that the train could not reach Athens.

Bad weather was not the only obstacle tht the *Simplon-Orient Express* encountered. An unpublished letter written by a traveller on 30th June 1919 between Venice and Milan relates a most unusual event. "The rake coming from Bucharest to Paris is held up at the Yugoslav frontier town of Subotica for sixteen hours, for lack of coal. (...) Questioned, the stationmaster could give no information about a probable arrival of coal and, letting it be known that this immobilization could last several days, the travellers decided to club together to buy a wagonload of wood offered to them for 4000 crowns. The train restarted two hours later, after a prolonged altercation."

But this was not the end of it! A second train was also deprived of its coal. Our traveller continues:

> As some of us had urgent business, we decided to do the same as the travellers in the preceding train, that is to say buy at our cost a wagonload of wood. Many of us were opposed to this. Two French officers – couriers – protested against this way of doing things, remarking, very wisely, that this procedure would become accepted practice, and there was no reason why the price should not be progressively increased. This is in fact what happened. Once the sum of 4000 crowns had been with difficulty collected, we were asked for 6000 crowns.

In the face of this unwelcome menace of racketeering, a Romanian, commandant of the police at Taquras, intervened on behalf of the Serbian general of the area, who forthwith appointed a French captain as military commandant of the station. After enquiry at the engine shed, it was learnt that the quantity of reserve coal was not enough for the locomotive. It was necessary to buy a wagonload of wood. M. Jacobson, a passenger from

Bucharest, volunteered to collect it. The Romanian commandant alone gave six hundred crowns to him. The stationmaster undertook to make sure the train would arrive at Vinkovci, a railway focal point north west of Belgrade. Leaving at twenty one hours (nine in the evening) the train reached the junction at four o'clock in the morning. "The sleeping car passengers continued to sleep, but the others had to leave the train and go to a hotel until 15 h. 50 mins, departure time of the express to Trieste". The cost of the second incident: 24 hours delay and a six thousand crowns supplement. Without delay, the passengers made haste to write down their protest demanding "a severe enquiry so that similar acts would not happen again, and that all the money illegally taken would be returned (to them)". An excellent example of "spontaneous" collaboration between the customers and a defaulting administration!

Rarely has a great express had to submit to so many vexations and given so much to dream about. The legendary train is going to "fire" imaginations, and soon inspire novelists and film directors with situations – often authentic – created by a hostile terrain, implacable bad weather, hundreds of kilometres of single track, and striking contrasts between the countries it traverses. But the *Simplon-Orient Express* plays its part, equal to any challenge: it is the umbilical cord of Europe.

The cars which made up the train for the most part were those of the pre-1914 *Simplon Express*. They consisted of a wooden framed body resting on a metal underframe or mixed timber and metal underframe (chassis). Their waist-line of brown teak was the 'livery' synonymous with luxury and comfort. But this rolling stock (R type) had suffered. It was time to think of renewing this fleet of cars, – although the last continued in service until 1964, – and to give the train the latest refinements of modern technique.

The first all-steel cars that appeared in 1922 were remarkable for their blue tint, lined in gold. The story goes on how these new colours on the cars of the Wagons-Lits Company came about. When the factory had finished the construction of the first car, and it had to go in the paint shop,[8] they hesitated to paint them the old brown colour of the teak cars. The chief of the workshops discussed this with his management who in turn consulted the Director, M. André Noblemaire. He remembered his *chasseur alpin* uniform (Alpine Light Cavalry), and he loved the dark blue decorated with gold braid. Why not, then, choose these colours? Dark blue, blue like the night, the gold like the rising sun. After all was that not the obvious epitome of a journey by sleeping car?

These new cars, weighing 53 tonnes, in which mahogany and poplar wood were used for the marquetries, had 16 berths, divided into compartments of one single bed, and four compartments of two beds (double), connected two by two by a large washroom conforming to the classic layout.

The entry into service of these new cars (type S), whose appearance was so different from the old cars, was officially devoted to their incorporation in the *Calais-Mediterranée* Express, which the public had soon christened Blue Train (*Train Bleu*). Little by little sleeping cars of this model were introduced in the other great trains, and notably in the *Simplon-Orient Express*.

The first all-steel dining cars with 42 and 56 seats, built on the same principle and equally painted blue, emerged from the workshops[9] in 1925. Thus completely homogeneous rakes of cars were built up. Later, in 1929, the construction of 'grand luxe' (LX) cars was reserved for the new *Train Bleu*.

---

115. *This heading which capped the* Simplon-Orient Express *timetable prospectus mentions the special motor boat service between the European and Asiatic stations at Istanbul, which the Bosphoros separates. Note also the C.I.W.L. motor car service between Rayak and Haifa providing the connection between the S.O.E. and the Palestinian towns. "This train includes a fourgon (van) with shower room" says the publication (bottom, right): a comfort appreciated by the traveller from London to Cairo.*

116. *On 15th February 1930 the C.I.W.L. gave a luncheon for the inauguration of the* Taurus Express, *served at the Hotel Tokatlian at Stamboul. The menu, printed in French and Turkish, was: Hors d'oeuvre, Sole Mornay, Poulet Ali Pacha, Carré d'agneau, Salade, Biscuits glacés, Fromages, Fruits, Café. (Sole, Chicken, Shoulder of lamb, Iced Biscuits, Cheese.)*

117. *In 1937 at Calais Maritime station the* Simplon Orient Express *is on the quay waiting for the passengers whose porters (ship's stewards) carry down the luggage from the ship which has just crossed the Channel. The daytime passengers changed trains while the train ferry only ran at night with special F-type sleeping cars (London-Paris, Night Ferry).*

118. *The* Simplon-Orient Express *in 1930, passing in front of Chillon Castle (Switzerland), hauled by a Swiss Federal Railways' Ae 4/7 engine (Built 1927, many of these "old-timers", as the Swiss call them, are still running in 1987. They often haul the Nostalgic Istanbul Orient Express.)*

8. Built at Leeds by Leeds Forge Co., Yorks, these cars were sent unpainted to Immingham, Lincs., where they were fitted out before shipment by train ferry from Immingham to Calais. It is believed the first one was sent over unpainted from Immingham; the rest were painted at Immingham, it is said. (Nos. 2641-2680).

9. Birmingham Carriage & Wagon Co. Ltd., Birmingham (Nos 2867-2881). Four are still in service. The first all steel dining car (no 2693) was built by Dyle & Bacalon, Bordeaux, 1925. Note by GB.

SIMPLON-ORIENT EXPRESS (1ʳᵉ et 2ᵉ Classe)

Quotidien entre (London) CALAIS-PARIS-ISTANBUL
et PARIS-LAUSANNE-MILANO-ZAGREB { BUCURESTI / ATHENES

Correspondances tri-hebdomadaire pour ALEP-NISSIBIN-BASSORAH, bi-hebdomadaire pour RAYAK-LE-CAIRE
Traversée du Bosphore de ISTANBUL (Sirkedji) à HAYDARPASA sur des vedettes spéciales
Service d'Automobiles de la Cie des Wagons-Lits entre RAYAK-HAIFA et des Chemins de fer de l'Irak entre NISSIBIN-KIRKUK
Wagons-Lits directs, 1ʳᵉ et 2ᵉ classes quotidien entre WIEN-BEOGRAD quadri-hebdomadaire entre WIEN-ATHÈNES PRAHA-ISTANBUL
et BERLIN-ISTANBUL, tri-hebdomadaire entre (London) OSTENDE-ISTANBUL et BERLIN-ATHÈNES
Réduction du prix de transport des bagages de Londres et Paris pour Istanbul, Bucuresti, Athènes et vice-versa
Voitures comportant des compartiments à une place   Ce train comporte un fourgon avec salle de douche

BEOGRAD — L'Université

ISTANBUL (Stamboul) — Mosquée de Suleymanié

DEJEUNER OFFERT
par la
Compagnie Internationale
des «WAGONS LITS»
à l'occasion de l'Inauguration du train
TAURUS EXPRESS

15 FEVRIER 1930

HOTEL M. TOKATLIAN
STAMBOUL

Until 1939, progress of all kinds was brought to the composition and the timetable of the *Simplon-Orient Express*, which ran in three directions:
- *Turkish Branch*: Calais-Paris-Milan-Belgrade-Nis-Constantinople (3,342 km);
- *Greek Branch*: Paris-Milan-Belgrade-Nis–Salonica-Athens (3,170 km);
- *Romanian Branch*: Paris-Milan-Vincovci-Timisoara-Bucharest (2,677 km);

and which, also included the following branches (with direct through sleeping cars): Ostend-Istanbul (via Brussels-Vienna-Budapest-Belgrade); Berlin-Istanbul or – Athens via Breslau (Wroclaw) – Budapest-Belgrade); Prague-Istanbul (via Galanta-Budapest-Belgrade).

These trains were beautiful, composed of four sleeping cars and a dining car; people wondered at the opulent look which the varnished teak gave them; the destination plates which gave birth to dreams, the soft interior which made Valerie Larbaud say that it was in a sleeping car cabin that he had tasted all the pleasures of life for the first time.

In the stations, during stops, the passers-by on the platform loved to look in the open windows at the glistening, stylish interior of the compartments with their mahogany partitions enriched with multi-coloured marquetries and ornamental bronze, veritable mobile boudoirs about to leave for the Orient.

This was the time when crowned heads, grand dukes, English lords, the highest political personages and all the east European aristocracy mingled together with American multi-millioinaires who travelled across Europe.

"I sing of Europe, its railways and its theatres" proclaimed Larbaud, the man who had "memories of towns like one had memories of love" and who could not resist this sumptuous journey across a fairytale, frontier-free world.

Larbaud was not the only one to worship this "cult of Wagons-Lits", to quote Jean d'Ormesson's expression: poets, writers and musicians have in their own manner sung the praises of the luxury trains, seeing there a quick and pleasant way of changing their place of residence while enjoying a real "high society life". The *modus vivendi* was facilitated by the fact that the trains only carried a limited number of passengers who, as on a liner, lost little time in getting to know each other. Intimacy only gets stronger between travelling companions in the course of conversations or meals taken together in the dining car, accomplices in the glimmer of the lampshades...

The conditions for putting the *Orient Express* and the *Paris-Prague-Warsaw Express* back into circulation in 1919 were made doubly difficult by objections of all kinds on the part of the German government: the bad state of the tracks, lack of coal, wear and tear of engines... This government, despite its agreement, did not see these trains pass over its territory with a favourable eye.

So it was decided to make a new *Orient Express* which avoided passing through Germany and which reached Vienna by Switzerland and Austria, using the route Basle-Buchs-Arlberg Tunnel-Innsbruck-Salzburg. After several months' trial, (February-June 1920), it was decided to establish this new train which carried the name *Suisse-Arlberg-Vienna Express* (Switzerland-Arlberg-Vienna Express). Starting on 20th June 1920, the *Orient Express* once more passed through Germany, but the occupation of the Ruhr in 1923 necessitated that it once again took the line through Basle, Buchs, and the Arlberg Tunnel and it was only on 3rd November 1924 that the political situation permitted it to take the classical route again through Strassbourg-Munich, not without leaving the Swiss Federal Railways with some regrets; they, however, had scarcely welcomed it favourably during this transitional period.

In May 1932, the *Suisse-Arlberg-Vienna Express,* in whose composition

119. *Y-type sleeping car No. 3704 built in 1931 by Gebrüder Credé, Kassel-Niederzwehren, Germany. First Class double cabin in night position.*

120. *The communicating door between two cabins, of this same car. (Note the camouflaged swastika-pattern upholstery on the arm-rest, not noticeable on the ladder in illustration 119, not bought intentionally by C.I.W.L.! Note by GB)*

121. *Sleeping car No. 3704 had 11 cabins, with 2 beds maximum, and a pantry.*

119

120

121

122

were sleeping cars for Bucharest and Athens, changed its name to become the *Arlberg-Orient Express*. A new *Orient Express* was born and its renown was not slow to reach that of its two elder brothers.

Running three times a week, the *Arlberg-Orient Express* became a real tourist train, giving great pleasure over some 500 kilometres of the most picturesque parts of the Alps. At the same time it benefitted from the infatuation with winter sports, which set up such a demand from December to February that it was necessary to run a train of sleeping cars every day to serve the ski resorts. The *Arlberg-Orient Express*, the *Oberland Express* and the *Engadine Express* ran united in the tourist season.[10]

The famous Vorarlberg and Tyrolean ski resorts were thus just one night's train journey away: Zurs, Lech, Oberlech, Saint Anton, Innsbruck with its satellites Kitzbuhel, Zell-Am-See.

The Arlberg-Orient Express was provided with 16-berth all-steel sleeping cars (Type S) divided into cabins of one or two beds. After the last war, 2nd class was introduced first on the central Europe sector, then little by little to the whole of the journey.[11]

An unquestionable complement to the *Orient Express*, operated on days when it did not itself run, the *Arlberg* was a fundamental transport implement for East-West communications. The length of the journey was: 21 h. 20 mins. for Paris-Vienna (1,467 km); 25 h. 25 mins. for Paris-Budapest (1,757 km); 47 h. for Paris-Bucharest (2,658 km); 61 h. 31 mins. for Paris-Athens (3,341 km).

At the time when the Germany of the Hohenzollerns was not hiding her ambition to become a great oriental power, the question of creating a *Berlin-Bagdad* luxury train often arose: starting from the Asiatic shore of the Bosphorus, it would penetrate into Mesopotamia, and, (why not?) beyond.

In Asia Minor the different railway networks were developed little by little, enabling a liaison to be made with those of Europe. A junction with the *Simplon-Orient Express* permitted southern Europe to profit from the role reserved by Germany for central Europe in the project, abandoned between Berlin and Belgrade with the defeat of the Second Reich.

The delegates of the railway administrations concerned in the *Simplon-Orient Express* met in 1925 at Baden-Baden the representatives (German) of the Anatolia and Bagdad railways, and of the French operating company of the Bozanti-Aleppo-Nissibin railway (the part of the Bagdad now in Syria) with a view to extending European-style passenger services beyond the Bosphorus.

Among the consequences of the Great War, the transfer of the capital of the new Turkey to Angora (Ankara), the conferring of the mandate for Syria to France and those of Mesopotamia (Iraq) and Palestine to Great Britain, made themselves felt quickly in the extension of great international communications.

10. *Oberland*: Calais/Paris-Chaumont-Belfort-Delle-Bern-Interlaken (Ost). *Engadine*: Calais/Paris-Chaumont-Belfort-Basle-Zurich-Sargans-Chur (-St. Moritz). *A.O.E.*: Chaumont-Belfort-Basle-Zurich-Sargans-Buchs-Arlberg-Orient.
11. The authors mean World War I. The A.O.E. also use Z type, 12 cabins, 1 or 2 beds, no communicating doors nor pantry. See page 109. Notes by translator.

123

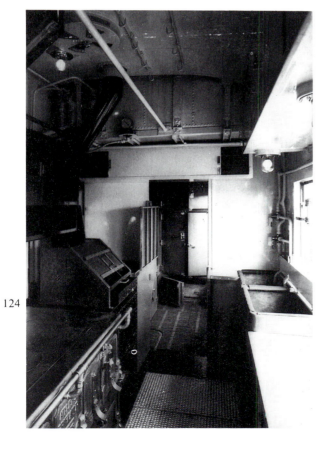

124

125

122. Dining car No. 3785, built entirely of steel (no marquetry) in 1932 by Cegielski Works, Poznan, Poland.
123. Its dining saloon, arranged for fifty-six covers, with fixed seating.
124. Interior of its kitchen, with coal-fired range, pantry side.
125. Insulation of the wine cellar by special materials.

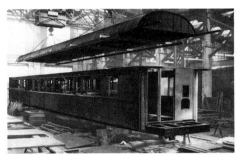

126. *Four different phases in the construction of a sleeping car in Simmering Works near Vienna (Austria): building-up the underframe, the roof, the body and the cabins.*
127. *Three menus: French (of the Est) (July 1925), Romanian and Hungarian (January 1930). A suggestion: "Passengers are asked, in their own interest, to lift their glass at the moment they are refilled." ... Among the drinks: "Nutritious medicinal beer".*
128. *Luggage Labels in 1920.*
129. *Map of the network of the* Simplon-Orient Express *and of the* Taurus Express *in 1930-1931, with their ramifications in Europe and in Asia. A family of illustrious trains.*

As Constantinople had ceased to be the seat of the Turkish government, this gave rise to the opinion that the town could no longer be the terminal point of lines converging on the Bosphorus. The Mandatory Powers in a part of Asia Minor extended their sphere of influence and took on new responsibilities. As for Turkey, she was no longer a great power, and her new legislative and economic establishments tended to bring her closer to European methods.

At this conference, it was decided that the agencies and stations situated on the route of the *Simplon-Orient Express* would issue direct tickets and accept luggage for the most important stations of the Asia Minor network; and that on this network, from 1927, luxury services, connecting with the arrivals and departures of the *Simplon-Orient Express* would start to function in the following directions:

A thrice-weekly sleeping car train named *Anatolie Express* (Anatolia Express) would be created between Haidar Pacha (Haydarpasa) and Angora (Ankara) via Eski-Chehir (Eskisehir). Length of the journey: 14 hours: a twice-weekly sleeping car service between Haydarpasa and Tripoli in Syria, via Eskisehir, Konya, Adana, Aleppo: about 58 hours for the journey of 1,728 kilometres.

For its part, the Wagons-Lits Company engrossed itself in providing a connection between Tripoli and Cairo, so as to offer its clientele an alternative to the sea route and to suggest round voyages.

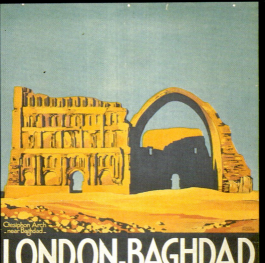

130. *London-Bagdad Poster by Roger Broders published in 1931 for the* Simplon-Orient Express *and* Taurus Express *services.*
131. *London-Cairo Poster published in 1930 for the London-Cairo service of the* Simplon-Orient Express.
132. Simplon-Orient Express *services Poster representing a view of Aleppo by Jean de la Nezière, published in 1927.*
133. Simplon-Orient Express *services Poster representing a view of Venice by Georges Dorival, published in 1921.*
134. Simplon-Orient Express *services Poster representing a view of the Acropolis, Athens by Jean de la Nezière, published in 1927.*
135. Simplon-Orient Express *and* Taurus Express *services Poster by André Wilkin, published in 1930.*
136. *Cover (front and back) of the Orient Express Folder with summer timetable 1929 illustrated with charcoal drawings enriched with pastel by S. Musson.*

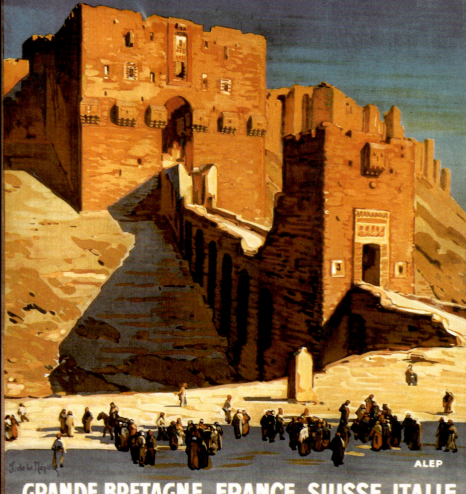

134

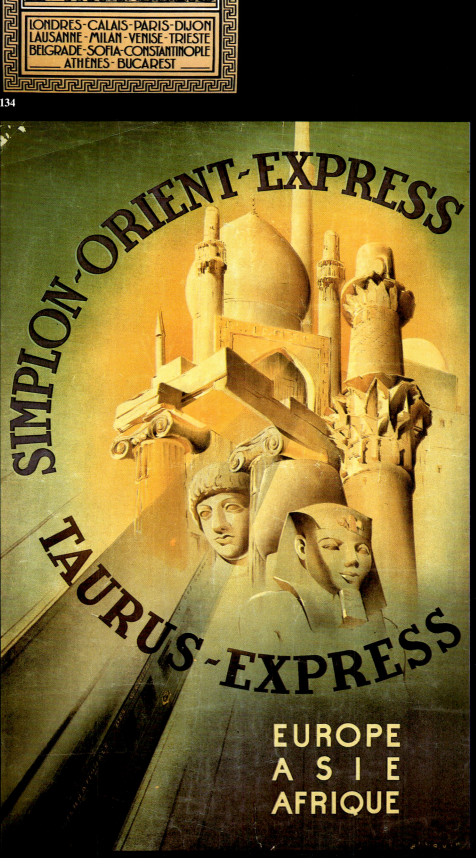

135

136

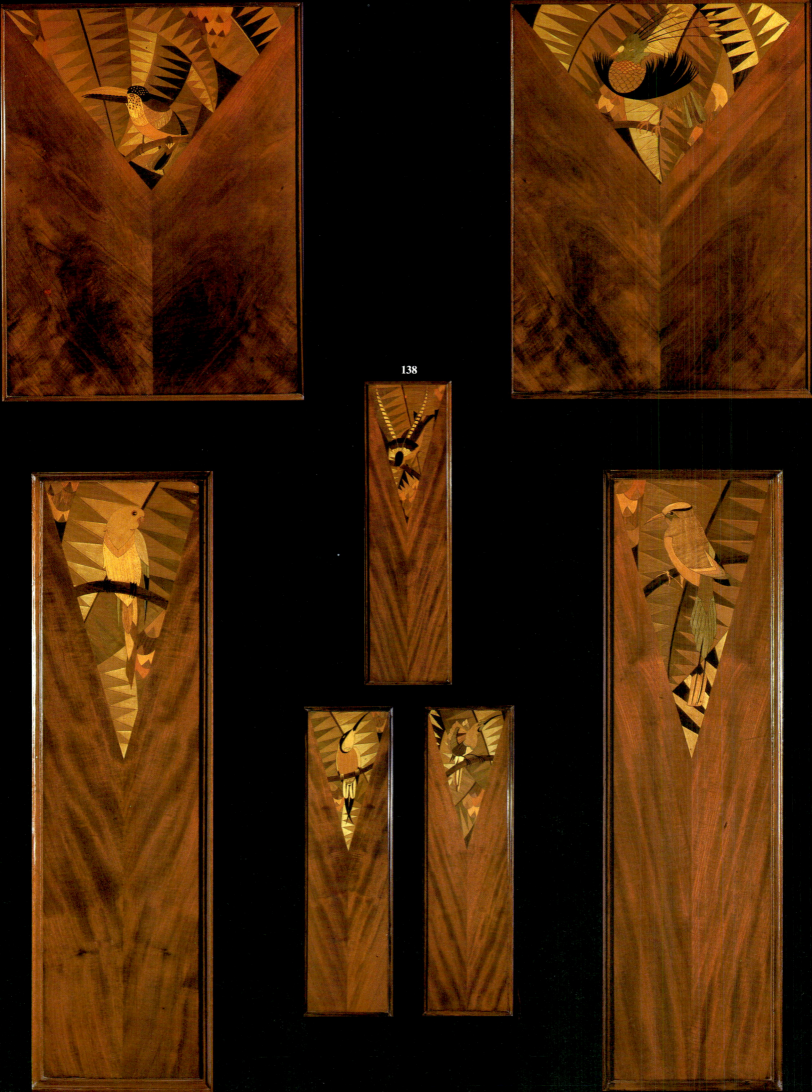

138

Between Tripoli and Haifa, where the Palestine Railways began, the lines not being continuous, it started a motor service which linked the two stations, connecting with the railway at each end. 10 hours were needed for this journey of 252 kilometres (some of it along the beach!)

From Haifa to Cairo, the standard gauge allowed a bi-weekly service to function which served Lydda (with connection for Jerusalem), Rafa and Cantara (El Kantara)[12]: length of the journey 14 hours, distance 610 km. Thus London and Paris would be linked by a land line with the principal Near East towns.

Would one be able to pass from Europe to Asia by a submarine tunnel under the Bosphorus? It seems that financial rather than technical difficulties opposed this venture. So a regular service of motorboats, placed under the control of the Wagons-Lits Company, was started between the Stamboul station (Sirkeci) and that at Hayderpasa. The timetable of the period provided nightstops at Stamboul or Haydarpasa since the Turkish administration would not allow night running in this region.

At the Vienna conference in October 1928 the C.I.W.L. obtained from the Turkish Railways delegate the suppression of these stops and the reduction of the Paris-Cairo journey by nearly thirty-six hours. Thus in the two years 1927 to 1929, innovations had been made to include Ankara in the list of capitals served by the luxury trains, to link Egypt to the European railway network, to facilitate access to Syria and Palestine, and lastly to anticipate much better relations with western Asia and Persia.

At a time when the airlines only offered a few possiblities for inter-continental journeys, these new railway services made a sensation. Future advances made new connections with Persia possible, besides the completion of the trans-Persian railway from Bendershahu (Bandarchah) on the Caspian and Chapour (Shahpur) on the Persian Gulf.

In 1929 Charles Loiseau spoke of "a very evident renewal of realism and even popularity in favour of a Channel Tunnel which has been displayed on the other side of the Straits of Dover"!

Charles Loiseau "takes note of public sympathy" given to this project and discerns there "a beginning of evolution in the British psychology"! The "sea serpent" which reappeared once again will not delude the Wagons-Lits Company, who will not wait for this hypothetical submarine passage to start a direct Paris-London sleeping car service a few years later, in 1936, thanks to the "Night Ferry"[13]. The desire to avoid any change of carriage made Charles Loiseau dream of a direct London-Cairo train which would use one tunnel under the Channel and another under the Bosphorus!

Charles Loiseau's dreams of tunnels have come true in 1987. The Channel Tunnel was set in motion perhaps finally on 29th July 1987 from Cheriton England to Frethun, France respectively near Folkestone & Calais. 35 km. The Bosphorus Tunnel is to be started from Yenikapi (Europe) to Sogutlusme (Asia) 9 km (2 km under Sea).

On 15th February 1930, the *Taurus Express* is officially inaugurated. It had a twice weekly service for Nissibin (Nisep), a weekly service to Mardine (Mardin), and a thrice weekly service to Rayak, for Beyrut (Beirut) and Damascus. At the same moment when the Taurus Express, on the Aleppo-Bagdad line, kept off her frontier, Persia which like all the countries suffered from the economic depression, decided to protect herself and promulgated laws on the monopoly of trade and the export of currency. So it was in a difficult climate that the delegate of the C.I.W.L. arrived in Teheran to negotiate agreements for setting up a motor service, which ran the connection between the Persian capital and Khanikin, contact point with the

137. Four examples of the marquetries of the sleeping cars built in 1922 by the Leeds Forge Co., Leeds (Great Britain), series 2641 to 2674 (see illustrations 93, 94). These were the first steel cars of the C.I.W.L. They have run in France, in Turkey and in Spain. The first, assigned to the Calais-Méditerranée Express and painted blue and gold, gave this train its name of Train Bleu.

138. Seven of the marquetries decorating the dining cars, series 3341 to 3360, built in 1928 by the Entreprises Industrielles Charentaises at Aytré-La Rochelle (France). A car of this series (No 3348) can be seen at the French National Railway Museum at Mulhouse. The decoration is by Nelson.

12. By teak C.I.W.L. sleeping car. To accommodate larger liners, the Suez Canal Railway Bridge was dismantled between the wars. Crossing by ferry, passengers completed the Kantara West-Cairo journey in a named C.I.W.L. Pullman, two were identical to Ibis (page 140).

13. Lasting until 1980. George Behrend & Gary Buchanan: *Night Ferry*. Jersey Artists (St. Martin, Jersey C.I.) 1985. Notes by translator.

139

(narrow gauge) line of the Taurus Express. To establish this service it was necessary to open a travel office at Teheran, and the installation of a foreign company was not welcomed. Tenacity, patience, and evolution of the political economy ended by conquering the difficulties, the economic interests of a connection between Persia and the West being obvious.

Tourism developed; the C.I.W.L. offered interesting reductions of 25-30% for groups of eight people on the sector London-Paris to Aleppo, Rayak, Tripoli, Kirkuk, Bagdad, Bessorah (Bassora)(Basra). The acceleration of the *Taurus Express* timetable reduced the time of the Haydarpasa-Tripoli journey to 45 hours from 15th May 1933. Comfort was improved by the arrival on 11th November 1936, of the first all-steel cars (type SG). Finally on 31st March 1939 it ran as far as Mosul and on 17th July 1940, it reached Bagdad direct.

The convention (from 1939 to 1972) between the administration of the Posts of the Irak State Ministry of Communications and the International Sleeping Car and Great European Express Trains Company (Wagons-Lits) was as follows:

> The C.I.W.L. undertakes to transport in its fourgons incorporated in the train named *Taurus Express* which runs in Turkey, Syria and Irak between Haydarpasa, Aleppo, Tel Kotchek, Mossoul and Bagdad all the postal mail-bags with foreign destination which are put on board by the Postal administration in Irakian territory, as well as those in transit by Irak from Iran, India, and beyond, as well as those of the administrations served by the S.O.E. and the *Taurus*.
> These mailbags will be carried by the fourgons included in the *Taurus Express* and its extension the *Simplon-Orient Express*.

The length of the journeys at that time were: Haydarpasa-Aleppo (Halab): 35 hours. Haydarpasa-Beyrut: 48 hours. Haydarpasa-Cairo: 3 days and a half. Haydarpasa-Bagdad: 4 days. Haydarpasa-Teheran: 5 days and a half. In total, the London-Cairo journey was made in the record time of seven days.

The route followed by the *Taurus Express* is of higher interest on the historic and touristic level. The line slips between the highlands of the Taurus chain before arriving at the famous Cilician Gates, which has seen the great conquerors pass by: Semiramis, Xerxes, Darius, Alexander the Great, Haroun al-Rachid, Godefroy de Bouillon, Ibrahim Pacha. A strangely beautiful countryside, the train crosses arid and volcanic regions before reaching the Taurus massif, crowned with snow. Intruding among gorges and ravines, thanks to numerous viaducts and tunnels, it proceeds to climb to more than 1,400 metres. Then the superb descent continues to Adana. The

139. *LX (Luxe)-type sleeping car of the series 3496-3555, built in 1929 by the Enterprises Industrielle Charentaises, at Aytré-La Rochelle (France). That bearing the No. 3507 was shown in Paris at the 1937 Universal Exhibition. While another, bearing the No. 3538 was assigned to the service of H.R.H. the Duke of Windsor from 1937 to 1940. A car of this same series (No. 3532 shown here at C.I.W.L. St. Denis works in 1977) is exhibited at the French National Railway Museum, Mulhouse. Seven cars of this type are actually in service in the Nostalgic-Istanbul – Orient Express, operated by Intraflüg Ltd., of Zürich. The marquetries decorating these cars are by the English decorator Nelson.*

140. *On this map which gives the itinerary of the* Taurus Express *and the* Simplon-Orient Express, *the timetable of these two trains is to be found for the years 1938-1939 as well as the weekly cadence of the various services.*

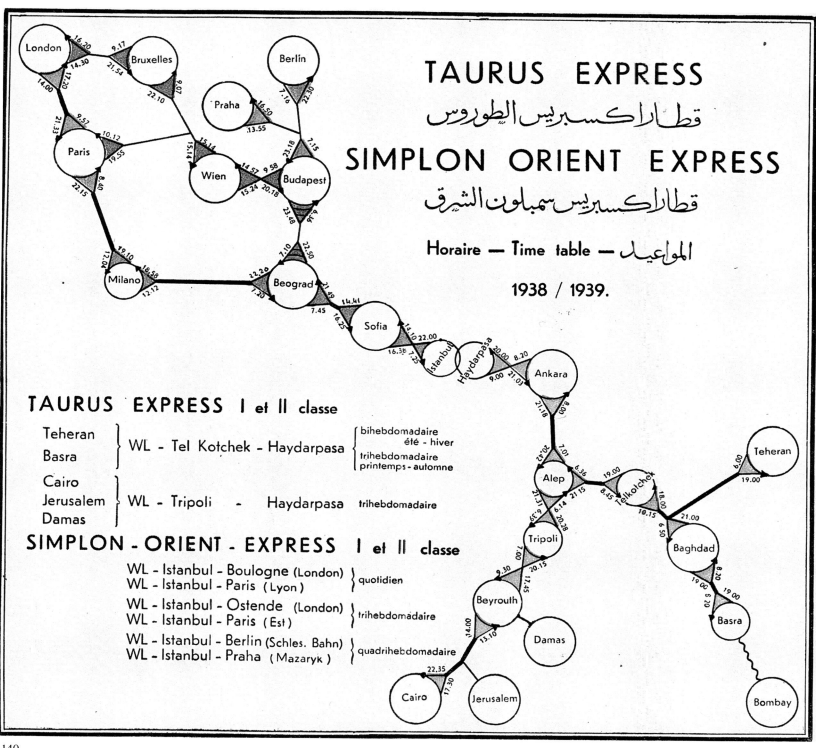

141. *1942: on the lines of Eastern France, the battle of the rails raged. Here a derailment was provoked near Port à Buisou Dumery.*

audacious programme started in 1930 was moving towards fulfilment, with the opening of a railway liasion with Egypt, India, and the Persian Gulf enabling a penetration towards the centre of Asia. A considerable stage had been cleared, securing a better knowledge of peoples and the establishment of economic and cultural exchange between East and West.

1939-1946
Another Battle of the Rails

More grievous, more troublesome for the European connections than the Great War, the Second World War will inflict deep, contagious and irreparable wounds on the *Orient Express*.

On the eve of the conflict, the *Orient Express* united a network of branches, unique in their conception, in conditions of highly evident comfort, and following a perfectly integrated timetable.

It had a western fork of which the two branches coming from Paris (Est) and Calais Maritime (via Amiens, Laon, Reims) joined up at Chalons-sur-Marne. The train afterwards served Strassbourg, Stuttgart, Munich, Salzburg, Linz, Vienna, Bratislava, Budapest and Bucharest.

At Linz, it had a central fork, receiving in addition the *Ostend-Vienna-Orient Express*, via Cologne and Frankfurt. Lastly it had an eastern fork at Budapest, to Belgrade, with sleeping cars going forward Paris-Istanbul, Ostend-Istanbul, and Berlin-Athens.

The *Arlberg-Orient Express* via Basle, Zurich and Innsbruck was made up of cars for Bucharest on the one hand, and Belgrade and Athens on the other.

Lastly, the *Simplon-Orient Express* joined the *Orient Express* at Belgrade. They followed each other a few minutes apart to Nis, where they forked either to Istanbul or to Athens.[1]

For a traveller who had the choice, the comparison of these three great axes, on leaving Paris, was arranged thus:

– *Orient Express*: Day A Paris-Est, depart 19 h. 55 mins. Day C Arrive at Bucharest at 12 h. 15 mins. Day D Arrive at Istanbul at 7 h. 25 mins. Arrive at Athens at 10 h. 16 mins. Time of the journey, 56 hours for Istanbul, 58 hours for Athens.

– *Arlberg-Orient Express*: Day A Paris-Est depart at 19 h. 55 mins. Day C arrive at Bucharest at 18 h. 32 mins. or 5 hours after the *Orient Express*. Day D Arrive at Athens at 10 h. 16 mins.

– *Simplon-Orient Express*: Day A Paris-Lyon depart at 22 h. 15 mins. or 2 h. 20 mins. after the *Orient Express*. Day D Arrive at Athens at 10 h. 16 mins. Arrive at Istanbul at 7 h. 25 mins.

In other words, on the whole of the journey Paris-Athens or Paris-Istanbul, whichever train was chosen, the journey time was the same. It was only on the intermediate connections, and of course the choice of towns, that the comparison could be made.

If we add some secondary connections, for example Munich-Milan, we see that the *Orient Express* is the sole example in the world of a train which is a family of trains. We also see how its functioning was tied to peace in Europe.

A peace more and more menaced, a train more and more fragile.

1. See illustration No. 207. In 1937-1939 the Athens cars were detached at Nis. The S.O.E., two fourgons, up to ten steel sleeping cars and a dining car (Lausanne-Trieste-Svilengrad) made a brave sight, to dream of through the war and not seen again in such length until 1976. The service was retimed and the teak Belgrade-Ristovatz dining car ran in train PA Nis-Salonica, reaching Nis in an ordinary train from Belgrade. Note by GB.

From March 1938, with the forced annexation of Austria to Germany by the Anschluss, the Reichsbahn (German State Railway) absorbed the Austrian Federal Railways and transferred all the Germano-Austrian contracts of the International Sleeping Car Company (Wagons-Lits) to the Mitropa. The Sudeten affair and the dismantling of Czechoslovakia extended this railway annexation.

The independence of Slovakia and the creation of the protectorate of Bohemia-Moravia, jeopardized the normal running of the *Orient Express* in this core of Central Europe of capital importance, by the territorial modifications, not to mention the strained political climate.

In the western sector, during the period called "the phoney war" (September 1939 to the beginning to 1940), the *Orient Express* was suppressed on the declaration of hostilities. By contrast, the *Simplon-Orient Express* continued to run luxuriously all the way to Istanbul and Athens, accepting, curiously at Belgrade, (Yugoslavia was neutral, then), some sleeping cars coming from Berlin... Certain portions (of the *Orient* and *Arlberg-Orient Expresses*) continued to function (Munich-Bucharest, Zurich-Bucharest), but mainly under German control.

After the invasion of France and the armistice of June 1940 (see illustration No. 76), the Wagons-Lits Company's services, amputated, reduced, and unpredictable, functioned under German control in Italy, in Serbia, in Croatia, in Hungary, in Bulgaria and in Romania. The sovereign of this last country, King Carol II who came to the throne in 1930, was one of the high personages who owe their salvation to the *Simplon-Orient Express* during this troubled period. Faced with German and Soviet pressure, he was forced to abdicate on 6th September 1940. The next day, he ordered his special train (two C.I.W.L. Pullmans full of works of art and jewellery) to be attached to the express. In a fourgon, his mistress, Magda Lupescu, had to disguise herself as a cook to flee, as she was detested by the Romanian people and her 15 year liaison with the king had provoked a State scandal. (They alighted in Switzerland).

In its turn, the *Simplon-Orient Express* was suppressed on 16th March 1942.[2] All the *Orient Express* network, split up and dismantled like Europe, was reduced to a few sleeping cars ensuring some limited international connections: Budapest-Bucharest, Budapest-Belgrade, Bucharest-Belgrade, Belgrade-Sofia, Sofia-Istanbul. The Mitropa operated its services as far as Salonica. Isolation and confiscation affected the men as well as the rolling stock, in particular the conductors, who could not abandon their cars, or the chefs de brigade.

Hitlerite Germany attempted to make an ersatz (imitation) *Orient Express* run in the form of a luxury train reserved for the Nazi elite, which should have illustrated the hold of Berlin on Europe. But very quickly, the passengers of this train came to know the dangers of the battle of the rails and the sabotage carried out by the Resistance. In the same way that the *Simplon-Orient Express* had itself been stopped by the partisans in Yugoslavia, the false *Orient Express* often had to be preceded by wagons loaded with stones, in case the line might by dynamited. Cut off from their base, halted, requisitioned (by Mitropa as well as the German Army), damaged and destroyed, the sleeping and dining cars of the *Orient*, the *Simplon* and the *Arlberg* were used to form trains for the military general staff headquarters and hospital trains, notably on the Eastern Front. Numerous Company staff, transformed into members of the resistance carrying documents or messages, where unmasked, arrested and deported.[3]

The regulars of this strange *Orient Express* went from Berlin to the Balkans via Vienna. The service struggled to be comparable to that prior to 1940 to please the dignitaries and important allies on board: the Romanian

---

142. *1941: the sabotage of the lines and the rolling stock by the Railway Resistance pushed the authorities to promise bounties to those who denounced the "saboteurs": a million (francs) for informing . . .*
143. *In spite of these rewards, the battle of the rails continued with heroism: the paralysis of the railway system in France efficiently delayed the occupiers' communications.*
144. *It was not without sadness and bitterness that the railwaymen destroyed or damaged the rolling stock, as seen here (engine No. 140 C 126 (2-8-0) derailed in 1943, at Bécon-Les-Bruyères, near Paris,) as a result of a "switching error of points".*

2. All conductors (to Bucharest as well as Istanbul) by then were (neutral) Turks, based in Milan, (formerly in Paris), so French conductors, allowed to work only to Milan, could work this train as well as others, and avoid forced labour deportation if unemployed. This was the origin of changing conductors, set out on *page. 125.*

3. Seven French conductors were shot for this. The Company managed to transfer some elderly teak sleeping cars from Yugoslavia to Spain, in 1943. Notes by GB.

PRÉFECTURE DE POLICE

UN MILLION DE RÉCOMPENSE

AVIS A LA POPULATION

Ces derniers temps, plusieurs attentats ont été commis contre les voies et le matériel des chemins de fer.

Ces attentats mettent en danger des vies humaines et notamment celles de milliers de travailleurs qui empruntent chaque jour ce moyen de transport ils interrompent les communications et compromettent particulièrement le ravitaillement déjà bien difficile dans la situation actuelle.

En conséquence, la population tout entière, dans l'intérêt général, est invitée à s'associer à la répression et même à la prévention de ces attentats.

Une récompense d'un million de francs est offerte à toute personne qui permettra d'arrêter les auteurs des attentats commis. La discrétion la plus absolue est assurée.

Il y a lieu de fournir tous les renseignements utiles à la Préfecture de Police (Direction de la Police Judiciaire — 36, Quai des Orfèvres. Téléphone : Turbigo 92-00, poste 557).

Marshal Antonescu, the Hungarian Admiral Horthy, the Croat Ante Pavelic, but also Admiral Canaris, head of the German secret service, and Franz von Papen, directing the Nazi espionage at Ankara. Exceptionally, some diplomats of neutral countries could use the train. In July 1944, one of these "privileged" travellers entered the German *Orient Express*. His name was Raoul Wallenberg. His poignant story is one more example of the part played by the train in spite of, and also because of, the war.

A month earlier, just after the Allied landing in Normandy, R. Wallenberg, a Swedish subject – therefore neutral – and a member of one of the wealthiest banking families of Sweden, met near Stockholm, the American Ambassador, Mr. Herschel V. Johnson, President Roosevelt's special representative on the Swedish Committee for refugees. A frank, gallant proposition was put to him:

"Are you willing to go to Hungary to save the surviving jews in the Budapest ghetto, menaced by the gas chamber and the concentration camps? The only way there is the Berlin-Budapest train"

After a time the American continued:

"Unlimited funds will be granted to you in the currency of your choice. That will depend on what you could carry. I ought to state precisely that, officially, the Swedish Consul-General at Budapest will know absolutely nothing about your mission for the benefit of the United States... Officially you will be Third Secretary, and I must remind you that, being neutral, even a purely humane activity could be compromising for your country..."

The Swede had already answered:

"If I can save a single person, I ought to try...„

Eight days later, with luggage which he could carry himself, Raoul Wallenberg crossed the frontier of occupied Denmark. The German and Hungarian money in his clothes did not exceed the permitted amounts. In his suitcases were more important sums, and above all, a list of anti-nazi Hungarians as well as members of the Horthy administration, secretly preparing negotiations with the Russians. Clearly this was not very wise, but the Swede counted on his diplomatic passport. He stayed only three days in Berlin, the time needed by his embassy to reserve him a berth in the phantom *Orient Express*.

The train, made up of three coaches, contained one sleeping car with a "Reserved" plate on the side, and the curtains drawn. On this summer night, Raoul Wallenberg was the only passenger not of german nationality. Equally

badly received by the officers of the Wehrmacht and a sarcastic civilian, the "diplomat" was as cautious as possible. The journey was interminable, with air raid alerts and stops to let trains of tanks and hospital trains pass by. After more than thirty hours and meals composed solely of black bread and stale sausages bought at buffets, the train finally rolled into Hungary. The sarcastic civilian suddenly became affable, explaining that he was the deputy of Riecke, the German Minister of Food. He slipped some bitter remarks into his conversation about the inefficiency of the German bureaucracy and spoke of the Allied progress in France. Wallenberg was on his guard: he was sensible; the civilian was really a Colonel in the Gestapo...

At Budapest, the Swede accomplished an extraordinary task and succeeded in saving thousands of Jews by placing them under Swedish protection.

October 1944. The Russian and Romanian troops were not more than a hundred kilometres from Budapest. Wallenberg's mission was completed. Marshal Malinovsky showed himself friendly towards him, but the sinister Beria, supreme head of the N.K.V.D., the political police, had other ideas about him. Arrested as a spy, Wallenberg was transferred to Moscow and shut up in the notorious prison of Lubyanka.

Peace returned; all trace was lost of the courageous Swede. During ten years, protests and appeals both American and Swedish came up against a hostile silence. It was not until 1956 that Mr. Gromyko, then Soviet Foreign Affairs Minister, informed the Swedish Ambassador in Moscow that he had recently learnt that Raoul Wallenberg had "died of a heart attack on 17th July 1947" without any other details. A natural or "accidental" death? One will never know. Only some of those who were saved thanks to him, remember this young man, dead at the age of thirty-four, who had risked his life for so many unknown people, in daring to take the most alarming of the *Orient Expresses*.

1945. Numerous services, suppressed in the summer of 1944, restarted in Romania (January), Bulgaria (January), Czechoslovakia (September). In Germany, it was in the month of August that a military train with sleeping cars and a dining car started to run from Paris to Frankfurt at the request of the American army. In addition, hospital trains using fifty cars, and military headquarters trains, notably for General Eisenhower, were also running. Little by little, as fast as they progressed into Germany, the Americans returned their rolling stock to the Company, expressing the wish that the

145. 25th August 1944: the German army capitulated. Paris was liberated. General de Gaulle met General Leclerc at Montparnasse Station (Paris).
146. 1945: the first survivors of the death camps here seen arriving at the Gare de l'Est, (Paris). The train, symbol of the deportation exodus, became the symbol of liberation.
147. 1947: the Railway Resistance is honoured at Strassbourg, where the railwaymen march past with a French flag decorated with a locomotive.

staff take up their functions which were very greatly appreciated. By contrast in Greece, in Hungary, in Yugoslavia and in Poland, the services could not be restarted, because of heavy destruction of the route and works, and of the railway rolling stock (i.e. engines).

On 27th September 1945, four and a half months after the German capitulation, the first civil international liaison was restarted on the axis of the *Arlberg-Orient Express*. The train linked Paris to Innsbruck three times a week.

The first peacetime journey is solemn. French army officers, S.N.C.F. and Wagons-Lits personalities are on board, on leaving Paris-Est. Swiss Federal Railway officials join them in Switzerland. Arriving in Austria, the train stops at each station decked out in flags. At Innsbruck headquarters of the French Zone of occupation, a military band and a guard of honour welcome the train. On 13th October, the wooden bridge over the Inn being strengthened, the connection is extended to Vienna, where the train is welcomed by the Mayor and the Austrian Minister of Transport. On all these cars is a panel: *Allied Forces*. This event, whose symbolism is obvious, marked the beginning of restarting the great European links, thanks to this vital artery. On the 8th January 1946, the *Simplon-Orient Express* sets off again as far as Venice, three times a week. On 7th October it became daily, but the liaison with Belgrade was only four times a week. On 1st January 1947, the sleeping car service reached Sofia, the terminus. Istanbul had to wait until March 1953 to be directly linked to Paris in a regular manner. The service for Athens was not re-established until 1950; indeed the Graeco-Yugoslav frontier was shut as a result of the British occupation of Macedonia.[4]

Lastly, the *Orient Express* was put back into circulation between Paris and Linz on 1st April 1946, then on 5th August from Paris to Vienna, with sleeping cars for Prague and Warsaw detached at Stuttgart; on 7th October, at the price of unprecedented efforts, "the *Orient Express* family" was run more or less normally, in a record time after the end of hostilities. Certainly there were still predicaments, and the disorder of temporary tracks. So the *Orient Express* was joined to the *Arlberg* between Salzburg and Vienna. And it was the *Arlberg* which ensured the services to Budapest. Moreover it was only on 9th May 1948 that this sector of the *Orient* was prolonged to Bucharest. And for Istanbul one must change trains at Sofia.

These efforts must be emphasised, for, inspite of the peace in Europe in the immediate post-war period, operations ran foul of multiple destruction and pilfering of all sorts. From June 1945, aided by the Allied military authorities, a search party examined and recovered rolling stock in running order, but often camouflaged and sometimes totally unrecognisable.

In the general inventory of the Company's fleet, one hundred and eighty-nine cars were never recovered, two hundred were heavily damaged but restorable, sixty were totally destroyed, and fifty, reaching the age limit, had to be withdrawn. At the detail level, the linen, the crockery, the glasses, the bedding and different accessories were all in short supply, (missing). Their renewal was the more difficult as numerous workshops of the Wagons-Lits had, clearly, suffered from the war.

The luxury of the king of trains and train of kings often appeared to belong to another age. The real luxury was to travel across ravaged Europe and delight in a meal that appeared sumptuous in these times of rationing. In spite of the peace, the ambience was grey. And other tensions would appear.

Bruised, injured but convalescing, the *Orient Express* had not finished suffering.

4. It was the communists who closed their frontier with Greece. The Bulgars did too, delaying the Istanbul O.E. which until 1976 passed through a small part of Greece. Note by GB.

1946-1962
The Train of the Cold War

Great victors of Nazi Germany, the U.S.A. and the U.S.S.R. are not on the same level. The American industrial and financial power was intact and reinforced on the military side by the possession of the atom bomb. Fearing a "capitalist domination" of central Europe, the Soviet government re-annexed the territories acquired in 1939 by the Berlin-Moscow pact, that is to say eastern Poland, the Baltic States and Bessarabia. At the same time the Soviet Union, which had extended itself in the Far East, increased its control of East Prussia and Eastern Europe by Red Army occupation.

And on 5th March 1946, Winston Churchill hurls his famous description at Moscow, accusing her of letting *an iron curtain fall on Europe*. The extension of communist regimes brings the two blocs face to face, and some major tensions are illustrated by the blockade of Berlin (June 1948-May 1949), the breaking away of Tito's Yugoslavia, refusing the tutelage of Moscow, the separation of Germany into two parts and the signing of the N.A.T.O. treaty (April 1949).

148

In a Europe broken in two by ideological, economic and military rivalry, the existence of the *Orient Express* and its branches was both a challenge and a necessity, bearing witness to the evolution of ideas and techniques.

149

In re-starting its pre-war journey on 1st June 1948, the *Orient Express* lost its label of luxury train. Crossing the socialist Republics of Hungary and Romania it had imposed alongside sleeping cars and dining cars ordinary seat coaches of first, second and third class. By way of compensation, the *Arlberg-Orient Express* received in 1949, a second class Pullman car. For such a train, it was a great novelty. It ran on the Basle-Vienna sector which escaped the democratisation enforced on the rest of the journey. One of these cars, No. 4127, built in England in 1927, gave a romantic feel to the train of Europe-in-crisis. It was equipped with fixed seats, some of which could be lowered, divided into two saloons providing in total, fifty one places. The interest in Pullman cars, in principle reserved for day journeys, was that they permitted a soft, comfortable journey, even in second class, in the midst of incessant and meddling controls, not to mention interminable stops at frontiers. These harassments were explained by the number of runaways trying to escape from the communists. At Vienna, occupied by the four victorious powers in 1945, the Soviet surveillance came on board the train to

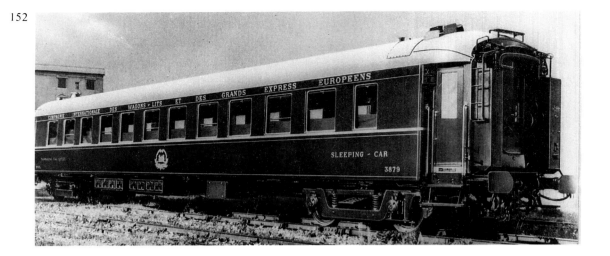

148. *Corridor of sleeping car No. 3879.*
149. *Single berth cabin.*
150. *The pantry with new plastic material imitating wood.*
151. *The lavatory at the ends of the car.*
152. *Y-type sleeping car No. 3879, built in Italy by the Ansaldo Works at Genoa in 1950. The corridor carpet and marquetries in the 'single' cabin, indicated that the Orient Express had begun a new adventure. There was once again confidence in the peace.*

hunt out the fugitives and the war criminals hiding in the toilets or in the narrow recesses of the cabins. The Allied Control Commission registered numerous complaints which only received vague excuses in reply, while silence – and freedom – was bought with watches, cigarettes and silk stockings... Even the wife of a top official of the Austrian Railways was scrupulously controlled as a "capitalist" because she travelled free in first class...

Until the "Prague coup" (25th February 1948), a powerful blow by which the communists made certain of absolute control of power in Czechoslovakia – and provoked considerable anxiety in western Europe – the capital of Bohemia was the turntable of traffic for the East. After the "Prague blow" the frequency of Wagons-Lits sleeping cars bound for the Bohemian capital was singularly reduced, to say the least. The conductors lived through dangerous hours and practically chained themselves to their cars, for fear of being arrested on the least pretext. Currency smuggling was discovered: one thousand five hundred dollars in the lavatory of a sleeping car, other greenbacks in the deep freeze of a dining car. The Czech police were not pleased; in case of fraud, the whole train was banned from running, that is to say put on a siding and all passengers lengthily interrogated. The repetition of these happenings baited the progressive litigation against the monopoly, given, by contract, to the Wagons-Lits Company. The "Iron Curtain" countries judged it too capitalist and prepared to abolish its presence on their territory. The agreements were denounced by Yugoslavia in 1947, Romania in 1948, Czechoslovakia and Hungary in 1949, Bulgaria in 1950. In all these countries, the C.I.W.L. internal services were rescinded.

Two *Life* magazine American journalists, Ray Rowan and the photographer, Jack Birns, tried the experience of the train during the Colder and Colder war. Their trip started badly: even the French or Swiss police and customs appeared for two hours while passports were examined under a magnifying glass. Some passengers, searched with care, were led into the offices where they were made to undress. The same procedure occurred at the Hungaro-Romanian frontier. At Lokoshaza, a halt for two and half hours: at Curtici, at five hour stop. The Vienna-Bucharest sector (about 1,300 km.) lasted thirty-five hours! The travellers, exhausted, noted with care that the bulbs were unscrewed three hundred times, the toilets visited twenty times and fifty people suspected.

On the line of the *Arlberg-Orient Express* an espionage affair unfolds, worthy of the best novelists concerning an action which will inspire Ian Fleming, creator of James Bond, the agent 007 who fights in the Istanbul-Venice train, with a Graham Greene-style atmosphere, grey and black, an alarming world where the tunnels are traps, and the wreaths of smoke a curtain of mystery.

One evening in March 1948, two American ladies, Lucille Vogeler and her sister, Wilhelmine Eykens, boarded the train, bound for the Tyrol where they were going to go skiing. The train left the anguished Vienna of the *Third Man* and rolled towards the Alps. Three hours later, in the middle of the night, the *Arlberg-Orient Express* stopped as ordered on the bridge of the river Enns, a tributary of the Danube, which marked the frontier between the American and Soviet zones. The policemen in red star caps woke up the passengers without consideration, hardly cast an eye on the two ladies' passports and circulation permits, very recognizable grey cards. A not very amiable corporal said immediately in very bad German:

"Your papers are not in order"

And, even less and less amiably.

"Get dressed and leave the train!"

With their cabin door shut again, the ladies dressed as slowly as possible. Mrs. Vogeler tried to simulate a pregnancy, her sister accentuating her unhealthy pallor with lurid make-up. "They hoped by this subterfuge to minimise the customary risk of such Soviet controls: rape."[1]

Ready at last, the corporal – very impatient – ordered them to take their luggage, four suitcases. Following the usual practice, the conductor helped them. On the platform, an officer, accompanied by a sergeant, gave the order to the train to move on.

In a barracks full of soldiers, where a stove smoked, the two ladies, who refused a drink, suffered various proposals, enforced with menaces. After four agonising hours, the travellers obtained permission to go to the nearby village of Saint Valentin, one and a half kilometres away. Curiously, they let them go. At the post office, they wished to telephone to General Keyes, American High Commissioner at Vienna. Impossible: they must have a written authorisation, signed by the Soviet Commandant of the zone. Finally, the employee agreed to sent an appeal telegram for help, addressed to General Keyes. While waiting for a train to Vienna, which should pass by at the end of the morning, the two ladies were interrogated by an English speaking Soviet officer, to whom they related their night's experiences. "Go back to Vienna, and never travel in the Soviet zone again", he said to them. The telegram had produced its results: the Soviet commandant at Vienna set up a rapid enquiry and announced that "the people to blame had been punished".

What went on? Mrs. Vogeler was the wife of a suspected spy. Robert Vogeler, aged thirty-six, was Vice-President for Central and Eastern Europe of the powerful International Telephone and Telegraph Corporation (I.T.T.). His parents were naturalised French and German Americans.

Resident in the American sector of Vienna since 1946, his incessant trips to Prague, Budapest, Zurich and Rome attracted attention to this man who was already considered a saboteur during the war because he had supplied the Soviets with bad quality telephone equipment. Robert Vogeler spent his time on the *Orient Express*: twenty three Vienna-Prague journeys, nine Vienna-Budapest trips. In August 1949 the Hungarian political police (A.V.H.) arrested him and interrogated him. An interrogation full of menaces and promises. If he talked... Accused of spying, his trial opened at Budapest on 17th February 1950. Admitting that he had "some illegal contacts" he was condemned to fifteen years in prison, but he was liberated in April, 1951.

1. E.H. Cookridge, *Orient Express* Random House, 1978.

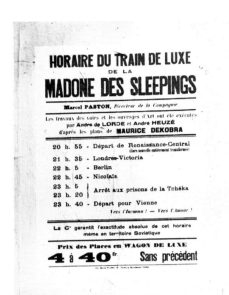

153. *The Renaissance Theatre poster in Paris during the "crazy years", for the play adapted from Maurice Dekobra's novel* The Madonna of the Sleeping cars. *The times of the different scenes are presented like a railway timetable book. 10,000 francs are offered, besides, to anyone who can prove that the scene-changing lasts more than 70 seconds.*

154. *The diorama representing the* Orient Express *on the front of the Renaissance Theatre made a sensation. By a mechanical function with lighting effects, the train seemed to be moving. According to contemporary witnesses, the effect was impressively realistic.*

This happy ending contrasted with the affair which began two days after the sentence of Robert Vogeler in Hungary, and what was, in reality, a second happening, dramatic this time.

On the morning of the 24th February 1950, the Austrian police discovered, alongside the line in Luz Tunnel, south of Salzburg, the mangled body of a man who evidently fell out of the train in the middle of the night. His face was unrecognizable. The enquiry established that it was thought to be the body of an American diplomat, Captain Eugene Karp, U.S. Naval Attaché at Bucharest embassy. He also travelled often in the *Orient Express* and the *Arlberg-Orient Express*. And it was in the train that he met his compatriot... Robert Vogeler. From neighbours to acquaintanceship, from acquaintances to friendship, the two men often travelled together, arranging to share a double compartment. When Karp – a batchelor – was alone, he stated that the surveillance to which he was subject could transform itself into delicate – and dangerous attention. A pretty blond Hungarian, who asked him if she could sit opposite him in the dining car was a hazard the *Orient Express* kept secret. On the second meeting in the train, Karp was on his guard. After the third, he made enquiries. The C.I.A. who thought Karp in danger, discovered that the pretty blond is none other than the mistress of Matyas Rakosi, Vice-President of the Hungarian Council of Ministers, secretary-general of the Hungarian labour party, a pure Stalinite. That such a woman should be burdened with amusing – and unmasking – him, proved that he was in hot water and in danger of death. The order to recall Karp was given by Washington on the day Vogeler's trial began. The diplomat tried to break loose from his emprisoned compatriot, took some documents to his wife's house, and on 23rd February boarded the Paris-bound *Arlberg-Orient Express*, where he dined in the dining car. After that he disappeared without trace and the conductor of his sleeping car was found drugged. Captain Karp had not returned to his compartment: the bed, normally unmade, had not been used. The escaping traveller must have had an evil meeting in a gangway bellows... Inside his pockets was found the dirk of his friend Vogeler, a sign of recognition agreed between them.

An accident due to fatigue, to drunkenness, to the classic error of mistaking the entrance door for that of the lavatory? The American counter-espionage service applied themselves without delay, to several experiments.

After an orderly search of the train in Paris, the experts threw a sack of sand, the same weight as the diplomat out of the same train at the same place. The sack fell intact into the ballast. So that it crushed itself against the side of the tunnel, two men had to use all their strength to overcome the pressure. A minute examination of the side of the tunnel revealed traces of blood, of flesh, and of clothing about the height of a man. The same day of the *accident*, Mrs. Vogeler received a telephone call. A resolute voice advised her not to forget this *accident* if she wished to see her husband again alive.

In the long and palpitating epic of the *Orient Express*, Captain Karp's is the only official death on this celebrated train. A romance in the best tradition of the suspense filled films about espionage. Captain Karp could not have been aware of what all regular customers know: *Dangerous to Lean Out*.[2]

On the southern axis, the *Simplon-Orient Express* restarted its service on 13th November 1945. The thrice-weekly journey was limited to Sofia until 30th April 1947. On that date the through Paris-Athens was still not re-established. The Yugoslav-Greek frontier stayed shut, British troops occupied Macedonia and the mountain line Salonica-Athens was out of service. The rolling stock of the S.O.E. at this time was made up of different types of sleeping car. From Paris to Brig (Swiss frontier), a sleeping car of the *grande Luxe* series, called LX 16 ran each day. Originally built in 1929 to convey ten passengers – the LX 10 were the most spacious and most beautiful sleeping cars in Europe – after transformation the LX 16 had six double compartments and four singles in the centre. It should be mentioned that two other LX 16 sleeping cars ran daily in the same train, one from Calais to Rome, the other from Paris to Rome. This stems from circumstances resulting from the progressive opening up of European connections. The Lugano timetable conference decided that, provisionally, the S.O.E. would be used for the link Paris-Rome-Florence which, in 1939 was provided by the *Rome Express*. Connection was made at Milan. A Z-type sleeping car ran four days a week in the S.O.E. from Paris to Belgrade, which had compartments of 12 beds, or 24 berths separated 2 by 2 by a partition designed with a kink in the form of a Z. Each compartment could, besides, be used as a single, for 12 passengers.[3] The same type of car was on the portion Paris-Svilengrad (Bulgarian frontier); on Paris-Istanbul, an S-type sleeping car was used, (16 berths, with intermediate washrooms). On Paris-Vienna, also four times weekly, a Z-type or an ST-type (24 berths) sleeping car was included. Lastly, of course, the S.O.E. ran a dining car daily on the sectors Paris-Dijon, Vallorbe-Milan, Milan-Lausanne, Milan-Trieste, Venice-Milan, Milan-Rome, Ljubljana-Belgrade, Sofia-Svilengrad. From Uzunkupru – the Turkish frontier – to Istanbul a Fourgon-Cuisine (Kitchen Van) was attached.

At the beginning of the 1950s, the S.O.E. remained pre-eminently a luxury train, with its maximum rake of seven sleeping cars offering first and second class cabins. The countries it traversed, less subjugated than the others by the Cold war, allowed a service of elaborate rolling stock with quality on board, and a very appreciated regular timetable. There were many good reasons for attempting to use it for various forms of smuggling... At the Swiss-French frontier, the French Customs officers, who knew, obviously, all the conductors regularly working the route, noticed a basket full of apples in the compartment where the man responsible for the car was putting his papers and the different documents entrusted to him by the passengers, in order. One official cried out: "You have some beautiful apples there!" – "Yes... when I saw them in Lausanne station, I could not resist buying them."

2. A plate fastened below the window in English and up to 17 other languages by C.I.W.L. on their cars.
3. Later certain Z cars were modified: Z 22 (22 berths and pantry), ZT (26 berths), ZS (30 berths), and Z3 (33 berths).

TYPES DE WAGONS-LITS

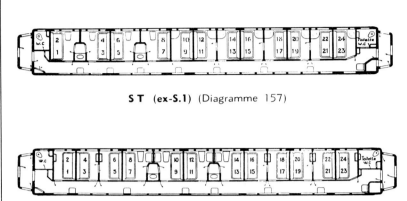

S T (ex-S.1) (Diagramme 157)

S T (ex-S.2) (Diagramme 113)

S.3 (Diagramme 141)

S.4 (Diagramme 70)

S G (Diagramme 127)

S G T (Diagramme 100bis)

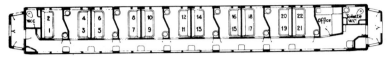

Z.22 (Diagramme 67)

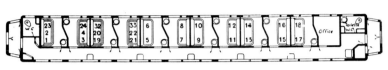

Z T (Diagramme 162)

Z S (Diagramme 53)

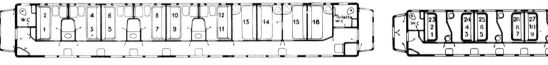

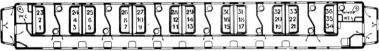

Z.3 (Diagramme 160)

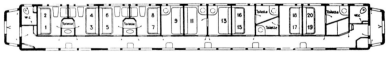

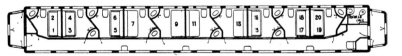

Lx.16 (Diagramme 144)

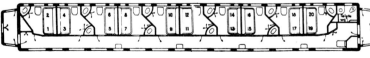

Lx.20 (Diagramme 144)

155. *In 1955, the International Sleeping Car and European Great Trains Company (Wagons-Lits) published a detailed description of its rolling stock. It was divided into four categories: sleeping cars (there were eighteen different types, of which the LX 16 and LX 20 offered 16 to 20 places for the Simplon-Orient Express according to the dispositions; also S4-Spain, SG & SGT — Taurus Express and Turkey, Z22-Orient Express &c, ZS-Denmark, Z3-Greece, F-England — Night Ferry, LJ — Spain, P — Stainless steel Budd-pattern shell introduced 1955, two-level small single-berth cabins: the uneven*

TYPES DE WAGONS-LITS

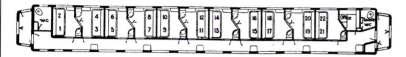

Y (Diagramme 84)

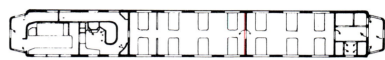

Voiture-Restaurant à 56 places

YT (Diagramme 161)

YUT : dans ces voitures-lits, les 4 compartiments 1/2/23 - 3 4/24 - 19/20/32 - 21/22/33 sont équipés de lits du type « universel »

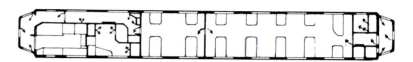

Voiture-Restaurant à 41 places (ex-VPC)

U (Diagramme 159)

Voiture-Pullman (1re classe)

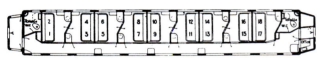

F (Diagramme 115)

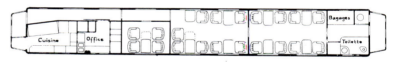

Voiture-Pullman-Cuisine (1re classe)

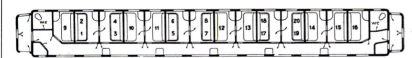

LJ (Diagramme 151)

Voiture-Pullman (2me classe)

P (Diagramme 158)

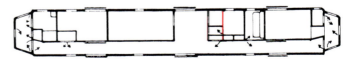

Fourgon

Les numéros impairs concernent les compartiments inférieurs et les numéros pairs les compartiments supérieurs communiquant 2 à 2 et auxquels on accède par les escaliers indiqués sur le diagramme.

numbers refer to the lower compartments, and the even numbers the upper compartments communicating 2 by 2 reached by the stairs shown on the diagram,) dining cars (of 46 or 56 seats), Pullman cars (of first and second class) with or without kitchen, and luggage vans (fourgons) with "birdcage" look-out in the roof (some were equipped with a shower installation). The great expresses (still) ran across an all-steam Europe, offering a very complete choice of accommodation.

Joining in the gist of this remark, the Customs man (was he a glutton or did he know how to find out things?) took possession of the basket and attempted to sniff the fruit. "But how heavy your basket is!" And, under the apples, ingots of gold appear...Classic scenario: a smuggler has 'bought' a conductor. Classic end: the conductor, dismissed, is sentenced, while the smuggler vanishes from life.

"Regrettable" behaviour is no joking matter – including attitudes to dress. A fifty-two page booklet, published by the C.I.W.L. in 1949 lays down, with exemplary detail *an instruction on uniforms and appearance of personnel*. It is the guide book to the great army providing the "luxury on rails" service, illustrated with very clear drawings. Summer and winter uniforms are inspected and described for the heads of the train, conductors, postmen (in the baggage vans), barmen, waiters and assistant waiters, cooks, washers-up and pantry boys, head cleaners, cleaners and fitters. All the hierarchy of the train staff evolved in shell-jacket (dolman), white round jacket (veste blanche), great coat (capote), smocks (blouse C.I.W.L.), waistcoat, wearing cap or 'kepi' (conductor's flat peaked headdress) with a remarkable uniformity. The arbiter of good travelling practice, this regulation states, for example, that:

> Staff provided with a uniform are normally subjected to wear a cap which is particularly obligatory on the station platforms. They salute their superiors carrying the right hand to the peak of this headdress. In the company offices as well as in the saloons of the dining and Pullman cars in whose interiors travellers are to be found, the staff always dress without their headgear on. (article 8).

Gold stripes, oak leaves and side tassels, black chin-straps with gold braid with two buckles, 21 mm and 5 mm brass buttons, peak, semi-lowered, 5.5 cm (wide), service number with figures 8 mm high: no staff dress detail is omitted for those running the grand European expresses who, at each turn of the wheel, share in the reconstruction.[4] The peak of this loyalty is measured on the uniform left breast pocket – except those of heads of the train – the insignia of length of service comprising the Wagons-Lits monogram (W and L intertwined) 28 mm high, and chevrons, one for five years, two for ten years, three for fifteen years, four for twenty years. The *Orient Express* has its old champions who defend the service, the comfort and the safety – in short, a tradition.

In 1951 catastrophic floods in Northern Italy cut the line to Domodossola at the southern portal of the Simplon Tunnel. The S.O.E. was diverted for a month by the Mont Cenis and Turin, to Milan.

More menacing than the bad weather, politics forced the train into other geographical acrobatics. In 1951 the Bulgaro-Greek frontier was shut. The train stopped, according to the notice – and local ill-will – "at Sofia or Svilengrad". However, in 1952 the Greco-Turkish frontier being re-opened, the train could reach Istanbul via Salonica – where one changed sleeping cars – and Thrace, instead of passing through Bulgaria.

Practically reserved for diplomats, the journey was long and risky. On this mountain line in the north of Greece, the communist guerillas threatened the train and it could only run from Salonica to Python (the Greco-Turkish frontier) during the day.[5] The travellers spent the night in the stationary rake, for discretion, in Alexandropolis station on the edge of the Aegean Sea. A wooden S-type sleeping car was still running in the S.O.E., built about 1925 with intermediate washrooms (16 berths). The crossing of Greek territory often took place with a detachment of soldiers, anti-mine wagons and an

156. *Four kinds of regulation dress. In 1949, the uniforms, dress and rules on board the great trains were set out in a small thinly-bound book, as detailed in the text and in the illustrations. Opposite, the uniforms and insignia of heads of the train, conductors, barmen, kitchen-porters-pantrymen, fitters and cleaners.*

157. *The most celebrated personage, surrounded by many stories, the sleeping car conductor with and without his black greatcoat and black cotton gloves over his puce-coloured uniform. He is still wearing the high neck collar. The chevrons on his chest mark his seniority in the Company, at the rate of one chevron for five years service.*

4. Staff, particularly Italians, were permitted to buy their own uniforms, provided they conformed to the details; hence the meticulousness of all the sizes. The result was often smarter than the Company-supplied clothes.

5. In his book "From Russia with Love", Ian Fleming goes via this route; the film does not. Notes by GB.

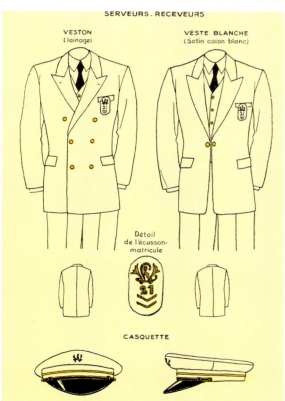

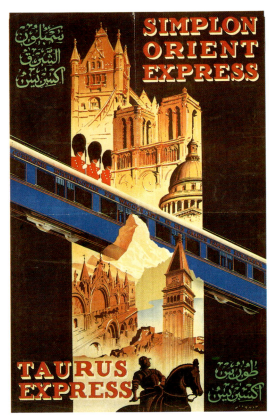

158.

158. Simplon-Orient Express *and* Taurus Express *Poster by Wilquin. The evocation of London and Paris on the one hand and of Milan and Venice on the other, as well as the Swiss mountains traversed by a sleeping car, makes no reference to the Asiatic journey of the* Taurus Express.

159. Simplon-Orient Express *Poster by Barbey, published in 1921. The southern painter Ziem was so famous at that period, for his evocations of Venice and Constantinople that the poster-painter contented himself here to reproducing one of the artist's pictures, mentioning very honestly "after Ziem".*

6. Interview for the French Television series "History of Trains", co-production Pathe-Cinema-TF 1 etc see footnote 7.

7. Interview for the French Television series "History of Trains", co-production Pathe-Cinema – T.F.1 by Daniel Costello. Consultants: Michel Doerr and Jean des Cars. Producer of the episode "Orient Express": Marie-Josephe Dubergey. Text published by Larousse. Preface by Michel Doerr, director of the French Railway Museum at Mulhouse, (now retired).

armoured coach with artillery. A curious luxury train which ran in the middle of a civil war, in an ambience of film adventures.

When Marshall Tito's Yugoslavia detached itself from the communist bloc, Belgrade played the role of turntable for liberty and migration. To stay on the *Simplon-Orient Express* is to set off towards the east. A French journalist, Philippe Daudy, a regular of the Cold War train remembers:[6]

> At a stroke, one is in another world. The apparition of the first uniforms, the first Red guards, the long Russian-style riding coats, the silence, the bareness, nothing for sale on the platforms, no little trolleys, an extreme politeness but a great void, no contacts, no converstaion, all that was most impressive. After the frontier, a second sleeping car was attached and, then, one sensed the notables of the (communist) party, their closed look, at the same time that numerous officers in uniform stood round us. In the dining car, the silver serving dishes were a little rough; they tried to maintain a form of decorum but the white round jacket of the waiter, a little lop-sided, brought to our minds all the falseness and illusion of these efforts.

While the train of anguish continued to run, the Balkans were flashed through by new natural offspring of the *Orient Express*, the *Balt-Orient Express* (Stockholm-Svilengrad), and the *Tauern Express*, named after the chain of Eastern Alps, in Austria. The line Ostend-Athens via the Tauern (Tunnel), entered service on 16th May 1953. This Nordic branch of the *Simplon-Orient Express* became the *Tauern-Orient Express*. The *Balkan Express* linked Vienna-Belgrade-Athens, starting on 21st May 1955, then Sofia and Istanbul. Politically, the Balkan Express allowed its passengers to go round Hungary and Bulgaria. Are all these new branches healthy signs? No, they are signs of fatigue caused by rising, ever-increasing nationalism and railway touchiness amongst each other. And little by little, the clientele changed. If an elegant world still went to Munich, Vienna, Lausanne, Milan and Venice, the rest of the journey was sad and wretched. To go further, the luxury class travel by air. Turks and Yugoslavs made up a crowd who escaped from a political regime and increasing unemployment. The great outskirts of Europe emptied themselves of a sub-proletariat, who came, clandestinely, with hope instead of real luggage, to make the factories of the free and rich towns work, for very low wages, certainly, but wages all the same. The dawns were painful, as Inspector Lievaux, retired from the frontier police, recalled:[7]

> The first emigrants were all Yugoslavs, who at the start were escaping from their country and the Tito regime. Very often these people had no passport and arrived hidden on the bogies of the coaches or in hiding places between the ceiling and the roof of the carriages. They were discovered on arrival at the international station of Vallorbe, and extracted from their hiding places. First they were rounded up, then sent back to the Swiss authorities, before being transferred to the international Committee for refugees, at Geneva, an organization which was in a position to determine if these people had the right to the status of refugees. For these people the West was the promised land. Given the conditions of life in their country, they regarded Western Europe as a region of abundance and employment. If they were rejected, they accepted the fact with a certain dose of fatalism. Discouraged, they stayed there, with their wives, their bundles, and their children; then, when the hour of return arrived, terrible scenes took place. Even for a police officer whose duty it is, to wake up people and children in the small hours of the morning, this sort of scene does not leave pleasant recollections.

At the end of the 1950s, numerous branches are cut off the *Orient Express*. If the Geneva conference (July 1955), the first summit meeting of the old wartime allies, let people perceive the attraction of detente, the insurrection of Budapest (October 1956) shook the world and the construction of the Berlin wall (August 1961) left it stupefied: the Cold War turned into ice. The Paris-

159

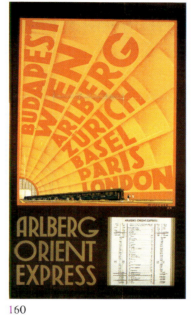

160

161

160. *Arlberg-Orient Express Poster* by Mitschek which gives the train timetable for 1937. Here the artist celebrates the imposing architecture of the great glass roofs of the European stations as much as the train. Only the names of the stages of the express seemed to resound under the vast canopy of glass and steel.

161. *Simplon-Orient Express Poster*. In front of the panorama of Constantinople, a British Guardsman and a person in Turkish costume present the great express's itinerary.

162. *The Orient Express*, hauled by a 241A (Est) 4-8-2 locomotive, passing the outskirts of Dormans on the Paris-Strassbourg line.

162

Budapest sleeping car was suppressed in 1959, then Bucharest. Vienna remained the frontier town between the East and the West.

The *Arlberg-Orient Express* included a daily sleeping car from Paris to Bucharest between 1957 and 21st May 1962. On that day the knell began to toll for the family of the prestigious train: stopped at Vienna, it lost its *Orient* label and is no more than the *Arlberg Express*, still running in 1984 (and 1987). Eight days later, the *Simplon-Orient Express* ran for the last time under this name. Its new title is the *Simplon Express* – as in 1906 – which will become *Direct-Orient*. A sad date for the luxury train of diplomats, of adventuring honeymoon couples, and of Europeans who persisted in going slowly to an Orient suddenly much less near. The suppression of the S.O.E. after forty-three years of fascinating and golden existence inspired Paul Morand to write a brilliant funeral ovation and an impressive epitome on the end of a fixed European idea. Certainly there existed a train with sleeping cars and a dining car from Paris to Istanbul, but it was no more than a phantom. To disfigure the rake, it sufficed to cut it off by successive interventions. Little by little, the magnificent blue cars lined out in yellow, flanked by the two gold lions of the monogram of the *Compagnie Internationale Des Wagons-Lits* had been replaced by less shiny coaches belonging to the networks of the popular democracies, and coloured red or green. This official end of the C.I.W.L. monopoly had removed all the raison d'être of the *Orient Express* and replaced it with a heterogeneous, envied, suspect train whose conditions of comfort left much to be desired, to say nothing about the instigated delays: the S.O.E. often had to yield priority to a goods train... In general, not including more than one or two sleeping cars drowned in the middle of very ordinary coaches, deprived of a dining car to enrich(?) the (station) buffets, it was repreived but condemned. Punctual Europe gives way to Europe in a hurry. She no longer travels, she moves about.

If the airliner has played an obvious part in this disappearance – dreadful or hoped for, according to opinions – because a flight of three hours replaces a journey of three days, politics also have a great responsibility for sentencing the train to death. Beyond the wear and tear of time, the rivalries of civilisation, indifference and technology are to blame: it is they who have killed the *Simplon-Orient Express*...

THE WRITERS AND THE ORIENT EXPRESS

Let us forgive Balzac, Flaubert, Musset, Theophile Gautier for having decried the railway. It took its literary revenge with the next generation of writers at the end of the XIXth century who have seen the *Orient Express* born.

Would it not have been more comfortable for the author of *La Comedie Humaine* to have reached Madame Hanska's house at Wierzhownia in a sleeping car, for Flaubert, with Maxime du Camp, to have made his Eastern journey in the *Taurus Express* and the *Sunshine Express*,[8] for Theophile Gautier to pursue his courtship with Griselle Grisi on board the *Simplon Express* sleeping cars, and for Musset to take this train to celebrate "The Venetian Night"? Look at Nerval who said he preferred a post-chaise to a train! What if he had used the *Simplon-Orient Express* to make his tour of Turkey, Syria and Egypt!

It is true that one had to await 1883 to travel comfortably by rail at last. Edmond About came back completely dazzled by his journey to Stamboul, inaugurating the *Orient Express*, and from the start of the celebrated train

8. C.I.W.L.'s luxury all-Pullman train, Cairo-Luxor, 1929-39 C.I.W.L.'s Club-car bars in their Cairo-Luxor-Aswan sleeping car trains of 1981 are the Sunshine's successors. Note by GB.

163

164

165

166

167

163. Margaretha-Geertruida Zelle, better known as Mata-Hari, a dancer born at Leeuwarden (Holland) in 1876, often travelled in the Orient Express more as an agent of the German information service than as a choreographic artist. Condemned to death, she was shot at Vincennes near Paris in 1917.

164. After the last war, the Fair of stars, a three day fete, took place each year in the Tuileries Gardens in Paris in aid of the Second Armoured Division of the French Army, the first to enter Paris in 1944, under the orders of General Leclerc. In June 1955, the C.I.W.L. agreed to build a "bridge of honour" which ended in a full-size mock-up of a sleeping car, in which the film stars, who co-operated in this display, were obliged to pass along.

165. During this Fair of June 1955, Marlene Dietrich, accompanied by Jean Marais acknowledge the cheers of their admirers.

166. In his turn, Eric von Stroheim, the great director, salutes the crowd.

167. In June, 1955, the Peking Opera company, passing through Paris, agreed to participate in this Fair of stars.

being put into service, poets and writers are going to appropriate these grand European expresses to satiate their whims. Huysmans rejects this infatuation with scorn. For him, the sleeping car is "a prison, the conductor, the jailer in the chestnut livery, the passengers resigned prisoners crammed together between the slender walls of a jail".[9] These sarcasms were greatly needed to counterbalance the concert of praises which were given to the great night expresses.

"Nothing commences with literature, but all ends with it, including the *Orient Express*" wrote Paul Morand, when one thinks of Bourget's first books, of *Cosmopolis*, of Barre's neurasthenic princesses in their "sleeping".[10] Valerie Larbaud, diletante globe-trotter, travels in a Europe whose frontiers are drawn aside before the *Orient Express*. His ode celebrates the miraculous muffled sounds of the luxury train. His inordinately rich A.O. Barnabooth notes in his intimate diary between Trieste and Vienna... in the bitter morning of Central Europe:

> Then when I am alone and feeling good, looking at my leather slippers which smell nice, the box on the carpet, the heavy copper ashtray, the glasses with the initials W.L. interlaced, and my body which I love, and a Muratti which exudes a long riband of blue smoke that rises towards the open window, dances to the rhythm of the train, hesitates a little, then mingles with the fresh air which the sun sweetens just now.[11]

He does not cease to marvel at this "aristocratic ease of moving about" and Emile Henriot also experienced this strengthening solitude of the sleeping car cabin:

> Rapture at starting! Here I am in my "single". Fifteen days holidays, what joy! But some fool soon said to me: "Why not go by air? It is much shorter, only four hours journey instead of twenty four..." The imbecile! When I would not give up just these twenty-four delicious hours for an empire, first happiness of the holiday, foretaste of liberty. Dream then of this forced repose, this relaxing, this leisure, this long night of cradled sleep, this long day of musing and staring at the countryside in flight, drifting across the windowpane, this compulsory immobility, this liberated self in the *farniente* (doing nothing) and perfect detachment of the mind, the absence of mail and the telephone, the divine silence. And self at last recovered, that dear me that one loses in business and work, found again like an old friend come back... What things I have to say to myself"[11a]

168

168. *The* Orient Express *running through the countryside near Chalifert, hauled by a steam engine. Ordinary coaches completed the rake which has lost its lovely unity.*

9. J.K. Huysmans, *De-tout*.
10. Paul Morand, *Le Voyage*. Hackette, 1964. French writers think the C.I.W.L. telegraphic address: "Sleeping" (legacy of Col. Mann) much more romantic than *"wagons-lits"* which is a Belgian barbarism – *"voiture-lits"* is correct French. So "Le Sleeping" appears throughout the original of this book.
11. V. Larbaud, *A.O. Barnabooth*, N.R.F.., 1922.
11a. E. Henriot, *La Rose de Bratislava*. Librairie générale française, 1959.

Elegy of the "single", Mac Orlan remembers:

> If all has been said on the song of the wheels or the rhythm of steamers on the high seas, much remains to be said on the mobile solitude of the cabins and compartments reserved for the use of a sole individual, well installed in this admirable comfort, who moves about day and night, adhering to the speeds indicated in the great timetables. The furnishing of these cabins is charming. A divan, a little table, a pocket-sized washroom. The little table folds away in front of the windowpane which resembles a screen. The countryside runs by like a film; the mysterious and gentle jazz fuses with the traveller's sensibility. This jazz is made up of several hundred wheels and a powerful whistle which dominates the memories... It was undoubtedly in one of these trans-european railway cabins that I chastised my feeling about visions of the future. The future was the next stop, unknown uniforms, *lumières* sometimes ice-cold *sols* frankly open, unforgettable songs with unknown words which made these people likeable.[12]

Bernard Frank has attempted to define in a word the impression that his sleeping car cabin left on him, and wrote:

> The sleeping car is an "undresser". Do not imagine you will find this word in your dictionary, even if it is by Littre. The "undresser" is my invention..
> To understand me, the sleeping car is childhood found again. During several hours or several days, the Company lets us dream "out loud".
> The sleeping cars of yesteryear with their noble, chained water carafes, their gilding, their red carpet, their marquetry, their panelling appropriate to a restaurant of the 1900s, are the most apt to arouse our imagination. Their foundation was the relaxation. One sleeps, one is in a Proust-style hotel bedroom, one does not stir, one wakes a thousand kilometres away...
> ... The world was bearable in days gone by, although it was an adventure, a long journey, a sparse success. Now it is no more than a cacophony, a waiting room for haggard tourists, we have had to invent tools which slide over the surface, which skim over the world without sticking to it. See little, see quickly, see without getting dirty or compromising ourselves, that is our slogan. One day Chardonne said to his friends: "If you love a woman, do not touch her". The sleeping car allows us to touch a country with tweezers.[12a]

It is so true that, during a journey in Italy, Jacques Chardonne wrote in a letter:

> ... and then I lay down, and I stayed in my bed until the next evening, my eyes on Italy, which went past before me like a magic lantern in the window. It was an Italy of yesteryear, without Italians, without vespas, without advertisment hoardings. A marvellous day. Afterwards, as soon as one left the sleeping car, it was hell, the little towns which are corridors of vespas, with their flyblown fruits, their terrible heat, their roads which stink horribly, this world finishes in congestion; it is no longer habitable. Returning to the sleeping car, the magic re-commenced.[12b]

This cult of the sleeping cars, to repeat an expression of Jean d'Ormesson in an article on Valery Larbaud, we find again in a request addressed to the Wagons-Lits Company by Paul Morand:

> I have slept in coaches hard and soft, in Russian and American couchettes, but nothing gave me the feeling of my country found once more, felt when I entered the moving home which the *Compagnie Internationale* put at the disposal of the "Friendly Syndicate of Wandering Jews"... If the *Compagnie Internationale* celebrates one day the jubilee of fifty years of service to its passengers, I would like it not to forget the bird of passage in its moving cage, the traveller militant and passionate, the horizontal wanderer who has always stayed faithful to it.[12c]

12 Pierre Mac Orlan, *Sentimentalité mobile*, in «Continents».
12a. B. Frank, *Reflexions sur le wagon-lit* in "La Revue de Voyages".
12b. Unpublished letter from Jacques Chardonne to Jean-Paul Caracalla.
12c. Paul Morand's preface to *"Sleeping Story"* by Jean des Cars, Julliard, 1976.

Alas, the C.I.W.L. could not fête this jubilee in which he believed so much. Paul Morand passed away discreetly at the beginning of the summer of 1976 when the Company was celebrating its centenary, in which the author of *Ouvert la nuit* (Open the night) certainly would have participated. When his ashes left for Trieste, Jean des Cars dedicated his *Sleeping Story* to him, which recounts the epic of the Wagons-Lits Company.

In *La Madone des sleepings*,[13] the best seller of the 1930s, Maurice Dekobra makes the most of the vogue of cosmopolitan snobbism of sleeping car travel. His heroine, Lady Diana, widow of Lord Wynham, former ambassador of His Britannic Majesty in Russia, shows from the very first pages of the book that she does not have a frigid aura. She hides nothing of her sexuality in confiding to the psycho-analyst Herr Professor Traurig, who lives in the Ritz, nor of her body in the course of a performance when she dances dressed as Eve. Nevertheless, she justifies her nickname:

> Doubtless you have heard that I have covered thousands and thousands of miles on the continental railway lines, and worn out the carpets of the Wagons-Lits Company. A Parisian journalist even called me "La Madone des sleepings" ... Sleepings with an 's', which is an English barbarism, unless you have already annexed this word on the other side of the Channel? And Madonna with a capital M, which is a euphemism full of irony, since I may have the profile of a Madonna but I have no more of the attributes... In truth I have roamed on the great European networks and I have lost many *billets-doux* between the pages of the A.B.C., the Indicateur Chaix or the German Fahrplan, and consigned the perfume of my suitcases and the secret of my confidential lingeries to Customs officers of every country.

All the palace hotels of the towns served by the *Orient Express*: the *Imperial* at Vienna, the *Hungaria* at Pest, the *Pera Palace* at Constantinople witnessed the eccentricities of the beautiful Lady Diana, depending on "the colour of the eyes of my neighbour in the compartment" said she. Like *La Garconne* of Victor Marqueritte, *The Madonna of the Sleeping cars* shows a certain provocative spirit, women are no longer confined to their part in the background, the novel ushers in the first examples of the liberalisation of women.

The chapter titles of *Orient Express*[14], the novel by Graham Greene follow each other like the station names in an international timetable: Ostend, Cologne, Vienna, Subotica, Constantinople. The characters pass each other in the corridors of the sleeping cars. More than the atmosphere of the train itself, the novelist looks at Europe at night as seen from the *Orient Express* to accentuate the mystery surrounding his novel's characters; the relevance of certain descriptions enables the reader to share this railway journey to the East.

Like Vladimir Nabokov who has so well described his sleeping car travels in the *Nord Express* of his youth, Graham Greene knows how to bring the enigmatic world of trains and stations to life.

In *"Murder on the Orient Express"*[15] the novel of Agatha Christie is limited to one sleeping car of the *Simplon-Orient Express*. Hercule Poirot boards the *Taurus Express* at Aleppo to reach Constantinople. The celebrated detective does not have the time to visit Santa Sophia whose beauty has been extolled to him. A telegram recalls him to London, where urgent business awaits him. So he leaves again hurriedly in the *Simplon-Orient Express* to get to the British capital. Monsieur Bouc, director of the Wagons-Lits Company, finds him a cabin in this abnormally full train. Between Vinkovci and Brod, when the train is blocked by snow, a cry rings out in the night. A crime has been committed. For Hercule Poirot, the enquiry

169. *The famous English novelist Agatha Christie, born in 1891 at Torquay has shared the glory of the luxury trains in siting one of her most famous detective stories in the* Simplon-Orient Express. *One of her favourite characters, the detective Hercule Poirot has to resolve a riddle, to which of course he finds the solution at the end of the journey. The novel was inspired by an incident which took place in 1929, when the* Simplon-Orient Express *was blocked by snow. Agatha Christie died in 1976.*

13. M. Dekobra, *La Madone des sleepings*, Cosmopolis, 1925 and Presses de la Cité, 1974.
14. Graham Green, *Orient Express*, Stock 1932.
15. Agatha Christie, *Murder on the Orient Express. La Crime de l'Orient Express*, Librairie des Champs-Elysées, 1934.

begins. The interrogations follow one after the other in the dining car and we make the passengers' acquaintance, all capable of being the assassins of Ratchett, the victim: the enigma is resolved when finally the train arrives at Belgrade. The sleeping car, microcosm of a small company of people apparently strangers to each other, is the excellent setting which gives to the novel's intrigue, that confined and mysterious atmosphere dear to the great English detective story writer.

1962-1977
The End of a Myth

The agony was going to last fifteen years. Fifteen years of hesitations, of starts, of hopes and of deceptions for the appreciators of authentic foreign travel and the lovers of the old Europe, persisting in prefering sleeping car travel, with its advantages and its disadvantages, to the temptation of the airliner whose success eventually became greater. Years of resigned struggle where progress in one condemned the other, as, a hundred and fifty years before, the diligent mailcoachmen whipped their horses to attempt to battle with the iron horse. A significant co-incidence: the progressive decay of the prestigeous train took place at the same time as the disappearance of steam traction in regular service for passengers in Western Europe. So much was swept away with the smoke...

The *Orient Express* watched its fall in popularity with the anguish of an old film star who had to face a new public. At first limited to Paris-Vienna (the second class seats coach, provided by the Hungarian or Romanian railways had been suppressed in the summer of 1961), the train was once more extended to Budapest in the summer of 1964. This decision was the result of insufficient capacity of the Hungarian Railways (M.A.V.) railcar set which ensured the link under the name of *Vienna-Budapest Express*. Even if the majority of the customers, in the west-east direction came from Southern Germany and Austria, there were, all the same, passengers who went further. One year later, in the summer of 1965, The Paris-Vienna sleeping car was itself extended to Bucharest four times a week. A permanent traffic continued between Romania, Hungary and Western Europe, even if it was abridged into a single sleeping car... sadly enclosed by very ordinary carriages for seats passengers.[1]

The *Simplon Express* was limited, as its name indicates, to a connection (from Paris) with Switzerland and Italy without going on to the East, nor to the Balkans... Actually at Milan, the train was cut in two. One part ran to Verona-Venice-Trieste, with an extension to Zagreb in summer. The other part ran to Florence, Rome and Naples.

If it had lost its eastern location, it had gained in speed – the obsession of the 1960s and 1970s – higher speeds were much more satisfying and easy to adhere to in France-Switzerland-Italy than beyond Trieste.

The new timetable fixed the departure from Paris (Gare de Lyon) at 19 h. 28 mins. and the arrival at Venice at 8 h. 51 mins. A dining car was in service between Paris and Dijon. In May 1967, in front of an increase in Yugoslav

170. *Scene in the famous — and marvellous! — Alfred Hitchcock film,* The Lady Vanishes, *produced in 1938 in a studio near London. A masterpiece of humour and railway suspense, with Margaret Lockwood (on left, facing front) and Sir Michael Redgrave (who in the photograph is holding the "nun"). Without ever being named, the pre-war Orient Express is the ideal setting for an espionage adventure, very well portrayed, where all the mysteries of the train are used. A great classic without a flaw, which proclaimed the future master of the cinema who would often use trains in his films. With the mock-up construction of a single coach, half sleeping car, half dining car, Hitchcock suceeds in giving us the illusion of a complete* Orient Express, *somewhere in the Balkans.*

1. The Paris-Bucharest sleeping car was cut back to Paris-Vienna again on 31st May 1987.

emigrant clientele, the *Simplon Express* was extended to Belgrade. The liaison Paris-Belgrade – depart at 19 h. 28 mins. and arrive at 23 h. 30 mins. the next day – was then ensured in twenty-eight hours. This progress was also due to the improvement of the Yugoslav Railways. The branch which went to Rome from Milan, left the traveller in the Italian capital at 12 h. 59 mins. Henceforth, travelling from Paris-Venice took only one night, a real night since it included the evening. The Milan-Rome route was soon supplanted by the *Rome Express*, and, in 1969, by the *Palatino*, with an improved timetable. Electrification worked wonders. It is from this date that the *Direct-Orient* truly took its place in the epic of the *train express d'Orient*.

The *Direct-Orient* set out from Calais for Istanbul or for Athens with a YU-type sleeping car with up to thirty berths, and a first and second class composite seats coach. The link was bi-weekly. The sleeping car was the only comfortable means of travel direct to the *Orient*, the other coaches being limited to local sectors. Complimentary rakes came to reinforce temporarily the skeletal composition of the *Direct-Orient*. Thus, at Nis, it divided itself into the *Marmara Express* (after the name of the Sea of Marmara, beside which the line runs in arriving at Istanbul) and the *Athens Express*.

What was this train like, the only one – the last – maintaining the railway connection between the Seine and the Bosphorus? It was like a Europe which lived more and more to the rhythm of desperate migrations. Turks, Greeks and Yugoslavs, looking for jobs in Italy, Switzerland, France and Germany, continued to pin their ultimate dreams on this train in which they crammed together, throughout the year, in the middle of their improbable bundles. In the other direction, they brought back money for their labour and the certainty of long-awaited holidays. For these families it mattered little that the *Direct-Orient* was the last pitiful, shameful child of an illustrious family. Above all, it was the cheapest means of covering two thousand or three thousand kilometres, and without excess baggage payments... As M. Didier Durandal, editor-in-chief of the great magazine *La Vie du Rail* wrote very reasonably: "The unique sleeping car of the *Direct-Orient* often has the appearance of a chilly little islet of western good living which has strayed among second class carriages full to bursting".

Between the worker customers and the back-packing youths in jeans who pass by there on their way to Katmandu, the journey was an ordeal which only fanatics voluntarily underwent. One of these people mad on railways was Dr. Fritz Stockl, author of the reference book *Rolling Hotels*,[2] a connoisseur who advised:

> ... One fact is certain, the train was long, heavy, slow (three nights in the train between Paris and Istanbul), its stops were numerous and irksome (an entire morning for the sector Lausanne-Brig) and the only dining car which for some time brought a smile to the faces of the gastronomes and other "starving" people between Milan and Venice had been suppressed... The solution remained for the latter "the attack on the buffets" or the "continental breakfast" tray of the sleeping car conductor".[3]

Thus the *Direct-Orient* ran...

The long train – it often exceeded five hundred metres long – heterogeneous, without luxury or prestige, remained, however, the number one international train of Europe, linking fourteen countries, thirteen railway administrations, and nine sleeping and dining car companies. Beginning in 1972, its improbable sloth pre-occupied all the authorities concerned. Assembled in September at the European timetable conference, the administrations examined its dossier.[4] An alarming dossier containing two main propositions. The first aimed to transfer the sleeping cars and the direct

Types of French steam locomotives that have hauled the Orient Express:
171. *4-4-0 Est Railway 220 No. 813 with Flaman double boiler, nicknamed 'camels'. Only forty engines of this class were delivered, between 1891 and 1895.*
172. *4-4-0 Est Railway 220 No. 2405, called 'speedy', in service from 1900.*
173. *4-6-0 Est Railway 230 No. 3175, a compound with Schmidt superheater, with front bogie for heavy express trains. This class was built from 1906 to 1925 and was called 'Le ten-wheel'. This engine was delivered in 1910.*
174. *4-6-2 Est Railway 231 No. 31007 (later 231 B 7) of 'Pacific' class, built between 1921 and 1923.*

2. Fritz Stockl, *Das Rollende Hotels*, Rudolf Bohmann Industrie und Fachverlag, Vienna, 1967.
3. Extract from *Eisenbahn* Austrian railway magazine, March 1977.
4. The European Timetable Conference comprises twenty-five railway networks. Their annual assemblies have the constant improvement of the timetables according to technical progress and commercial obligations, as objectives.

seats coaches: Paris-Athens, Paris-Istanbul, Paris-Sofia and Milan-Athens to the *Simplon Express*. The second proposed to bring these carriages back onto two trains conceived specially for the Paris-Balkans traffic on the basis of two departures in summer and only one departure in winter per week. These measures, envisaged by the Swiss Federal Railways and which were a menace to the existence of the *Direct-Orient*, were not adopted. But in 1973 an important mission was conferred on M. Bailleux, an official of French Railways (S.N.C.F.) to attempt to find solutions to the tardiness of the train's despatch. The official points of view could be divided into two groups. British Railways (because of the connection at Calais), the S.N.C.F., the Swiss Railways (S.B.B.) and the German Federal Railways (D.B.) wished, above all, that the length of the journey might be reduced, either to two nights plus one day, or to two days and a night. On the other hand the Italian, Yugoslav, Bulgarian, Turkish and Greek Administrations wanted the comfort – very limited apart from the sleeping cars – improved by replacing the second class seats coaches with couchettes. From divergences to disagreements – where is the fine unanimity of the past century? – these conferences ended on the refusal of one or other of the members to support the costs of the service. Even those most anxious to maintain a France-Balkans train, that is to say Greece and Turkey, were scarcely enthusiastic about the real share of the operation. A loss-making operation whose balance sheet grew more and more negative, and which was made worse, after 1974 by cheap air fares for Paris-Athens and Paris-Istanbul. Between 1972 and 1976, the rate of occupancy of the two sleeping cars fell by twenty per cent. One traveller in five went the whole way. They amounted to four hundred and seventy on Paris-Istanbul-Paris and five hundred and seventy-eight on Paris-Athens-Paris. Among them some unhurried businessmen, immigrant workmen and tourists hoping to defend an archaic way of travel, certainly, but one which kept its charm and its mystery. Twelve locomotives between Paris and Istanbul, ten from Paris to Athens, four types of electric current (1,500 V D.C., 25kV 50 Hz, 15kV 16⅔ Hz A.C. and 3000 V D.C.) and more and more diesel traction with the disappearance of steam (335 km from Svilengrad to Istanbul, 787 km from Skopje to Athens) are the things which fascinate the few gentle maniacs of railway pleasure... And what a falling off of standards for the "European services of sleeping cars and dining cars" as announced in the timebook in the summer of 1974 when Jean des Cars had an unprecedented journalistic experience, being the first great reporter working, incognito on board the *Direct Orient*. He remembers:

171

172

173

174

> I was in service from Paris to Venice, wearing the legendary chestnut-brown uniform. The car for which I was responsible, No. 3625, type Y, was very jaded under its scaly paint, and with its coal-fired boiler. It was built in France in 1930 by the *Enterprises Industrielles Charentaise* at Aytré, La Rochelle. I was going to Istanbul in "E.I.C. – style"... even if, transformed into a type U sleeping car, it now carried the number 99 and offered 33 berths with eleven compartments convertible into single, double or tourist.
>
> From Venice to Belgrade, the conductor was a Yugoslav, from Belgrade to Sofia he was a Bulgar, and his service was, from all points of view, limited, since the sector was crossed by day. Lastly, from Sofia to Istanbul, the conductor was a Turk, very devoted, and I had permission, exceptionally, to assist him. As much to inform my first passengers as for my personal information, I had consulted the timebook greedily, which made me dream.
>
> I had then, noted – and announced! – the different means of refreshing oneself: C.I.W.L.T. tray-meal service from Milan to Trieste, Yugoslav buffet car from Belgrade to Gevgelija, Turkish dining car from Kapikule to Istanbul. Alas! None of these cars was included in my train. After breakfast, warned by passengers armed with sandwiches and flasks of wine, who knew that the *Direct Orient's* passengers

were truly very badly treated, I bought provisions in Yugoslavia. It was the *Exodus* on rails. But the atmosphere was extraordinary, and the countries crossed magnificent. After three trying nights, we arrived at Istanbul... eight hours late! Happily I was in no hurry and this heroic journey will stay unforgettable.

In the winter of 1976-1977 the *Direct Orient* observed the following theoretical timetable, effective in France, Switzerland, and Italy, becoming more and more elastic as gradually it approached the Orient. Day A; depart from Paris-Lyon at 23 h. 53 mins. Day B: Lausanne: 7 h, Milan: 12 h. 55 mins., Venice: 17 h. 14 mins., Trieste: 21 h. 09 mins. Day C: Zagreb: 3 h. 01 mins., Belgrade: 8 h. 16 mins., Sofia: 18 h. 23 mins. Day D: Istanbul: 8 h. 25 mins.

This journey of 3,055 km. was accomplished in "about" 55 h. 30 mins... The commercial speed was set up thus:
  Paris-Milan: 821 km. in 13 h. 0.4 mins., an average of 62.83 km/h.
  Paris-Venice: 1,018 km. in 17 h. 23 mins., an average of 62.58 km/h.
  Paris-Belgrade: 1,981 km. in 33 h. 10 mins., an average of 58.79 km/h.
  Paris-Istanbul: 3,055 km. in 55 h. 32 mins., an average of 53.73 km/h.
  Paris-Athens: 3,242 km. in 58 h. 42 mins., an average of 53.74 km/h.

Observe that in the Istanbul-Paris direction, the length of time was even higher: 58 h. 01 mins., an average of 52.43 km/h, and that Athens-Paris was a little shorter (!) than Paris-Athens: 57 h. 31 mins., an average of 54.85 km/h.

The multiplicity of stops provided for – sixty eight stations from Paris to Istanbul, sixty-three from Paris to Athens – the stops unprovided for – assorted trolleys, faulty couplings, other trains on the line – added to customs procedures where suspicion vied with a bureaucratic obsession, made this international train the slowest in the world.

In the north, the *Orient Express* left Paris Est at 22 h. 15 mins., reached Munich at 8 h. 26 mins., Linz at 12 h., Vienna at 14 h. 25 mins., Budapest at 19 h. 38 mins., Bucharest the next day at 12 h. The 2518 km. were run in 36 h. 45 mins., an average of 68.50 km/h rising to 86 km/h between Paris and Vienna. Most of the carriages do not go beyond the Austrian capital and the Paris-Bucharest sleeping car, MU-type with 36 berths, ran four times a week (once a week 1986-1987).

The *Arlberg Express* left Paris at 22 h. 40 mins (as in 1987), served Zurich at 7 h. 19 mins., Innsbruck at 12 h. 0.5 mins., Zell-Am-See 14 h. 25 mins. and Vienna at 19 h. 45 mins. The train took nearly five hours longer to run from Paris to Vienna, but it is essentially used by skiers in the Swiss and Austrian Alps.

Lastly the *Simplon Express* left Paris-Lyon at 19 h. 28 mins., reached Venice at 8 h. 34 mins., Trieste at 10 h. 56 mins., Zagreb at 16 h. 23 mins. and Belgrade at 22 h. 0.8 mins. The 1,985 kilometres of the run were covered in 26 h. 43 mins., at an average of 74 km/h. (28 h. 36 mins. in 1987), between Paris-Venice (1,088 km) the average rose to 86 km/h. Compared to the *Direct-Orient*, the *Simplon Express* which used the same itinerary, took seven hours less.

It was, then, the extreme sloth which condemned the *Direct-Orient* in the spring of 1977. At the timetable conference, the chopper fell. The hundreds of kilometres of single track on the eastern part of the journey, the interminable stops due to crossings (waiting for a train coming the other way) and the financial ill-will of the Balkan systems killed the moribund train. The news astounded the amateurs: the last departure of the *Direct Orient* was announced for 19th May 1977 in the Paris-Istanbul direction and the 22nd May in the Istanbul-Paris direction. First known to the specialists, the information was let loose on the world press, dominating dozens of television

175

and radio channels. Six months before the last trip of the asthmatic old train, the beds, the couchettes, and the seats were reserved, taken by storm. From Japan, from the United States, from Canada, tickets were taken for the last journey: the end of a giant, the end of an era, the end of a dream. The catastrophe, foreseen by experts for five years, excites the imagination, makes the nostalgia bubble, often with grave historical and technical mistakes which has fabricated a supplement to the legend having little to do with reality.

To speak of the end of the *Orient Express* was at once true and false. What was true was the end of the link Paris-Istanbul and Paris-Athens in direct through coaches. Henceforth a change at Belgrade was necessary. What was false was to confuse the suppression of the *Direct Orient* with the *Orient Express* itself. Actually the *Orient Express* Paris-Vienna-Budapest-Bucharest still continues, and this confusion is partially explained by the absence of a well-established link between this axis and the Golden Horn. The Austrian National Tourist Office (in Paris) published a press release rectifying the truth and recalling that it sufficed to look at the timetable to learn that the *Orient Express* still left Paris-Est at 23 h. 15 mins.; this contradiction, like all contradictions, was not taken into account by incorrigible lovers of the past. The ignorance and lack of curiosity of certain journalists is very culpable... An astonishing paradox: the *Orient Express* still lives and, at the same time, one weeps for its disappearance!

The Gare de Lyon, at Paris, on Thursday 19th May 1977. Since late afternoon this imposing building with its famous tower on the end, twin sister of Big Ben, had been abnormally overrun by an impatient crowd. This evening the Station of the Sun was truly the station of the Orient. Travellers came from another continent, journalists interviewed the last wearer of a képi, everyone gets ready, whether a simple sweeper, or a dazzling television presenter: Camera crews go on board, others will film the departure or the arrival. The last departure, the last arrival, the last thrill. This evening, the *Direct-Orient* resembled a district cinema whose demolition starts tomorrow.

175. *Gare de Lyon (Paris) one evening in July 1974 at 23.00 hours. The passengers of the Direct-Orient Express did not know that the conductor of sleeping car No. 3625 was none other than Jean des Cars, great reporter and historian, employed incognito after having followed the regulation theoretical and practical probation. Disguised in the uniform, he was the first journalist to live the adventure and the profession of a man dreamt about for a century.*

176

176. *Thursday 19th May 1977, Gare de Lyon in Paris. A panel, already nostalgic, announced the last departure of the* Direct-Orient Express. *In spite of its "Rapide" character, it was suppressed mainly because of its sloth, in particular in Bulgaria, Turkey, and Greece. It was the end of an era, the end of the direct sleeping car link between Paris and Istanbul, and Paris and Athens. By contrast it was not, as the world press repeated, the end of the* Orient Express *so far as the train bearing that name was concerned. What matter: the tears flowed, weeping for a myth.*

177, 178. *Booked up six months before, the last sleeping car, modern and without soul . . . had been taken by storm for this historic journey from the Seine to the Bosphorus. Previously forgotten and despised, the* Direct-Orient Express *now attracted an exceptional revival of crowds and curiosity. Too late, alas . . . But the stoic conductor marked up the presence of his passengers.*

5. Series of Daniel Costelle. Producer of the episode: Marie Josephe Dubergey. The six films, of great quality, have had much success, and they have been shown in twenty countries.

The notice invites the crowd, but as the celebrity looks like death, it is too late...

Of all the television channels present, Jean des Cars particularly remembers two whose work was remarkable: the French co-production T.F. 1 – Pathé-Cinema on the history of trains whose episode *Orient Express*, in the course of being filmed all over Europe, found a moving scene here.[5] And, elsewhere, the Flemish channel of Belgian Television (B.R.T.) had the original idea, without precedent, of devoting all the evening, from seven-thirty p.m. to midnight to the train. Animated by Robrecht Willaert, a real professional, the transmission was run live from the Algerian Salon of the national historical monument, the celebrated *Buffet Le Train Bleu* restaurant. From Brussels the service put out live sequences and film on the history of the train, its adventures, its gastronomy, its songs; even a live competition was organised; a competition between fathers, who, surrounded by their children, hastily had to build a miniature railway circuit. The good old *Direct-Orient* whom the crowd have not noticed for a long time, provoked some unforseen reactions. But without hope...

In the hall, two hours before the rake had backed in, the sleeping car passengers camped on the platform. Some, very well informed, were provided with refreshments and thermos bottles. Others were astonished that they have neither fanfare, nor red carpet, nor champagne. They ran to buy a bottle, tepid, which exploded, frothy and frivolous on this nostaglic occasion.

At 23.16 the assault was made, the fortress was truly vulnerable. The sleeping car conductor, the lucky (?) one assigned to this last departure was overrun: as usual, the fascination was above all in the west-east direction. Istanbul-Paris, curiously, was less of a dream...

The sleeping car was really tasteless. It no longer wore the celebrated night blue livery with yellow bands, nor the leonine arms. Sign of the times, it was without distinction, in this grey-blue, with the white band which is worn by sleeping cars bought little by little by French Railways (S.N.C.F.), in pursuance of the European "pool". Sleeping car No. 99, formerly 3824 of type Y, built in 1939 at Nivelles (Belgium) has memories – thirty-eight years, millions of kilometres – but they have effaced it, vulgarised it. The *Direct-Orient* was a little more false: it had no true relationship any more with its ancestor. What did it matter? In the corridor, the champagne flowed. In the next coach, there was less jostle. And some drawn, unshaven faces asked what all the fuss was about. Those who took the *Direct-Orient* as the obligatory train of the "leprous" outskirts of Europe could not regret its burial.

At the rear of the train, one could read, for the last time, the plaque covetted by the enthusiasts:

23 h. 56 mins.
DIRECT ORIENT
Rapide 225
1st and 2nd class,

the couchette and sleeping car signs, 1st and second class. And the enumeration of the principal stations: Dijon, Dole, Mouchard, Frasne, Vallorbe, Lausanne, Vevey, Montreux, Martigny, Sion, Brigue, Domodossola, Stresa, Milan, Venise, Trieste, Belgrade. Branch to Gevgelija and Athens, branch to Dragoman, Sofia, Istanbul.

On the flank of the coaches, the destination plates, scaly and hardly shining, will be unscrewed and coped with by the very organized, patient collectors. One read there: DIRECT-ORIENT MARMARA EXPRESS. Paris (Gare de Lyon)-Dijon-Vallorbe-Lausanne-Simplon-Milano (C)

(Centrale)-Verona-Venezia-Trieste-Villa Opicina-Sezana-Zagreb-Beograd-Nis-Sofia-Istambul. This last orthography, a spelling whim was inspired from the name of the old town of Stamboul.[6] Does the *Direct-Orient* know where its going? A sadly historic journey: the route of the Orient will, tomorrow, be cut.

At the head of the train, the engine No. 2 D 2 9102 waited in its green livery with white streak, for the honour of pulling the condemned train away from Paris.

People embraced and photographed themselves in front of it. Stationmaster and conductor posed in front of the two venerable direct coaches, the others only going part of the way. Faithful to its bad reputation, the *Direct-Orient* was late... from the start! It waited for the Calais-Milan coaches and at 23 h. 56 mins., nothing happened. Time could suspend its running. 24 hours, or 0 h. in railway terms. 0 h. 5, 0 h. 10 mins... It was not until 0 h. 13 mins. that the sleeping car finally commenced to grind.[7] Handkerchiefs waved on the platform where the television had asked the waiters of the Buffet to pose in their long aprons of the Belle Epoque. Seventeen minutes late, the *Direct-Orient* slipped out of the sleeping station at a time when its "brothers" the *Orient Express*, the *Arlberg Express* and the *Simplon Express* had long since left. Seventeen minutes late: this delay allowed the phantom train to bring its effective departure back to Friday 20th May instead of Thursday 19th. A reprieve for our inevitable tear.

Seventeen minutes of mercy before the oblivion...

THE ORIENT EXPRESS, STAR OF THE CINEMA

With their long runs, their night travels favouring adventures and all tastes, the thrill of crossing frontiers, and their cosmopolitan clientele, the international expresses could not fail to influence the cinema. And the *Orient Express* has added a supplement of magic and fascination in the vision inscribed in a compartment window of imposing countrysides. Was this not, in the end, just like a film on a screen?

In the silent epoch, the *Orient Express* was little used by the Seventh Art. With the talkies, it obtruded on various films, major or minor, but always emphasizing its importance in communication between men. It is thanks to Graham Greene's famous novel that it appeared in the projection room of obscure cinemas. *Orient Express* has been filmed three times. The first version, dating from 1934, was produced in the United States by Paul Martin, a German producer of Hungarian origins, with Heather Angel, Norman Foster and Ralph Morgan. In 1944, a first remake was made in Germany by Victor Tourjansky, a white Russian emigrant, a former assistant to Abel Gance. Lastly in 1954 a third film relating the same story came out of the Italian studios thanks to Carlo Ludovico Bragaglio, with Silvana Pampanini and Henri Vidal. Three producers, three different nationalities, three countries; one more proof of the multinational character of the train.

But it was just before the war that the *Orient Express* got its high ranking credentials in the cinema in the excellent *The Lady Vanishes* produced by Alfred Hitchcock in 1938 and which proclaimed his total mastery over railway suspense, amongst other forms of suspense. This film, this masterpiece was Hitchcock's greatest success commercially and in reviews, before 1940, and marked the summit of the producer's English period. The action, the entertainment and the humour were so greatly appreciated, that they made Hitchcock decide to leave for Hollywood.

The Lady Vanishes was also a fête of technical prowess: it was entirely filmed in a little studio in Islington, London, with just one carriage to

177

178

6. C.I.W.L. plates were always spelt correctly. See illustration 175. Note by GB.
7. The same evening and also at 23 h. 56 mins. it was the last departure of the Paris-Athens. The car was No. 3821 also type Y of 1939: One year earlier, 20th May 1976.

represent the train, half sleeping car, half dining car. The paradox is that there is no mention at any moment, neither in the picture nor the dialogue, of the *Orient Express*. Not a single time is it named, and its destination plates are invisible. However, there is no doubt about this ghost train. It left from the Tyrol and ran towards a western port which could be Venice. A spontaneously light and whimsical journey but rich in matters which are well understood. Only the *Orient Express* could serve as an ideal frame for a spy thriller of 1938 and very precise remarks make reference to the rise of nazism and the risks of imminent war. It is notable that Hitchcock deliberately jumbled up the train's tracks: the only precise information, the dining car No. 2593, is itself false, as, due to the First World War, some cars were never built and this serial number, like others[8], were never used. In ninety minutes *The Lady Vanishes* became a classic, still appreciated today. Let us add that the two gentlemen wearing a spotted bow tie and a club tie and only concerned to reach London in time for a cricket match, were played by the same actors two years later. In *Night Train to Munich* (English title: *Night Train*), which appeared in July 1940 under the direction of Carol Reed, it was again a story of escape from the Nazis thanks to the famous train which was related.

After some allusions in secondary films made after 1945, it was in 1963 that the *Orient Express* made its very brilliant return, thanks to Terence Young in *From Russia with Love*, second film of the prolific adventures of James Bond, the celebrated agent 007 in Her Gracious Majesty's secret service. A prototype of the spy film, well constructed, gripping, a third of whose rapid action takes place in the train from Istanbul to Venice.

Inspired by the book by Ian Fleming – which John Fitzgerald Kennedy considered as one of his ten favourite works – the film had a perilous shooting scene. Bad weather in Turkey caused the budget to overrun by two hundred thousand pounds excess on the one million nine hundred thousand pounds provided for. The crew moved to Scotland, where a helicopter accident during the acrobatic sequences, wounded Terence Young and his assistant (stand-in?) Michael White, happily not seriously. As for Pedro Armendariz, who played the part of Kerimbey, the head of the British network in Istanbul, he waited for the end of the film to end his days: he was struck down by a cancer... The sleeping car used, with brio in the brawling scenes, was not a mock-up but the authentic No. 3893, type Y, built in Belgium in 1948 and really allocated to journeys in Turkey.[9]

The film has also become a classic, a model of adventure which was possible without too many sophisticated gadgets, and a perfect example of the historic and diplomatic status of the train. However, in his book, the creator of Agent 007 wrote that the destination plate of the *Orient Express* is the most romantic in the world, which is true. But the writer and the film-makers made the classic mistake here: of course the plate in question was not that of the *Orient Express* but of the *Simplon-Orient Express*, which moreover, had unfortunately just been suppressed. What counts is that, on platform No. 3 one feels "the tragic poetry of departure".

The same technical mistake occurs again in the famous film *Murder on the Orient Express* produced by Sidney Lumet in 1974, whose outdoor shots were filmed on a line in the snowy Jura at the end of the winter. The interiors were partly produced in France and the Landy workshops station, to the north of Paris,[10] was transformed into the European station of Istanbul (Sirkeci). The composition of the train was also whimsical. If the Fourgon (luggage van) No. 1283, built in England in 1928 had indeed run in the *Simplon-Orient Express*, by contrast no Pullman car, not even first class, was ever included in the *Simplon-Orient Express* in the 1930s. That which one saw in the film,

179, 180. *In Sydney Lumet's film* Murder on the Orient Express, *made in 1974, Landy station near the Porte de la Chapelle in Paris was transformed into Istanbul Station. It is a luxurious reconstruction of the East, (Near and Far). Note the error in the 1930s composition of the train: the Pullman car seen here (No. 4163), lit like a brilliant jewel-box, never ran in the* Simplon-Orient Express *but in day trains like the* Cote d'Azur *(Paris-Marseilles-Nice-Menton) which gave its name to this type of Pullman car.*

8. Numbers never used appear on the mock-ups in the film *Rome Express*, too. Was this obligatory, to make everything fictitious?
9. Above its windows, the film immortalises the words: Avrupa Surat Katalari Ve Beynelmilel Yatakli-Vagonlar Sirketi, the C.I.W.L. title in Turkish, see Illustration No. 91.
10. Stabling point for the *Night Ferry* and the *Nord Express*, starting from Paris-Nord. Notes by GB.

carrying the number 4163 was built in France in 1929 of the type "Cote d'Azur".

It is the place where the detective Hercule Poirot assembles all the passengers, all suspects, after the crime imagined by the great Agatha Christie, and where, very spectacularly, he reveals the truth to them. *Murder on the Orient Express* was the first film putting back in fashion, sumptuously, the luxurious atmosphere of travel between the two wars and the worldly intrigues cooked up by the novelist. The latter, who knew the *Simplon-Orient Express* well, as she had often taken it, was inspired by an authentic incident on departure, namely the train being blocked by snow for several days. However, in spite of a very clever distribution and dazzling numbers of actors – Ingrid Bergman won an Oscar for best supporting role, the stationary train deprived the film of the part of its atmosphere created by movements, speed and noises when the train is running. The enquiry, in the closed-in car, respecting the unity of time and place, allows the producer to recapture the force of one of his famous films, Twelve Angry Men.

The revival of nostalgic interest for this train explains the aggressive French title of *Sherlock Holmes attaque l'Orient Express*, a puckered translation of *The Seven per cent Solution*. This *Seven per cent Solution* is the cocaine dose which Sherlock Holmes takes when he is in a sullen mood. The scenario of this film, produced in 1979 by Herbert Ross, is by the talented Nicholas Meyer, after his novel which was a homage to, and very interesting imitation of, the work of Conan Doyle. In a very rousing railway scene, where we meet the sleeping car of an oriental pasha who travels with his harem and Dr. Sigmund Freud, the authors greatly amuse themselves. The film was shot in Vienna and London, but the rolling stock has absolutely nothing to do with reality. It is a steam train, still in service on the preserved Severn Valley Railway in the Midlands![11] But besides remarkable actors (Laurence Olivier, Vanessa Redgrave and Joel Gray, notably) it is an exercise in successful style. That is the essential. Alfred Hitchcock often declared: "There is something more important than logic, it is imagination".

At the cinema, the *Orient Express* is never neutral. Most often, it is the symbol of implacable dramas linked to the train route, pretext of murders and tribulations in a disquieting symphony of steel and mahogany. All the spies on earth rendezvous on it to exchange State secrets, all the lovers dream of meeting and embracing a traveller there. And it is so very famous (and seductive for the script-writers!) that, like a favoured extra, one of its discreet appearances is enough to set the cameras turning. Thus in *Avec la peau des autres* (With the skin of others), Jacques Deray's clever French espionage film, the action at Vienna, where Lino Ventura lives, unfolds with the arrival of the *Orient Express* "which is always on time". Quite the opposite to the light – and elaborate – tone of the hilarious American comedy which George Cukor produced in 1973: *Travels with my Aunt* is a glittering fantasy where a conventional nephew pursues an eccentric aunt. The film is inspired by another novel of Graham Greene, this time tender and delightfully optimistic. On departure in Paris-Lyon station his hero stretches out on his bed seductively and says to the viewer, enraptured, overwhelmed by the sense of adventure: "After all, I am on the *Orient Express*!"

At the cinema, indeed, anything could happen in this train. The *Orient Express* deserves an Oscar for 'change of surroundings'.

179

180

11. Dining car No. 2975 and Sleeping car No. 3916 (type Y) with an assortment of continental steam engines and ordinary coaches, are available for film-makers in Britain, on the Nene Valley Railway, Peterborough. Note by GB.

Since 1977
Nostalgia on Rails

We have buried it a little quickly. The illustrious train is like the old film stars who make their farewells several times, and, sometimes, start a new career after having announced retirement... A few days after being considered dead, the Paris-Istanbul train lives again.

Friday, 27th May 1977. The last *Direct-Orient* has left the Gare de Lyon barely a week before, but, in the brand new Bercy station, a few hundred metres from the fateful platform, a merry crowd celebrates the departure of a special train: the *Orient-Express-Citroen*. The great make of car has decided to reward fifty head salesmen and their wives, for their efficiency at selling cars, by offering them a genuine railway cruise. What a contrast with the shabbiness of the last departure of the *Direct-Orient!* Here, the platform disappears under the red carpet of great occasions, an orchestra pours out a flood of ambience, a cocktail party enables the good champagne flow. Citroen has done things well by hiring a train composed of six MU-type sleeping cars offering first class cabins, a Pullman car, three dining cars, a shower car, a bar car and a cinema-car where four films will be shown. The happy winners find in their compartment blue and orange bath robes with the Citroen and Wagons-Lits company crests on them, some books on the famous train and some little presents... The Presidential brigade surpasses itself in cooking and service, from the boiled eggs for breakfast to the spaghetti simmered by the chef, M. Orlandini, for the night-birds. Elegant menus, printed in English lettering, are an apt invitation for the V.I.P.s to the delights of the dining car. Half the prize-winners make the outward journey and the other half the return, the two groups joining up in Istanbul for three days. Successful in all respects, the journey was enlivened by the presence of Jean des Cars who answered all the questions raised – and they were many! – both going and coming back. The itinerary was that of the *Simplon-Orient Express,* with agreeable stops at Venice, Belgrade and Sofia. And the "Simplon dance" during the twenty minutes in the long tunnel (20 km) will remain memorable!

The event was at the same time spectacular and discreet. Spectacular because it appeared in defiance[1] to the administration who had sent the *Direct-Orient* to the museum of Remembrance, discreet because it only carried invited guests.

181. *Since 1982, the* Venice-Simplon-Orient Express *linked London and Venice via Paris three times a week from spring to autumn until 1985: with 1930s sumptuous rolling stock, an audacious risk. In the early morning the train slips across the Alps towards the Italian Lakes. All the poetry of the honeymoon journeys of yesterday has been retrieved. From 1986 the route was altered to the Arlberg twice weekly, once weekly in winter.*

1 Allegedly because it did not pay through underpatronage, the real reason for ending the *Direct-Orient* sleeping car was failure to agree on it by the railway administrations, one discovered some years later. Translator's notes.

This initiative was the "Parisian" sequel to another astonishing show of defiance which had seen the light of day in Switzerland, and which marks the return of the positive poetry of travel.

On the heights of Zurich, Mr. Albert Glatt, director of a travel agency, was troubled from the spring of 1976 by the progressive and irretrievable abandoning of a luxury railway link to the Bosphorus. Heartbroken to see the beautiful cars condemned, he decided to buy them up, restore them gradually, and make them run in the form of train cruises where nostalgia would be the tryst. Tenacious, audacious and precise, clad in his inseparable tartan cap, in October 1976 Mr. Albert Glatt organised a journey, already legendary, which by about two months coincided with the International Sleeping Car (Wagons-Lits) Company's centenary. This rolling stock, saved at great cost from demolition, and now private property, gathered together sleeping cars of Type LX 16 for sixteen passengers only (compared to 36 in the most modern cars), which had been in service on the Blue Train *(Train Bleu)* and the *Nord Express*, two Pullmans of *Cote d'Azur* type, a shower car (seven cabins functioning continuously), a modern dining car while awaiting a period car to be put in order, and a Swiss Federal Railways luggage van with reserve kitchen and wine cellar.

From the beginning of this new adventure, life on board the train conceived by Mr. Albert Glatt was worthy of eulogies. The composition of the train, identical throughout the journey, allowed the brilliant, luxurious and privileged atmosphere of bygone days to be recaptured, whether it was the detail of the menus, on which one could read, as tradition requires, that it had been "prepared by the chef, Monsieur X, and presented by the maitre d'hôtel, Monsieur Y"; or even the appreciable number of people concerned with the comfort of the passengers – twenty stewards, conductors and a doctor for ninety six passengers – all combine in a journey in time across the history and geography of old Europe. A gala dinner by candle-light, in black tie and long dress, steam locomotives brought out again with pride to have the honour of hauling this nostalgia on rails: it is certainly Mr. Albert Glatt and his well organised team who has put the first "retro" *Orient Express* back into fashion.

In the spring of 1977, five journeys were run under the label *Arlberg-Orient Express* (Zurich-Innsbruck-Ljubljana-Belgrade-Sofia-Istanbul) and under the label *Simplon-Orient Express* (Lausanne-Milan-Venice-Ljubljana-Belgrade-Thessaloniki-Paleofarsalos-Athens). Only the crossing of France was absent from the original itinerary. Since then, the purchase of further old cars, their sumptuous restoration conforming to the decor of the period, and the quality of the food, have made this train, now called the *Nostalgic-Istanbul-Orient Express,* synonymous with an unforgettable journey. Complementing these cruises at fixed dates in spring and autumn, with the same rolling stock the Intraflug agency organises circular tours in France (with visits to the great vineyards of Champagne and of Bordeaux, and of the Chateaux of the Loire), day trips in Pullman cars across the Swiss Alps, or for example on the spectacular Tenda pass mountain line from Zurich to Nice, with the outward or return journey possible by air.

Successively, this most nostalgic of trains has run from Zurich to Istanbul (1976), from Zurich to Athens (1977 and 1978), from Paris to Istanbul via Milan, Trieste and Belgrade (1981), from Paris to Istanbul via Munich, Vienna, Budapest and Bucharest (1982) and on a combination of historic itineraries in 1983 for the centenary journey of the *Orient Express* on a great European circuit using the routes of the *Orient*, the *Arlberg* and the *Simplon*.

182

183

184

185

186

182. *Evening dress is indispensable for this dinner in the Dining cars of the Venice-Simplon-Orient Express, one evening in 1984. This former C.I.W.L. car has been restored according to the designs of the decorator Gérard Gallet.*
183. *A single cabin which communicates with another cabin forms a small appartment in the centre of an LX car of the Nostalgic-Istanbul-Orient Express.*
184. *The mahogany corridor serving the cabins of an LX car whose charm has been immortalised by the poet Valery Larbaud.*
185. *The washroom of an LX car cabin of the Nostalgic-Istanbul-Orient Express is hidden behind this curved double door.*
186. *The Nostalgic-Istanbul-Orient Express here hauled by a (Swiss) steam locomotive, is made up of sleeping cars, Pullmans, dining car, bar car and showers car. A necessary comfort for a journey of more than three days in 1987. (Compare illustration No. 72)*

187. *The all-steam Nostalgic-Istanbul-Orient Express running towards the Orient. Albert Glatt, President of Intraflug Ltd., and owner of the train, truly passionate about the railway phenomenon, strives to obtain engines of the Belle Epoque from the railway administrations of the countries crossed.*

Some brilliant stops in addition (like the Opera at Vienna for example) have led this train to be considered a palace on wheels, whose maintenance is carried out while the passengers are "on land".

The *Nostalgic-Istanbul-Orient-Express* organises few advertised journeys. Most often the train is leased on charter to travel agencies or companies.

Actually the train is made up thus:

— *Three Pullman cars* built in 1929 by the Aytré works (Entreprises Industrielles Charentaises) of "Pullman Côte d'Azur" type. They comprise Car No. 4149 decorated by René Prou and withdrawn in 1971, Car No. 4158, decorated by René Lalique withdrawn in 1972, and Car No. 4161, also decorated by Lalique and withdrawn in 1972, after having been equipped with air-conditioning and allocated to the *Mistral* (Paris-Nice) until 1969.

These three cars each provide 28 seats in comfortable armchairs, spread between two coupés, with doors, each with a table of four covers, a large saloon with one table of three covers and four tables of two, and a small saloon with one table of one cover, one table of three, and two tables of two covers. Belonging to a series of thirty-four cars, they were part of the two hundred and eleven Pullman cars which were all put in service between 1926 and 1931 by the International Sleeping Car and Great European Express Trains Company. Five of them are still authorised to run in international traffic, three of them are the property of Intraflug A.G.[2]

— *A dining car* No. 2741, built in 1926 by De Dietrich at Luneville, Lorraine. Allocated to the *Sud Express* (Paris-Madrid-Lisbon, French portion, Paris-Irun) it was one of twelve very comfortable saloon cars with twenty-four armchairs. In 1949 it was converted into a dining car and ran until 1977 between Irun and Lisbon. Today, arranged with twelve tables for four, it provides 48 leather seats, and in 1981 has been repainted in the colours which it wore in 1926 (chocolate and cream); its range still functions on coal. Its superb marquetries are all the original ones.

— *A Bar Car* No. 4164, built in 1929 at Aytré and decorated by Lalique. Initially a First Class Pullman car type "Côte d'Azur", it was converted in 1951 into a saloon-bar, painted blue, allocated to the *Train Bleu* (Paris-Ventimiglia) and sold to the S.N.C.F. (French Railways) in 1962. It provided 16 seats in the bar, and 24 in the dining saloon, and its bar was, until the end of the 1960s as elegant as that of the Ritz. Here one met Coco Chanel, Sacha Guitry and all the high society fleeing from the fogs of the North to the

2 During 1987, Wagons-Lits have restored at least one more. They still own the other two.

Mediterranean sun. Bought by Intraflug in 1980, restored by the Wagons-Lits workshops at Vienna-Inzersdorf, it has been refurnished with red leather armchairs and a piano which bestows a "retro" ambiance to warm one's heart. It has seats for 30 without counting the standing passengers who encourage the pianist and hum the airs which one hears in a fashionable bar. No food is served there but the drinks flow continuously!

– *Six sleeping cars*, type LX 16 built in 1929. No. 3542 (Aytré), decorated by Prou, in service in the *Pyrenées-Côte d'Argent*, was withdrawn in 1976. No. 3537 (Aytré), allocated to the *Paris-Mediterannée Express* was later on the *Train Bleu* until 1969 and withdrawn 1976. No. 3472 (Metropolitan-Cammell Carriage & Wagon Co. Ltd., Birmingham) decorated by Maple, at first on the *Calais-Mediterannée Express*, the first name of the *Train Bleu* until after war, to which it was allocated until the winter of 1969. No. 3475 (Metropolitan), decorated by Maple, worked to the same destinations. The same goes for Nos. 3480 and 3487 (Metropolitan) decorated by Morisson and withdrawn in 1975. These cars, which were the most luxurious model ever built by the Wagons-Lits Company, have four individual compartments, linked two by two with a communicating door – the summit of luxury! – and six double compartments of which four are linked in pairs, and two are non-communicating. Total: sixteen beds.

– *One sleeping car*, type LX 20. No. 3551 (Aytré), decorated by Nelson, originally allocated to the *Pyrenées-Côte d'Argent* and withdrawn in 1973. It has eight double compartments linked in pairs, and two non communicating double cabins. Total: twenty beds.

– *The presidential car* No. 3554. This dining car, built at Aytré in 1927, was transformed and allocated to the train of the French President of the Republic in 1955. The Presidents René Coty, Charles de Gaulle and Georges Pompidou received important personages there, such as H.M. Queen Elizabeth II, H.M. Baudoin I King of Belgium, and Nikita Kruschev. Menaced by demolition, this car has been saved by an association of defenders of whom Jean-Paul Caracalla, Jean des Cars and Gerald Maurois were members. Its historic value is immense, because its long table which can welcome eighteen guests came from the first official French train for President Felix Faure in 1894. The original kitchen still functions on coal. Restored, the car was re-inaugerated in the spring of 1983 on an excursion from Zurich to Zurich, around the Lake of Constance, with the *cuisine* prepared and served by the staff of the famous Swiss chef Max Kehl, of *Chez Max*. Because of its individual character, this car is allocated to journeys of a gastronomic kind.

– *A shower car* No. 4013, initially a 1st class Pullman "Golden Arrow" type built at Birmingham in 1926, was transformed in 1966 by the Wagons-Lits workshops at Rome. Specially designed for tours it includes seven cabins, a water-boiler room, a pantry and two compartments for the stewards. Functioning at all times, passengers can refresh themselves at any hour; towels and soap are provided. This car, which belongs to the C.I.W.L.T., is hired by Intraflug.

– *A luggage fourgon* No. 1283. Built at Birmingham (by Metropolitan) in 1928, with, at that time, a shower compartment and a cage for dogs, it was part of the *Simplon-Orient Express*. Discovered in the suburbs of Paris, and destined for the scrap-heap, it has been converted in 1981-1982 into a fourgon for provisions equipped with electrical equipment, deep freeze, refrigerator, auxiliary kitchen, wine cellar, reserve linen, food cupboard, etc. With its legendary look-out (bird-cage),[3] this van – today very rare – completes the general profile of the *Nostalgic-Istanbul-Orient Express*, whose composition

3 This fourgon was the one used in the film "Murder on the Orient Express", 1974.

is, obviously, variable, and subject to the needs of the journey, with, if necessary extra cars (Rheingold saloons No. 24506 and 24507 of 1928,[4] Pullman Cars Nos. 4151 and 4159 hired from the C.I.W.L.T.).[5] Two sleeping cars are added to it for the staff. These comprise 32 people (for a maximum of a hundred passengers) divided into two crews: the Presidential brigade (1 chef de brigade, 2 chefs, 1 cook, 2 commis, 1 maitre d'hotel, 6 waiters, 1 barman) and the Staff of Intraflug (1 Train Captain, 1 travel guide, 1 engineer, 1 fitter, 3 cleaners, 1 housekeeper, 8 conductors, 1 shower-car steward, 1 pianist, 1 Swiss doctor).

With an average composition of fifteen cars, all built between 1926 and 1929, a length of 350 metres and a weight of 700 tons which need double-heading on mountain routes, the *Nostalgic-Istanbul-Orient Express* is an authentic railway aristocrat, and its arrival in the shadow of the minarets of the Blue Mosque with a steam engine dressed with flags and spitting black scrolls, while the folk dances replace the rhythm of the coupling rods, is an extraordinary occasion. The innovation for the spring of 1984 are Paris-Vienna-Paris journeys with different outward and return routes and stops at Strasbourg, Heidelberg and Salzburg. Great luxury over a relatively short distance is surely a means to dream that one day, one evening, one will make the great journey to the Bosphorus.[6]

One year after Albert Glatt had put his *Orient Express* network back on the rails, the world of collectors and lovers of nostalgia fixed their eyes on Monte Carlo. At midday on Saturday, 8th October, 1977, the elegant capital of the smiling Principality was invaded by journalists, by cameramen and by more discreet people for a very original auction sale which was without precedent: the sale, organised by Sotheby Parke Bernet of five cars, in byegone days jewels of the Grand European Expresses. Six television chains and the greatest newspapers gave world coverage to this unusual auction sale.

The day before, these five cars had formed a special train from Nice to Monaco, in which H.R.H. Princess Grace had taken her seat for a breakfast during the journey of about sixty minutes travelling at very slow speed: 25 km/h! It was made up of the Pullman No. 4163 of 1929; the sleeping car LX 16 No. 3489, allocated to the *Simplon-Orient Express* in 1946-1947; the sleeping car LX 16 No. 3548 of 1929, requisitioned by the staff of the German Army from 1941 to 1945, and had been part of the *Simplon Orient Express* in 1946 and 1947; the sleeping car LX 16 No. 3542 of 1929; and lastly the dining car No. 2741 of 1926, built for the *Sud Express*. The fact that two of these cars had really been in the composition of the *Simplon-Orient Express* made people write and report, once again wrongly, that "the Orient Express had been put up for auction"! After death, the booty.

These auctions were swift, although there was one moment of dispute when an Englishman, too discreet, and constrained by the television cameras, did not show his intentions in time. In less than half an hour, the cars had changed their fate. The centre piece was the Pullman, gone for 360,000 francs to a mysterious Parisian, M. Piccard, who bought it, as well as a sleeping car on behalf of H.M. Hassan II, King of Morocco. But it was between two other bidders that the battle was fought. The first was Albert Glatt, who carried off the dining car for 290,000 francs. The second was an American, Mr. James Sherwood, of whom we are going to hear further. He bought two sleeping cars, the first pieces in a gigantic game of reconstruction of a luxury *Orient Express* in regular service.

---

4 Ex-Mitropa.
5 A new Golden Arrow-type Pullman car No. 4080 has just been added to the fleet of the *Nostalgic-Istanbul-Orient Express* in 1987. This Pullman, built in 1927 by the Leeds Forge Co. (Leeds, England) had been transformed into a dining car at Budapest in 1937, then re-arranged as a Pullman with kitchen in 1964, in Spain. Totally restored at the C.I.W.L.T. works at Ostend, it is actually the only Pullman of its type to run.
6 Some Zurich-Istanbul trips are arranged each year in September. Under the name *Semper Oper Pullman*, a rake of day cars formed of Pullmans, operates the Zurich-Frankfurt-Dresden service for Opera lovers in October and November. For all the exciting journeys organised by Mr. Glatt and his team, ask for details from Intraflug A.G., Taegernstrasse 12A, CH-8127 Forch, Zurich, Switzerland. Telephone: 010-411-9801772. Telex 828518 IFZCH. Sumptuous brochures are published each year "Travels with the great luxury express trains of the world". Very enticing, they show how Mr. Glatt has become an expert in luxury trains, surpassing even the limits of his own *Orient Express*, with notably the journeys of a *Trans-siberian* special, "the only luxury train in the U.S.S.R."

188. H.P.H. Princess Grace of Monaco, opposite the Director General of the C.I.W.L., is "machine-gunned" by the photographers before having breakfast between Nice and Monte Carlo.

189. Before the exceptional auction sale of the C.I.W.L. cars which took place at Monte Carlo in October 1977, Jacques-Bernard Dupont, Director General of the Company, invited some personalities to take part in a short journey between Nice and Monte Carlo at breakfast time. The cars, which are going to be sold by the auctioneer Peter Wilson, Chairman of Sotheby's, had to make this ultimate journey before changing ownership.

190. Albert Glatt, President of Intraflug Ltd., the first to want to resuscitate the Orient Express in all its pomp, receiving, from the hands of a C.I.W.L. conductor, the keys of the car which he had just bought at the Monte Carlo auction sale: the dining car No. 2741, built in 1926.

Totalling 1,450,000 francs, the five cars were saved from the demolishers blow-torch by the ivory gavel. One felt that, sooner or later, these cars, having become private property, were once more going to run again, and that was the essential thing. And Mr. Sherwood announced without delay that he intended to organize a 'retro' train from London to Venice. It was the beginning of an extraordinary adventure.

President of the very important *Sea Containers Ltd.*, James Sherwood brought all his financial support to the realisation of this audacious project, so opposite to the sad fashion of democratisation and commonplace travel. His wife, Shirley, was equally involved in this gamble, and assisted in carrying out deep searches for the rolling stock, dispersed through Europe, which could be saved. The investigation, the work, and the organisation of this train lasted nearly five years.

The figures give the scope of the enterprise, known henceforth under the name of *Venice-Simplon-Orient Express* (V.S.O.E.) whose first departure to the city of the Doges took place on 25th May 1982. At this date, the investment had been eleven million pounds sterling. This applied notably to the repurchase and the absolutely sumptuous restoration of eight British Pullman cars as well as two luggage vans, on the one hand, and of twelve sleeping cars, two dining cars, one Pullman car, one bar car, and two cars for the staff on the other hand.

The originality – and the interest – of the V.S.O.E. is, first, the existance of a double train for the whole of the journey.

The sector London-Folkestone-London is made exclusively in British Pullman cars superbly restored. Sumptuous in its livery of chocolate and cream, the rake is composed of splendid examples of Pullman services beyond the Channel which made the reputation of great trains such as the *Golden Arrow*, the *Brighton Belle* and the *Queen of Scots*. These cars were equally allocated to movements of the Royal Family, for short journeys, notably in the south of England. Some had the honour to carry heads of States, heads of governments and other VIP's on the occasion of the Coronation of H.M. Queen Elizabeth II, in 1953, and of visits of Presidents of the French Republic, Vincent Auriol in 1950 and Charles de Gaulle in 1960, and at the funeral of Sir Winston Churchill in 1965.

These cars, which follow, have the characteristic of carrying an individual name – instead of a number – which is a custom reserved for the Pullmans of Great Britain.

– *Audrey:* built in 1932 at Birmingham, allocated to the *Brighton Belle* (the oldest all-Pullman service in Europe, which goes back to 1881). Damaged in 1940, she had the honour to carry Sir Laurence Olivier and others up until the disappearance of this luxury train in 1972. Vandals also stripped her. Restored, her marquetry panels are exceptional.

– *Cygnus:* built in 1951, ran on the *Golden Arrow* London-Dover-London from 1951 until the suppression of the train in 1972. In 1976, she ran on a steam operated private line, the *North Yorkshire Moors Railway*. Used in the film *Agatha*, which relates the life of Agatha Christie (with Vanessa Redgrave and Dustin Hoffman, directed by Michael Apted).

– *Ibis:* built in 1925, placed in service in Italy (under the number 52) from Milan to Venice, in the *Deauville Express* in 1927 among others. In the *Golden Arrow* from 1930 to 1952, after having been a stationary restaurant for the Royal Navy. On the London-Southampton boat trains from 1952 to 1963, bought back from Birmingham museum in 1981.

- *Ione:* built in 1928, included in several boat trains and on the *Queen of Scots,* a prestigeous train linking London (Kings Cross station) to Glasgow and Edinburgh, and Royal trains with Scotland as their destination. Withdrawn in 1968 and purchased for private journeys, she was bought from the Birmingham museum in December 1982, and boasts sumptuous flower-pattern marquetries.

- *Minerva:* built in 1927, decorated in Edwardian motifs, allocated to the *Golden Arrow* from 1951 to 1961, in the invited guests train from Dover to London on 30th May 1953, at the time of the Coronation of Elizabeth II.

- *Perseus:* built in 1951. In service on the *Golden Arrow* from 1951 to 1972. On 27th April 1956, she carried Marshal Bulganin and Mr. Nikita Kruschev at the end of their official visit to Great Britain. Bought back by Sea Containers (James Sherwood) in 1977.

- *Phoenix:* built in 1952 at Brighton (by the Pullman Car Company itself) using the underframe (chassis) of the car *Rainbow* (built 1927, destroyed in an accident-fire in 1936). In the *Golden Arrow,* then allocated to official trains for Her Majesty the Queen Mother, and General de Gaulle. Bought in 1973 by the French Mercure hotel chain, she was converted into a stationary restaurant near Lyon. Bought by V.S.O.E. in 1980, repatriation on an enormous lorry was very tricky: she even stopped, wedged under a railway bridge! It was necessary to let down the tyres of the lorry!

- *Zena:* in service in 1929, her decoration is an art deco triumph. In March 1950 the French President, M. Vincent Auriol savoured on board "fillets of sole Zena" and addressed, on the back of the menu, a message of congratulation to King George VI.

- *Lucille*[7]: built in 1928 for the *Queen of Scots*. In the *Bournemouth Belle* 1963-66.

Lastly, this train is completed by a superb luggage van, which, in 1943 was used for the transport of . . . carrier pigeons!

One needs to add that these cars, perfectly restored — one would say like new — at the Carnforth workshops are not the only British Pullmans acquired by V.S.O.E. Others could be, eventually, placed back in service. Their actual capacity comprises 2 kitchens (in Ibis and Ione) and from 20 to 26 seats. Total: 194 passengers. The length of the journey on British territory is one hour and a half, and a luncheon or copious tea, included in the ticket, is served on board by stylish staff.

At the maritime stations of Folkestone and Boulogne, the passengers, who do not have to concern themselves with their luggage, go on board a ship of the Sealink British Ferries Company, travelling in a reserved saloon. Duration of the crossing: one hour and fifty minutes.

The second train, also, is sumptuous, very long (401 m), and heavy (944 t. without the locomotives) and its regular circulation in France, Switzerland, Austria and Italy is a *tour de force* and an event in the history of luxury railway journeys.

The timetable is carefully arranged to permit the nostalgic travellers to spend some thirty-two hours on board, to make practical connections with the great business capitals, and to take the time to savour the full pleasure of a journey in the manner of former times in the shining cabins, at the bar, in the deep Pullman armchairs, with details such as the morning newspaper (in English), fresh croissants for breakfast, a service of quality, taking into account the consideration shown by the staff of the dining cars and Pullman, and a refined cuisine headed by Christian Bodiguel, awarded the international Gastronomy's golden fork.[8]

The continental rolling stock of the *Venice-Simplon-Orient Express* is made up of the following cars, bought back for the most part from the C.I.W.L.T. — *Sleeping car* No. 3309, type S1, built in Belgium in 1926,

---

7. *Lucille* joined the train in 1986.
8. The V.S.O.E. has changed its itinerary for a longer and more picturesque journey. Henceforth (from 1985) it uses the route of the Arlberg-Orient Express which traverses Switzerland, Austria and then Italy by the Brenner Pass.

decorated by René Prou. From 1928 to 1939 it was part of the Orient Express on all its branches. After having been requisitioned in Germany from 1942 to 1945, then put back on the Orient Express (Paris-Prague) in 1946, before it was based in Lisbon in 1958, for the *Sud Express*. Withdrawn from service in 1971. Number of beds: 24.

– *Sleeping Car* No. 3425: type S1, built in England in 1929. Has run in the *Orient Express* (Boulogne-Karlovy Vary), the *Arlberg-Orient Express* (Paris-Chur) and the Simplon-Orient Express (Istanbul-Milan). In 1940 it ran from Istanbul to Lisbon.

The successive allocations of these two cars, which originally had eight 'single' cabins and four doubles, gives an idea of the international career of this rolling stock, traversing very different countries and over millions of kilometres.

– *Sleeping Car* No. 3473: type luxe (Lx), built in England. In 1929, decorated by Morisson. Ran from Calais to Vintimille (Ventimiglia) in the *Train Bleu*, then, in 1937, from Paris to Niegoreloje, via Berlin, in the *Nord Express*. After a return to the *Train Bleu*, it finished its first career in the *Simplon-Orient Express* in 1961.

– *Sleeping Car* No. 3482: type luxe (Lx), built in England in 1929, decorated by Maple. In the *Train Bleu*, the *Nord Express*, the *Rome Express* and the *Simplon-Orient Express* until 1961. Last services: Madrid-Santander *(Costa Vasca Express)* until 1971.

– *Sleeping Car* No. 3483: type luxe (Lx), built in England in 1929, decorated by Morisson. In the *Train Bleu*, the *Rome Express*, the *Nord Express*, and in 1948, in the S.O.E. In Spain from 1973 to 1977.

– *Sleeping Car* No. 3525: type luxe (Lx), built in France in 1929, decorated by René Prou, with his elegant stylised flowers. In the *Train Bleu*, the *Pyrennées-Côte d'Argent Express* (Paris-Biarritz), the S.O.E. the *Rome Express*, then Spain.

– *Sleeping Car* No. 3539: same characteristics as the previous car, used by the American Headquarters from 1945 to 1957 in the *Mozart Express* (Strasbourg-Vienna).

– *Sleeping Car* No. 3543: same characteristics. One of the first cars bought by James Sherwood at the Monte-Carlo sale, in 1977.

– *Sleeping Car* No. 3544: same characteristics — with supplementary toilets, very spacious, but an even more astonishing history. Stationary during the war at Limoges, it was used as a bawdy house (brothel), before becoming part . . . of the Royal Train of the Dutch Royal Family. A social ascent!

– *Sleeping Cars* Nos. 3552, 3553 and 3555: type luxe (Lx), built in France in 1929 and decorated by Nelson. Various allocations from the *Nord Express* to the *Sud Express* and on the S.O.E.

– *Dining Car* No. 4095: built in 1927, type "Étoile du Nord (North Star)". Initially a second class Pullman kitchen car. Allocated to the *Edelweiss* (Amsterdam-Basel-Lucerne). Before transformation it had 38 seats, after the work, 36.

– *Dining Car* No. 4110: former second class Pullman, with kitchen, built in England in 1927. Formed part of the *Danube Express* or *Danubiu-Pullman-Rapide* which crossed Roumania from Bucharest to Constanza, on the Black Sea and was, as we have seen, the first embarkation port for the maritime sector of the *Orient Express*. This service, of very great luxury, was well known in all central Europe. After transformation, it ran in Portugal and in Spain, notably between Cadiz and Seville. Today it has 36 places against 38 formerly.

— *Dining Car* No. 4141: former first class Pullman kitchen car, built in 1929 in France and decorated in the "Côte d'Azur" style by René Lalique, of translucent beauties very engrossed in a bacchanalian orgy... It was, among other services, in the *Golden Arrow (Flèche d'Or)*. Before its re-arrangement, it had 20 seats, today it has 35. However, a recent modification has allowed an optional bar to be used. This option requires the removal of 5 seats, that is to say the table for 4 and that of one person situated near the former kitchen.

— *Bar Car* No. 3674: formerly a 56 seat dining car, built in France in 1931, allocated to the *Trains Transatlantiques* (Ocean Liner boat trains) *Paris-Le Havre,* then in the first rakes of the fast train, the *Capitole* (Paris-Toulouse), this car has been entirely rennovated by the French decorator Gerard Gallet, the designer also of the plates, silverware and upholstery-cloth on board the *Venice-Simplon-Orient Express*. This ensemble of objects and accessories on board the train, can also be bought. They comprise, with the very elegant annual diaries, the *Collection Venice-Simplon-Orient Express*, directed by Paul Bianchini. Note that the bar car today presents a new appearance nearer to the saloon cars of America at the beginning of the century than to the European bar cars of the Crazy Years of the 1930s. But its comfort and the softness of its tones are very successful. And there is a piano, equally highly appreciated...

The cars, restored at the Ostend and Bremen works, represent a summit of railway luxury for rolling stock which is, on average, over half a century old. Two sleeping cars of 1949 are added to them, for the staff. Dressed in pre-1914-style uniforms, the staff from Boulogne to Venice comprise forty people, made up of non-railway hotel staff: a train manager, a head conductor, a maitre d'hôtel, a head barman and two barmen, three head chefs, six waiters, five cooks, four pantrymen, a fitter, a cleaner and eleven conductors, and... a pianist. They are assisted by "ground staff": twenty-eight people for the maintenance of the train.

The *Venice-Simplon-Orient Express* links London to Venice twice a week from spring to autumn, once a week in winter. Depart from London at 11 hours from Victoria Station, depart from Paris Gare de L'Est at 21 h. 05 mins. Arrive at Venice the next day at 19 hours.

On the continental portion, on average three hundred drinks, ninety bottles of wine and and thirty bottles of champagne are served. During the first season, from 25th May to 31st December 1982, the V.S.O.E. carried 21,000 passengers of whom 39% were British, 36% were Americans, 12% were French, 9% were Italians, 2% were Japanese, 1% were Belgians and 1% were Australians.

Certainly a part of the journey — the continental part — appears to suffice for savouring this pleasure of different travel. This is a mistake. Only the full journey (taken by 81.3% of the passengers in 1982) allows one to know the joys of the progressive pleasure, thanks to this double train, though one never meets the other. An experience which one must experience: each departure of the V.S.O.E. resembles a honeymoon journey: magnified by the posters of an exceptional artist, Pierre Fix-Masseau, who has known how to find again — and modernise — this evocative expression of the 1930s.[9]

In the light of the success obtained by the companies operating the *Venice-Simplon-Orient Express* and the *Nostalgic-Istanbul-Orient Express*, the Compagnie Internationale des Wagons-Lits at du Tourisme has put back into circulation a rake of old rolling stock, intended to commercialise special trains. At the moment six cars are grouped under the name *Orient Express:* the dining cars Nos. 2979 and 2869 built by *Officine Meccaniche Italiane (Reggio Emilia)* in 1927.[10] Two Pullman cars Nos. 4151 and 4159 built by

9. Venice-Simplon-Orient Express, Paris: 11 Rue de Surène, 75008. Tel: (1) 47 42 36 28. Telex 649387 VSOEP. Italy: Via Turati 18, 20121 Milan tel: (2) 6572344. Telex 312344 SC ITA 1. London. Sea Containers House, 20 Upper Ground, London SE1. Tel: (01) 928 60 00 Telex: 8955803. New York. One World Trade Centre, Suite 1235 N.Y. 10048. Tel: (212) 938 68 30. Telex: 645446.

10. No 2869 was built by Birmingham Railway Carriage & Wagon Co. Ltd., in 1926. Note by GB. See note 9 page 82.

191. *This goods forwarding company has not hesitated to take the* Orient Express *as the emblem of speed for publicity purposes. Note the fantasy sleeping car and the unorthodox destination plates.*

192. *On the back of a dining car bill, a traveller, the Marquis of Beauvoir declares "never to have eaten as good a steak, and which was also cooked to a turn (à point), neither at* Paillard's *nor the* Café Anglais *nor at the* Savoy". *Ought not this note, entitled "Complaints", to carry the words "and compliments"?*

11. It is planned that in 1988, the *Golden Arrow* will run with steam traction Paris-Boulogne-Paris with the *N.I.O.E.* Pullmans, and *V.S.O.E.* British Pullmans London-Folkestone-London.

12. Read the interesting articles of M. Didier Durandal in *La Vie du Rail* Nos. 1900, 1901 & 1902 of 30th June, 7th & 14th July 1983.

Entreprises Industrielles Charentaises at Aytré (France). The first has decor by René Prou, the second decorated by René Lalique. Two bar cars complete the rake, both of them built at Aytré in 1929, the first, decorated by René Prou, the second by René Lalique with the famous glass bouquets of flowers. Another Pullman car, No. 4156, dating from 1929 and decorated by René Prou, ought to emerge from the restoration workshops soon.

Alongside the nostalgia on rails which Messrs. Albert Glatt and James Sherwood offer us — who knows if, one day, their trains will not unite occasionally to reconstitute an extraordinary London-Istanbul[11] — the "ordinary" *Orient Express* continues its discreet career, every evening from Paris to Budapest, and, alternatively Bucharest. Certainly it does not benefit from any publicity, from any promotion, no film star is photographed there, and it scarcely inspires tour operators. Not sentimental enough? Without doubt, but it also in its own fashion expresses European history and only the connisseurs really know what this train which appears on the indicators of five countries under the number 263 is.[12]

A train which persists in maintaining railway and human relations between west and central Europe, a contact, still maintained between men despite their differences, even political opposition. A connecting link express on, approximately, the first itinerary of 1883.

It is the ultimate proof that its history is not yet completed. De luxe, or ordinary, yesterday's or today's, it still fascinates us. For a hundred years, the most exciting of nostalgic journies invites us to dream, in wishing us, at each departure:

–Bon Voyage...

191

Appendix

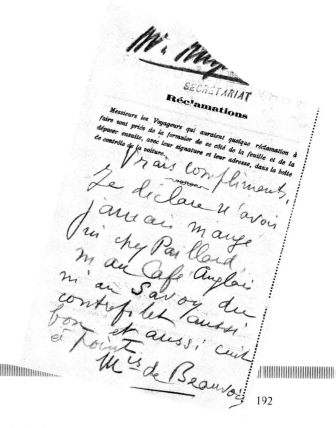

THE GREAT HOURS OF THE ORIENT EXPRESS 1882-1987

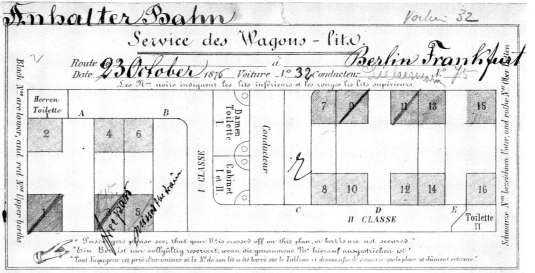

193. *The engagement of one of the first sleeping car conductors, on 15th March 1876.*

194. Carte diagramme *(berthing list)* of car No. 32 (built in 1874 at Berlin by Eisenbahn Bedarfs-Aktiengesellschaft), dated 23rd October 1876.

10th October 1882
The Paris-Vienna rail axis, greatly used, justifies the placing of a luxury train in service, the *Train-Eclair, Lightning Train*. It links the two capitals, 1,350 km. apart, in 27 hours 53 minutes, four hours less than the ordinary train. It is the first international luxury train.

Spring, 1883
Georges Nagelmackers, a Belgian Engineer, Founder-Director General of the Compagnie Internationale des Wagons-Lits, and promoter of the first European sleeping cars, negotiates agreements with the administrations of the French Est, Alsace-Lorraine, Baden, Wurtemberg, Bavarian, Austrian-Hungarian and Romanian systems. Object: to extend the Lightning Train to Constantinople

5th June 1883
The *Train Express d'Orient* makes its inaugural journey, a rehearsal which its creator considers indispensable. Actually, this train is the first in the world to run across eight countries, exclusively composed of sleeping cars, vans, and a dining car suppressing the meal stops. The itinerary links Paris (Strasbourg station, today Gare de l'Est), Strasbourg, Munich, Vienna, Budapest, Bucharest, Giurgiu. This last place is a Romanian port on the Danube, terminus of the concessions obtained by M. Nagelmackers. Here, the passengers use a ferry and then a train of the *Danube Black Sea Company (Austrian Eastern Railway)* as far as the seaport of Varna. From there a crossing on the Austrian Lloyd liner takes them to Constantinople. Duration of the Paris-Constantinople journey: 81 h. 30 mins., thirty hours less than in an ordinary train. Departures from Paris: Tuesday and Friday. Departures from Constantinople: Saturday and Tuesday.

4th October 1883
First official journey, with important guests, political personalities and journalists. The rolling stock, specially built with bogies will remain in service until 1898. The passengers get back to Paris on 16th October. A new era begins. International travel is born.

March 1884
The International Sleeping Car Company takes the title Compagnie Internationale Des Wagons-Lits Et Des Grands Express Europeans.

145

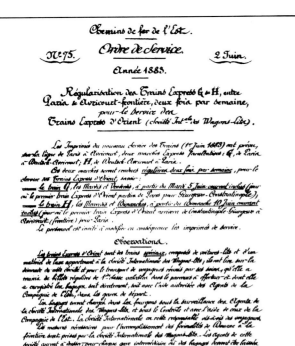

196. *The Train Express d'Orient daily Paris-Vienna timetable of 1st November 1885 in French and German, extended to Belgrade once weekly. It mentions that passengers must pay for their reservations telegrams.*

1st June 1884
Daily service between Paris and Budapest. The fourgons (vans) of M. Nagelmackers replace those of the Est Railway.

1885
Once a week a train ensures a link for Belgrade and Nis, with a mailcoach – diligence sector (335 km) – organized by C.I.W.L. – from Nis to Plovdiv via Sofia, then a connection by train from Plovdiv to Constantinople. It is the first incursion of the *Orient Express* to the south of the Balkans. The first official passenger in it is Prince Alexander I of Bulgaria.

12th August 1888
The Paris-Nis line is extended to Salonica. Nis becomes an important junction south of Belgrade. The Paris-Sofia line is completed.

195. *Service order of the Est Railway, 2nd June 1883, 3 days before the first departure of the Train Express d'Orient. The order states that the trains are special, will go twice weekly each way, that the C.I.W.L. looks after all luggage except at intermediate stations where it must be signed for by the Est Railway personnel, and that C.I.W.L. deliver it at Paris. It also states the first train from Avricourt frontier to Paris will be on Sunday 10th June 1883.*

197. *Shame on conductor Laesker who allowed a passenger to board without a ticket (Berlin-Paris service)! He was dismissed from the Company on 31st August 1883.*

1st June 1889.
The section Budapest-Belgrade-Sofia-Plovdiv is completed. The Paris-Constantinople journey, entirely by train, is a reality. Duration: 67 h. 35 mins for 3,186 km without change of carriage.

1891
The *Train-Express d'Orient* becomes officially the *Orient Express*, "the" train of Europe.

31st May 1891
Near Cerkeskoy (Turkey), the train is attacked by bandits. Plunder: £50,000 sterling and five German hostages, released for a £8,000 sterling ransom.

12th September 1892
The train is put in quarantine at the Turkish Frontier because of a cholera epidemic. Only the diplomatic bags are carried, with great precautions.

1894
The Compagnie Internationale des Wagons-Lits (C.I.W.L.) opens some Grand Hotels for the passengers of the train: the *Bosphorus*, the *Summer Palace Hotel* and the *Pera Palace*. First class return fare: £58 sterling. Second class, for servants accompanying their masters: £44 sterling.

1895
The line Paris-Giurgiu-Varna is opposed by a line ending at another Black Sea port, Constantza, further north. When the Romanian Railways complete Fetesti Bridge over the Danube, Constantza replaces Varna. New cars are ordered and a branch is inaugurated, starting from Belgium with the *Ostend-Vienna-Orient Express*, first "family" extension of the *Orient Express*.

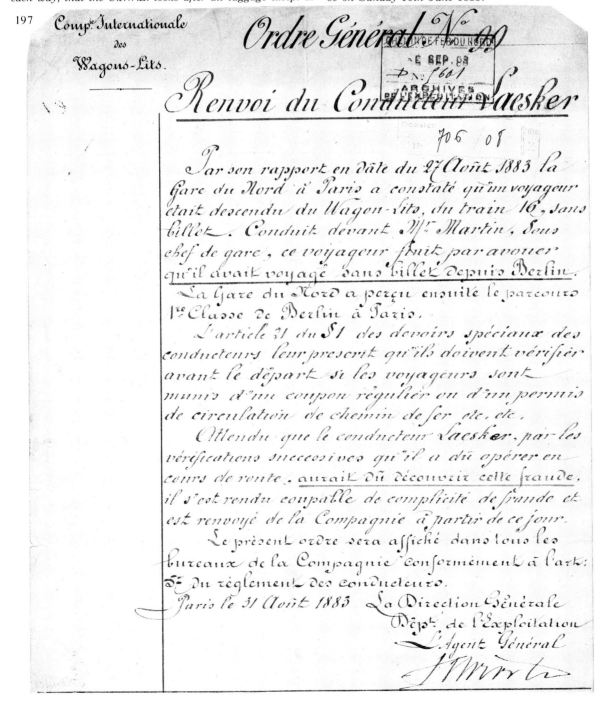

1897
The line abandons Simbach (Austria) to the advantage of Salzburg.

1901
A Paris-Karlsbad (today Karlovy Vary) sleeping car is placed in service.

1906
Creation of the *Simplon Express* (Calais-Paris-Milan) after the piercing of the Simplon Tunnel, the longest in the world (nearly 20 km) linking Switzerland to Italy.

1907
New rolling stock. The name of the train appears in brass letters alongside the Company title C.I.W.L.

1908
The *Orient Express* celebrates its 25th anniversary. The *Simplon Express* is extended to Venice.

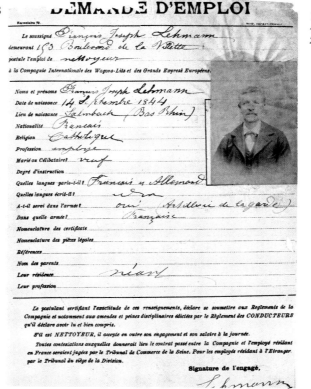

198. *A cleaner's application for employment at 4 francs a day: Francois Joseph Lehmann, 25th April 1876.*

199. *The great newspapers noted in their worldly memorandum page, the famous travellers who took the great luxury trains. "Their Majesties the King and Queen of Wurtemberg, going to London, will take the luxury train "Orient-Express" on the 18th May". Signed by the Direction Generale, 17th May 1897.*

201. *Timetable of the* Express d'Orient, *daily between Paris and Vienna, weekly for Bucharest, bi-weekly for Constantinople (February 1900).*

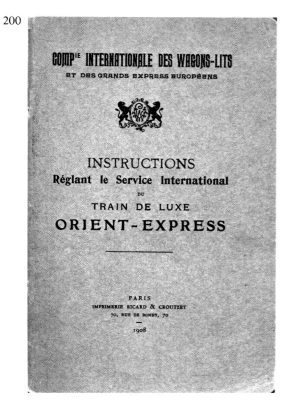

200. *Instruction book regulating the international service of the* Orient Express *(1908).*

1909
Daily service Paris-Budapest, bi-weekly Paris-Bucharest-Constantza and tri-weekly Paris-Budapest-Sofia-Constantinople. So the *Orient Express* runs on two different itineraries in the Balkans, but under the same name. The Constantza line is 2,747 km long, that to Constantinople 3,043 km. The junction is outside Budapest. A point to note: the southern axis is the only one that links the Seine and the Bosphorus by train. Duration: 76 hours; the journey of the northern route, with the ship, lasts 63 hours.

4th August 1914
The war stops the train.

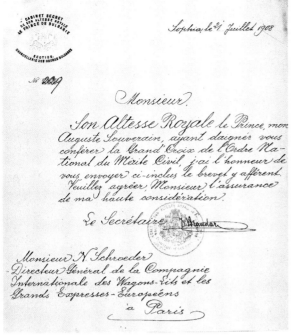

202. Letter from H.R.H. the Prince of Bulgaria's secret Cabinet sectretary, informing Napoléon Schröder, Director-General of the C.I.W.L., that the "August Sovereign" deigns to confer on him the Grand Cross of the civil Order of Merit.

203. Report of Chef de brigade Ch. Kammerer on the progress of the train *Orient Express*, 15th May 1912. Note that as well as the staff list, the functionary must indicate if any 'personages' boarded during the journey. This crew appear to have changed trains at Avricourt frontier and returned to Paris on 16th May, something said not to have happened before World War II.

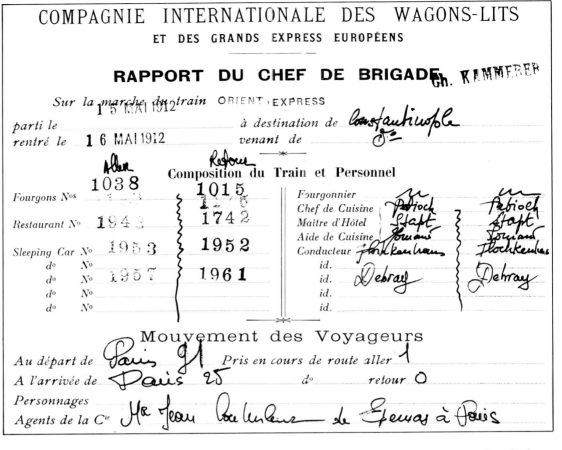

1916-1917
It is replaced by the *Balkan-Zug* (Balkan Train) which links Berlin to Constantinople with rolling stock confiscated from the C.I.W.L. by the German rival, the Mitropa.

February 1919
Creation of the *Train de luxe militaire* (Military luxury train) reserved for VIPs (personalities), and officers, under the control of the French Minister of war. Route: Paris-Linz-Vienna-Warsaw-Linz-Prague-Bucharest.

11th April 1919
Creation, provided for by the Treaty of Versailles, of a new train, *Simplon-Orient Express,* or *S.O.E.* It stops at Trieste where the passengers take sleeping cars for Bucharest, Athens, or Constantinople. The Danube bridge being destroyed, Budapest was reached by a ferry.

Autumn 1919
An international conference wishes to re-start the *Orient Express* and extend the *S.O.E.* to Turkey.

1st May 1920
The *Train de luxe militaire* retrieves its name *Orient Express* but the service is suspended until the month of June, due to the lack of coal. Hungary refuses to haul the train through that country.

20th June 1920
Operation of a train Boulogne-Paris or *Ostend-Vienna Express.*

July 1920
Start of the *S.O.E.* departing from the Gare de Lyon (Paris). This southern line passes by Dijon, Lausanne, Milan, Venice, Trieste, Belgrade. One sleeping car diverts to Orsova and Bucharest. Some travellers must club together to buy coal in Yugoslavia!

1921
The German railways refuse to take the dining service organized by the C.I.W.L., substituting for it that of the Mitropa. Some sleeping cars ensure the link Calais-Constantinople and Ostend-Constantinople, via Basle and Milan. The *S.O.E.* runs complete in one sole train from Calais to Vinkovci, meeting point of a secondary line to the north west of Belgrade, capital of the new kingdom of Yugoslavia. At Vinkovci, two sleeping cars are directed to Bucharest, while the rest of the train – three sleeping cars, a dining car and a fourgon (van) continue to Belgrade. At Nis, a further junction to Constantinople or Salonica and Athens.

1923
The Germans refuse to haul the *Orient Express* through their country when Belgian and French troops occupy the Rhineland: the train is diverted by Basle, Zürich and Innsbrück.

November 1924
The *Orient Express* restarts from Paris (Gare de l'Est) via Munich, but Switzerland calls it the *Suisse-Ariberg-Vienne Express* from the name of the Arlberg Tunnel (Austria) on the Zürich-Innsbrück line. This tunnel, 10,250 km long, was opened in 1883.

1925
Beginning of electric traction between Munich and Salzburg.

1926
First metal cars – of steel – built for the *Orient Express*. These cars, whose livery is blue with gold letters, made their first appearance in 1922.

1929
The *Orient Express* Paris-Vienna-

204. Agreement concerning the operation of the Simplon Express of 1912. The railway administrations concerned — the Nord Company, the P.L.M. Company, the Italian State Railways and the Swiss Federal Railways — have signed this protocol as well as representatives of the C.I.W.L., which had to pay the legal costs.

COMPAGNIE INTERNATIONALE DES WAGONS-LITS
1922

205. *Memorandum-book of instructions regulating the Simplon-Orient Express service, published in 1922, also concerning the provision of fuel supplies as well as the visits of customs and police on the journey Calais-Paris-Constantinople, and the towns in which victuals for the dining car would be brought on board.*

206. "*I am very satisfied with the luncheon which has been served to me this morning, 1st November 1924*" (signed) J. Joffre. The conqueror of the Marne wrote this on the back of his dining car bill. Marshal Joffre drank his half-bottle of Bordeaux (claret) and a bottle of Evian (mineral water). M. Chardon (Section Toulouse), chef de brigade of the dining car, has devoutly kept this evidence of satisfaction.

Budapest-Constantza restarts its service with sea transport on to Istanbul, the new name for Constantinople. Because of a snow storm, the *S.O.E.* stays immobilised in Turkey. It does not reach its terminus – Constantinople – until after... five days of delay! A world record!

1930
The service is, once more, interrupted.
Start of the *Taurus Express*. Starting from Istanbul, this train is the connection of the *S.O.E.* The *Taurus* runs towards Teheran, Bagdad, but also towards Beyrut, Haifa and Cairo. At Istanbul a special ferry links the European station of Sirkeci with the Asiatic station of Haydarpasa. Europe and Asia are henceforth linked by rail.

12th September 1931
In Hungary, on Biatorbagy Viaduct, the *Orient Express* is attacked by terrorists. Twenty deaths are counted. The assailants will be hanged. Among the surviving passengers are important Airwaymen, delegates to an early International Air Transport Association conference at Bucharest, returning to France and Britain after setting up the rival airlines.

22nd May 1932
The Paris-Istanbul service is reorganized. The *Orient Express* alternates with the *Arlberg-Orient Express* via Basle, Zürich and Innsbrück. The *Orient Express* has a daily service, as does the S.O.E. The *Taurus Express* ensures connections tri-weekly with Syria, Palestine and Egypt; bi-weekly with India by Basra, the Persian Gulf and the ships to Bombay. Beginning of electric traction between Basle and Salzburg and between Hegyeshalom and Budapest. The *Orient Express* "family" is full.

1933
Electric traction Stuttgart-Munich.

4th September 1939
Interruption of the *Orient Express* but the S.O.E. continues, as do the sectors Munich-Bucharest and Zürich-Bucharest.

7th September 1940
King Charles of Romania (Carol) takes refuge in Switzerland, thanks to the S.O.E.

207. *Composition of the* Simplon-Orient Express *on departure from Paris, during the period 14th May to 29th June 1931, with the principal timetable.*

16th March 1942
Interruption of the S.O.E.

27th September 1945
The *Arlberg-Orient Express* or *A.O.E.* (Paris-Innsbrück) re-starts its service.

13th November 1945
The S.O.E. restarts its service from Paris to Istanbul. Alongside the sleeping cars it includes ordinary coaches, called seats coaches, the first blow to its quality of luxury train.

8th January 1946
Tri-weekly service of the S.O.E.

7th October 1946
Daily service of the S.O.E. The *Orient Express* is put back in circulation, with a sleeping car for Prague.

1947
The *A.O.E.* is extended to Bucharest. At the Istanbul conference, creation of a *Balt-Orient Express* to ensure the Scandinavia-Balkans link. The trains include some sleeping cars Oslo-Prague and Stockholm-Belgrade.

1st June 1948
The *Orient Express*, which has lost its luxury train label, restarts its service Paris-Budapest-Belgrade-Bucharest.

End of the C.I.W.L. contract in Romania.

1949
Suspension of the service Paris-Budapest-Belgrade. End of the C.I.W.L. contracts with Czechoslovakia and Hungary. A Pullman car Basle-Vienna is incorporated in the *A.O.E.* (until 1957). Prague-Sofia-Istanbul sleeping cars are put into service.

1951
The *Orient Express* is diverted from Bratislava to Hegyeshalom to avoid Czechoslovakia. Re-opening of the Greek frontier: the S.O.E. runs once more from Paris to Athens.

1952
Electric traction Salzburg-Vienna. The sleeping cars of the S.O.E. are stopped at Sofia or Svilengrad following the closure of the Bulgaro-Greek frontier.

1953
The Paris-Istanbul service is thus constrained to avoid Bulgaria and pass by Salonica and Greece, since only the Graeco-Turkish frontier is open. But the northern part of Greece is dangerous at night, because of bandits. The passengers sleep in the train in Alexandropolis station.

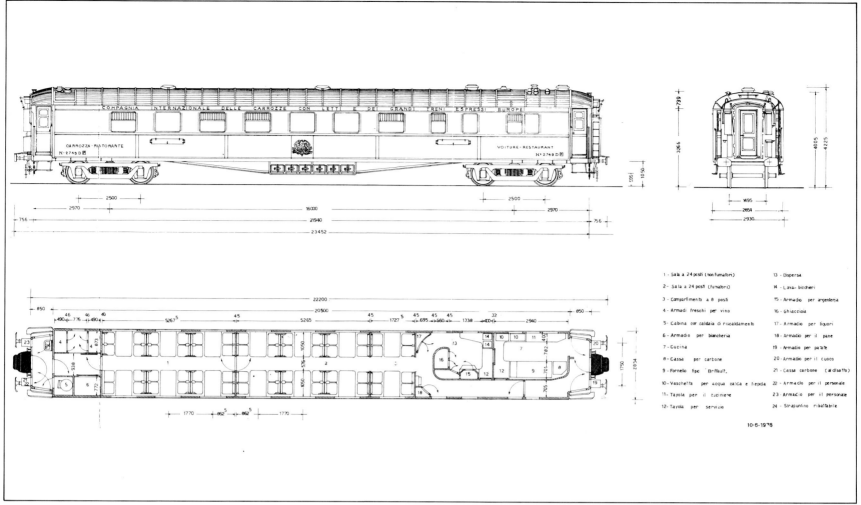

1954
The *S.O.E.* again takes the line by Sofia, coupled to a goods train.

1956
The *Orient Express* is stopped at Budapest. Electric Traction Kehl-Stuttgart.

1959
Suppression of the Paris-Budapest sleeping car.

21st May 1962
Re-organization of the services. Suppression of the *S.O.E.*, replaced by the *Direct-Orient Express*, including numerous ordinary coaches, from Paris to Istanbul. Suppression of the *A.O.E.*, replaced by the *Arlberg Express* Paris-Vienna. Electric traction Paris-Strassbourg.

1964
The *Orient Express* gets back the Paris-Budapest sleeping car.

1965
The service is extended to Bucharest three times a week. It is still in force in 1984.

1966
With the electrification of Strassbourg-Kehl, the Paris-Vienna line is entirely electrified.

1967
The Compagnie Internationale des Wagons-Lits loses its title "et des grands express européens" for "et du tourisme" (not painted on the cars). The old title has been in official use for eighty-three years. The abbreviation of the new one is: C.I.W.L.T.

1970
End of the C.I.W.L.T.-Turkey contract but a special agreement permits the Paris-Istanbul sleeping car to continue to run.

1976
Electrification of the sectors Vienna-Hegyeshalom and Budapest-Lokoshaza. Suppression of the Paris-Athens sleeping car. In Switzerland Mr. Albert Glatt, a Travel Agent, starts to buy cars of the LX series and organizes a *Nostalgic-Orient Express* in the form of a train cruise departing from Zurich to Istanbul or Athens, and on the lines of the Simplon, the Arlberg and the line of the North, by the Danube. Grand luxury service on board and steam traction in Yugoslavia and Turkey.

20th May 1977
Actual last departure of the Paris-Istanbul sleeping car of the *Direct-Orient*.

22nd May 1977
last departure of the Istanbul-Paris sleeping car. These two events, whose echo

208. *Plan and elevation of dining car No. 2749 built in 1926 by Officine Meccaniche Italiane, Reggio d'Emilia (Italy), series 2749-2773 — actually the property of a Swiss collector.*
209. *Evolution of the different C.I.W.L. logotypes from 1876 to 1969.*

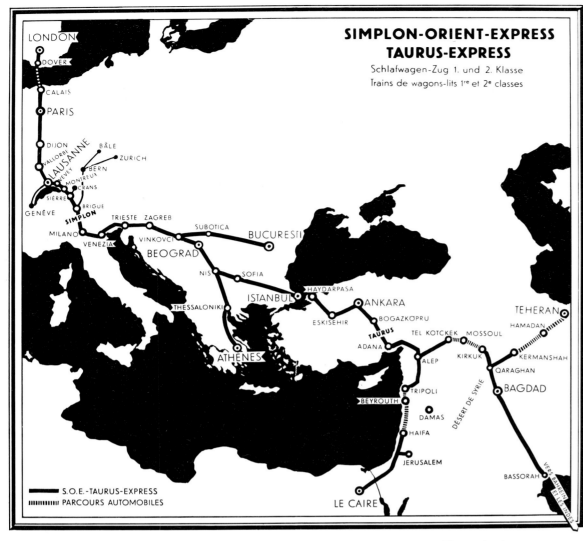

210. *Map of the* Simplon-Orient Express *with its three branches: Bucharest, Istanbul, Athens, and of the* Taurus Express: *Istanbul-Haydarpasa, Aleppo, Cairo and from Aleppo to Tel Kotchek (C.I.W.L. Rest House) in the direction of Bagdad and Basra. (Extract from a C.I.W.L. folder of 1938).*

is world wide are improperly called "the end of the *Orient Express*". The point in question is an error, grave and repeated. Actually, what is suppressed is the direct sleeping car liaison Paris-Istanbul-Paris. Henceforth a change is imposed at Venice or at Belgrade. By contrast, the *Orient Express* still runs from Paris to Budapest and alternately, to Bucharest. It almost makes the inaugural route journey of 1883.

October 1977
Auction Sale at Monte Carlo, the first of its kind: five cars are bought by the King of Morocco, Mr Albert Glatt and Mr James B. Sherwood, President of Sea Containers Ltd. H.R.H. Princess Grace of Monaco takes breakfast in the special train from Nice to Monte Carlo, composed of the five cars. Start of electrification in Romania.

1978-1980
Pursuit of purchases and restoration of sleeping cars, bar cars and fourgons by Mr Albert Glatt on the one hand, and by Mr James Sherwood on the other hand.

25th May 1982
First departure of the *Venice-Simplon-Orient Express* from London-Victoria Station. An enterprise which has cost eleven million pounds sterling. The sector London-Folkestone-London takes place in British Pullman cars, sumptuously restored. After the crossing of the Channel by boat, in a reserved saloon, the sector Boulogne-Paris-Lausanne-Milan-Venice and back is ensured by LX sleeping cars, magnificent, and sometimes in an adapted style (bar car). The regular service provides two departures weekly London-Venice and three departures Paris-Venice. An all the more remarkable initiative since it is a question of a private train employing hotel staff.

Autumn
Development of the journeys of the *Nostalgic-Istanbul-Orient Express*. Publicity tour of France, cruises in Europe. Restoration of the cars, rigourously conforming to their original decoration. Service ensured by highly qualified brigades of the C.I.W.L.T. Appreciable detail: the train includes a shower car.

4th October 1983
Centenary of the *Orient Express* Each of the two trains of Mr Glatt and Mr Sherwood operate a "historic" journey, the first combining the axes of the *Orient,* the *Arlberg* and the *Simplon,* the second from London to Venice.
The *Orient Express* phenomenon is fashionable. Besides these two luxury trains in the style of the 1930s (that of Mr Glatt, the *Nostalgic* is the only one which may go to Istanbul), the "ordinary" *Orient Express*, that which goes to Budapest and Bucharest follows practically the same route as a hundred years ago. The press ignore it. Wrongfully: it is there that it all began...

Spring-Summer 1984
The *Nostalgic-Istanbul-Orient Express* runs nine journeys Paris-Vienna and equally nine journeys Vienna-Paris. Outward via Strassbourg, return via Salzburg and Heidelberg. Service provided by the prestigeous Presidential brigade of the C.I.W.L.T. who in normal times serve the chiefs of state and illustrious guests invited to France.

(See page 156).

211. *Metal sieves and cullenders like all kitchen utensils had to be found a place in the order cupboards of the pantry.*
212. *The "Chinese" strainer was part of the equipment of the dining car kitchen.*
213. *White wicker cork basket. Used to ensure corks did not slip onto the floor, provoking vexatious accidents to the dining car staff.*

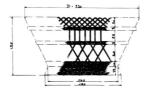

Fig.2. Corbeille à bouchons.
(en osier blanc) Diamètre moyen des brins - 2,5 environ.

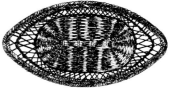

Fig.3 et 4. Corbeilles à fruits.
(en osier blanc) Diamètre moyen des brins - 3mm environ.

THE DINING CAR

First journey on the *Train Eclair de Luxe (Lightning Luxury Train)* (Paris-Vienna, 10th October 1882).

At this time the kitchen Chef "composed" his menu and took delivery of commodities at the central store of the Company.

In front of his coal-fired "piano", whose thin plume of smoke pointed out to passengers the presence of the dining car, the chef prepared his sauces, his assistant trimmed the meats, and his pantry boy washed the vegetables.

The kitchen equipment, besides the shining copper saucepans included all the indispensible utensils for the good of the service. Their dimensions were calculated in relation to the reduced space in which the staff worked.

This meal service, called "classical", which required the presence of numerous employees, has been abandoned, little by little, for economic reasons. (Railway meal service has double the net cost of a stationary restaurant).

On a practical level, the suppression of the dining car, replaced by tray meal catering at every seat, allows an extra carriage to be added to the train without increasing its weight. The brigade, customarily made up of 7 to 8 people is replaced by two or three hostesses or stewards, who only intervene to reheat the dishes in the ovens, distribute the trays and drinks, and put the money in the till. Another formula is that of the grill-express car, which offers continuous dining in the form of self service, allowing a greater number of passengers to refresh themselves.

In trains where no refreshment service is provided, the perambulating salesman passes with a mini-bar trolley, offering sandwiches, cakes and hot or cold drinks.

Classical meal service continues to be offered on *Trans Europ Expresses* (and some *EuroCity* services which have replaced them from 31st May 1987).

Rail catering today is simple and subdued. Railway gastronomy can only be carried out in the sphere of special trains, on request, or in the dining cars of the private companies, the *Venice-Simplon-Orient Express* and the *Nostalgic-Istanbul-Orient Express* (see Chapter X).

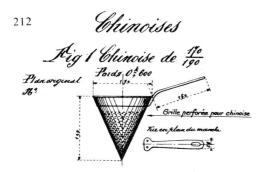

INVENTORY-TYPE OF DINING CARS

SILVERWARE	From 48 to 56 Seats	From 36 to 43 Seats	From 24 to 34 Seats	Bulgarian Cars 18 Seats	Russian Dining Cars
Coffee Pots	2	2	2	2	2
Vegetable serving dishes	4	4	4	4	4
Egg Cups	12	10	6	6	8
Desert Knives	100	80	50	36	40
Table Knives	150	120	80	50	80
Coffee Spoons	60	40	30	20	40
Desert Spoons	56	42	34	20	36
Soup Spoons	80	50	40	36	50
Desert Forks	56	42	34	20	36
Table Forks	120	80	60	50	80
Cruet Stands with cut glass small decanters and stoppers	2	2	2	1	2
Tea Trays	6	4	4	3	2
Oval Dishes	8	6	4	3	6
Round Dishes	8	6	4	3	6
Salt Cellar Spoons	10	8	6	6	10
Cream Pots	12	8	4	4	10
Salt Cellars, plated	1 per table	1 per table	1 per table	6	1 per table
Soup Tureens	—	—	—	—	12
Soup Ladles	—	—	—	—	12
Ice Buckets	3	3	3	2	3
Salad Spoons and Forks	2	2	2	1	2
Sugar Basins with Lids	6	4	2	2	4
Metal Plated Tea Pots	3	3	2	2	2
Pepper Mills	4	4	4	2	2
Saucers with handles for holding Tea Glasses	—	—	—	—	12
CHINA					
Plates	200	180	120	100	150
Individual heat-proof Egg dishes	10	8	6	6	5
Salad Bowls	3	3	2	2	2
Coffee Saucers	60	45	30	30	40
Breakfast Saucers	60	45	30	30	40
Coffee Cups	60	45	30	30	40
Breakfast Cups	60	45	30	30	40
Porcelain Tea Pots	3	3	2	2	2
Porcelain Mustardpots, with spoons	16	14	12	6	6
Radish dishes	12	10	8	12	10
GLASS					
Water Carafes; with Stoppers	8	6	4	4	12
Water Glasses	60	45	30	30	40
Wine Glasses	25	20	15	12	20
Graduated Liqueur Glasses	40	36	30	6	—
Lemon Squeezers	2	2	2	2	—
Tea Glasses	—	—	—	—	36
Vodka Glasses	—	—	—	—	20

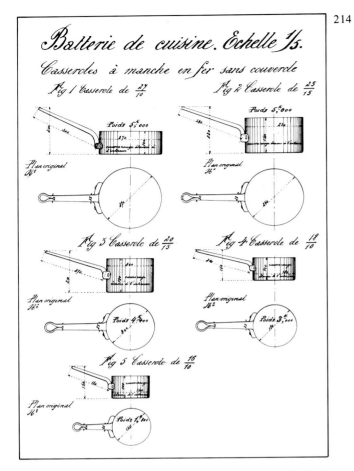

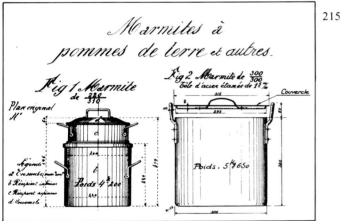

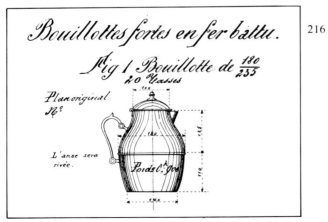

KITCHEN UTENSILS	Dimensions	From 42 to 56 Seats	Bulgarian From 24 to 36 Seats	Russian Cars 18 Seats	Dining Cars
1. TIN-LINED COPPER ITEMS					
Bain-Marie, Steamer with handles	0.20/0.17	2	–	–	–
	0.18/0.16	–	1	1	1
	0.16/0.14	–	1	1	1
Saucepans with inverted lids and handles	0.30/0.22	1	–	–	–
	0.27/0.20	–	1	1	1
	0.25/0.19	1	1	1	1
Saucepans with iron handles	0.27/0.10	1	–	–	–
	0.25/0.15	1	1	1	1
	0.20/0.15	–	1	1	1
	0.18/0.10	2	1	1	1
	0.16/0.10	–	1	1	1
Saucepan Lids	0.29	–	–	–	–
	0.25	1	1	1	1
	0.22	–	1	1	1
	0.18	1	1	1	1
Ovens	0.44/0.27/0.24	1	–	–	–
	0.42/0.23/0.22	–	1	1	1
Pot spoon, tinned	0.13	1	1	1	1
Round Steamer with inverted lid	0.38/0.38	1	–	–	–
	0.33/0.31	–	1	1	1
Mould for Charlotte	0.17/0.11	2	–	–	1
	0.14/0.10	–	2	2	1
Roasting slabs	0.52/0.42/0.09	1	–	–	–
	0.52/0.33/0.09	–	1	1	1
Stewing dishes, with handles	0.38/0.10	2	–	–	–
	0.35/0.10	–	1	1	1
	0.30/0.08	–	1	1	1
Oval roasting dishes	0.40/0.26	2	1	1	1
	0.36/0.24	–	1	1	1
2. CAST IRON ITEMS					
Kettles	20 tasses	1	1	1	1
Chinoises strainers		1	1	1	1
Ordinary Spoons		4	4	4	4
Soup Spoons		1	1	1	1
Skimmers		1	1	1	1
Coffee percolators with rim underneath	5 litres	1	–	–	–
	3 litres	1	1	1	1
	1 litre	1	1	1	1
Wire Whisks		1	1	1	1
Ordinary Forks		4	4	4	4
Three-pronged Toasting Forks		1	1	1	1
Potato Steamers	0.20/0.20	1	1	1	1
Colanders with handles		1	1	1	1
Frying Pans	0.36/0.26	2	1	1	2
	0.31/0.22	1	1	1	–
	0.22	1	1	1	1
Cheese graters		1	1	1	1
3. DIVERSE UTENSILS					
Jam Knives		1	1	1	–
Meat Hooks		2	2	2	2
Coffee Grinders		1	1	1	1
Mincing Machines		1	1	1	1
Chopping Boards		1	1	1	1
Butter Curlers		1	1	1	1
Sieves		1	1	1	1

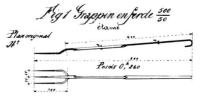

214. Kitchen utensils in tin-lined red copper, indispensible for simmering.
215. Covered saucepan-pots (steamers) whose volume has been calculated relative to the number of passengers likely to occupy the dining car.
216. The kettle for boiling tea- or coffee-water. In a 56-seat dining car, a kettle for 20 cups was sufficient.
217. Toasting fork, skimmer, whisk, spoons minutely counted, found their place in a pantry drawer.

GLOSSARY (C.I.W.L. Terms)

Bat flanc : Sleeping car conductor's folding berth in corridor, extension of his corridor armchair.

Bourdaloue : Chamber-pot. Derived from the name of an XVIIth century preacher, whose very long sermons obliged the faithful to take intimate precautions...

Brise-bise : Blanketing material in a long strip, partially covering the corridor windows of sleeping cars, and dining saloon windows, against condensation. Often folded, could be unfolded to cover them completely in snowy weather.

Calo : Coal-fired boiler for the heating and the hot water for the washbasins.

Chassis : Window. Sometimes means window-frame.

Chef de Brigade : Person responsible for the staff of the dining saloon and the kitchen. In bye-gone days: Train Manager of Luxury Trains, in charge of all staff in dining, sleeping cars and fourgons.

Chef de voiture : Head conductor of several accompanied sleeping cars, each with their own conductor.

Clef carree : Square key (see illustration 190). To open compartment, cupboard and pantry doors, etc.

Clef a coeur : Old-type door key: to open the two doors to the corridor, and sometimes the cupboards.

1er commis : Person responsible for the dining car wine cellar and for making out the bills.

2e commis : Dining saloon waiter.

Commis Officier : Person who assists the pantryman as well as the dining saloon waiters.

Conducteur : Person responsible for all aspects in a sleeping car in which he travels, including passengers.

Convoyeur : Person responsible for accompanying one or several empty sleeping cars.

Liseuse : Bedside mural reading lamp at the head of each bed.

Nettoyeur : Person responsible for cleaning, and making up the beds of a sleeping car. (Also in charge of empty car from carriage sidings to starting station, where he assists conducteur until train leaves).

Serveur-Receveur : Barman; formerly the term now ascribed to *1er commis* on classical dining cars.

Serie : Service of luncheon or dinner (First, Second, Third and Fourth).

Travées : Tables for four persons and two persons.

Voiture-Buffet : Buffet car, arranged for simplified, à la carte, hot or cold meals: can accommodate from 10 to 36 persons.

Voiture différée : Car banned from a train. (Stopped by some defect).

Voiture haut le pied (H.L.P.) : Car running empty, without passengers; the term also used for a sleeping car conductor or other member of travelling staff, moving about in service without a car. (French Railway term : Loco.H.L.P. = Light engine.)

BIBLIOGRAPHY

Novels

Edmond About, *De Pontoise à Stamboul*, Hachette, Paris, 1883.

Agatha Christie, *Murder on the Orient Express*; Fr. translation *Le Crime de l'Orient Express*, Librairie des Champs Elysées, Paris, 1934.

Graham Greene, *Orient Express*, Stock, Paris, 1932.

Maurice Dekobra, *La Madone des Sleepings*, Paris, Cosmopolis 1925 and Presse de la Cité, 1974.

Historical Studies

George Behrend, *Grand European Expresses, the Story of the Wagons-Lits*, George Allen & Unwin Ltd., London, 1962.

Roger Commault, *Georges Nagelmackers, un pionnier du confort sur rail*, La Capitelle, Uzès, 1966.

Dr Fritz Stöckl, *Rollende Hotels*, Rudolf Bohmann Industrie und Fachverlag, Heidelberg & Vienna, 1967.

George Behrend and Vincent Kelly, *Yatakli-Vagon: Turkish Steam Travel* Jersey Artists Ltd., Jersey, Channel Islands, 1969.

Werner Sölch, *Orient Express. Glanzzeit und Niedergang eines Luxuszüges* (Splendour-time and decline of the Luxury Trains), Alba Bucherverlag, Düsseldorf, 1974.

Jean des Cars (with the collaboration of Roger Commault), *Sleeping Story*, Preface by Paul Morand, Julliard, Paris, 1976. (French Text).

E.H. Cookridge, *Orient Express*, Random House, New York, 1978.

George Behrend, *Histoire des Trains de Luxe, de l'Orient Express aux Trans-Europ-Express*, Office du Livre, Fribourg, 1977. *History of Trains de Luxe, from the Orient Express to the High Speed Train*, Jersey Artists Ltd., Jersey, 1982 / *Luxury Trains, from the Orient Express to the Trains à Grande Vitesse*, Vendome Press, New York 1982. (Translations in German & Dutch).

M. Wiesenthal, *La belle époque de l'Orient Express*, Geocolor, Barcelona, 1979.

Derck Campbell, *1883 The Orient Express 1983*, New Horizon-Transeuros Ltd., Great Britain, 1983.

Shirley Sherwood, *Venice Simplon-Orient Express*, Weidenfeld and Nicholson, London, 1984.

Die blauen Schlaf-und-Speisewagen, Eine Geschicte der Internationale Schlafwagen Gesellschaft, (The Blue Sleeping and Dining cars, a history of the International Sleeping Car Company), Alba Bucherverlag, Düsseldorf, 1976.

PRINCIPAL SOURCES OF DOCUMENTATION

Contracts

Protokoll über die Verhandlungen der am 28-29 Dezember 1882 in München abgehaltenen Konferenz über Einrichtung eines Luxus-Schnellzüges swischen Paris und Giurgewo (Protokoll about the proceedings of the Munich Conference held on 28th-29th December 1882 about the arrangement of Luxury Expresses between Paris and Giurgewo).

Traité entre la Compagnie des chemins de fer de l'Est et la C.I.W.L. pour la création, entre Paris et Giurgewo de trains rapides spéciaux destinés à développer les relations directes entre Paris et Constantinople, Paris le 17 mai 1883. (Agreement between the Est Railway Company and the C.I.W.L. for the creation, between Paris and Giurgewo of special express trains intended to develop direct connections between Paris and Constantinople, Paris, 17th May 1883).

Protokoll über die Verhandlungen der am 8-9 Februar 1889 in München abgehaltenen Konferenz über Einrichtung der Orient Expresszüge (Protokoll about the proceedings of the Munich Conference held on 8th-9th February 1889) about the arrangement of the Orient Express Trains).

Traité concernant les trains de luxe circulant entre Paris et Constantinople et entre Paris et Constantza. *(Express d'Orient)*, Paris le 5 mai 1899. (Agreement concerning the luxury trains running between Paris and Constantinople and between Paris and Constantza. *(Express d'Orient)*, Paris 5th May 1899).

Traité pour l'organisation d'un train spécial *(Orient Express)* entre Paris et Bucarest, Giurgewo ou Kustendsche, Paris le 19 août, 1891 (Agreement for the organisation of a special train *(Orient Express)* between Paris and Bucharest, Giurgewo or Kustendsche (Constantza), Paris, 19th August 1891).

218. *In a memorandum-book including the Services Orders concerning the Orient Express, the design of the luggage label for this train is precisely laid down, as to its shape and dimensions (110 × 150 mm.)*

Traité concernant la circulation du train express international *Simplon-Orient Express,* Paris 16 Octobre 1919. (Agreement concerning the running of the international express train *Simplon-Orient Express,* Paris 16th October 1919).

Traité concernant le train de luxe Orient Express, mars-avril 1925 (Agreement concerning the luxury train *Orient Express,* March-April 1925.)

Press

Le Figaro : Georges Boyer, *L'Orient à toute vapeur,* 20th October 1883.

L'Europe Nouvelle : Charles Loiseau, *Le nouveau transcontinental Simplon-Orient Express,* 30th July 1927.

L'Akcham : article on the rescue of the *Simplon-Orient Express,* blocked by the snow, Constantinople, 11th February 1929.

Rail et Route : Pierre Renon, special number on the C.I.W.L. (1951).

La Vie du Rail : Pierre Renon, *L'Orient Express,* 11th October 1959.

La Vie du Rail : Roger Commault (with the collaboration of Maurice Mertens). *La C.I.W.L. à 75 ans* (1876-1951).

Transmondia : Roger Commault, *L'Orient Express à 75 ans.* September 1953.

La Vie du Rail : Cinquantenaire du tunnel du Simplon (1906-1956), July 1956.

Files

Account of the journey of Georges Nagelmackers and Maurice Aubert by the Comte de Berlaymont (1868). Unpublished.

Meetings for the elaboration of commercial questions concerning the train *S.O.E.* (1919-1920).

Internal C.I.W.L. conference on the *S.O.E.* (1919).

Mitropa lawsuit against Austria (C.I.W.L. archives) 1917-1928.

Report and enquiry of the Secretary-General of the C.I.W.L. into the diplomatic incidents in 1914. Unpublished.

Route note-books of 1918 of M. Bourguet of the Compagnie internationale des grands hôtels. Unpublished.

Instruction-book on the uniforms and dress of the staff (C.I.W.L. 1949).

Reports of the chefs de brigade. Unpublished.

Reports of the conductors, Unpublished.

Special instructions to the C.I.W.L. conductors of the *S.O.E.*

Minutes of the timetable conferences.

Correspondence concerning the 25th anniversary of the *Orient Express.*

Circulars concerning the composition of the *S.O.E.*

Diverse correspondence of passengers, famous or unknown. Unpublished.

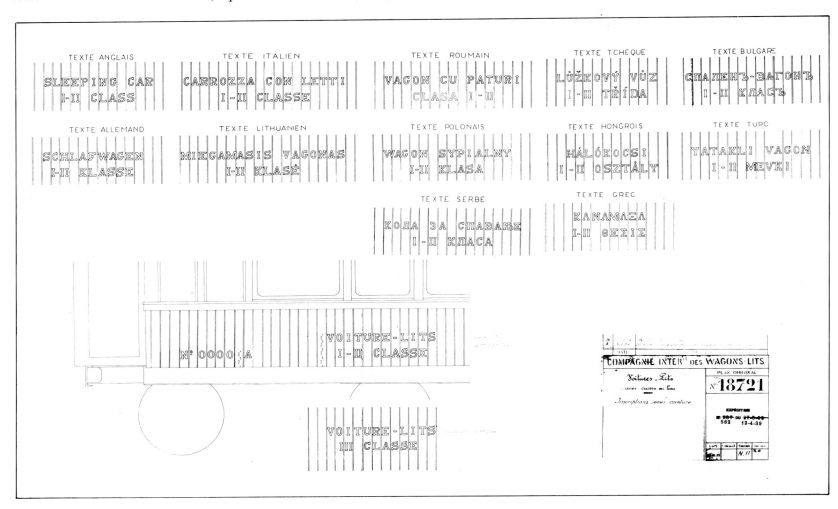

219. *Plan No. 18721 gave the different C.I.W.L. Directions and Divisions, the type and dimensions of the letters which should appear on teak sleeping cars. On the plan one can see the position of each letter in relation to the wooden laths which adorned the sides of the cars.*

July 1986
The *Nostalgic-Istanbul-Orient Express* celebrates its tenth anniversary by running the *Midnight Sun Pullman Express* (called in America the *Polar Express*) from Zurich to Narvik via Hamburg, Copenhagen, Oslo and Stockholm. The train has now visited every European country with standard guage tracks.

31st May 1987
The Paris-Bucharest sleeping car of the *Orient Express* is withdrawn. Only one second class seats coach of the Romanian Railways or Hungarian Railways makes the through journey. The sleeping car is cut back to Salzburg, – Vienna in winter – and a Romanian Railways sleeping car runs Vienna-Bucharest.

CONTENTS

1. The Audacious Monsieur Nagelmackers.   11
2. 1883-1889. The Birth of a Giant.   19
3. 1889-1906. The First Belle Epoque.   39
4. 1906-1914. A Rival from the South: the *Simplon Express.*   *53*
5. 1914-1919. The *Orient Express,* War Victim.   63
6. 1920-1939. The Crazy Years of the *Simplon Orient Express.*   *69*
7. 1939-1946. Another Battle of the Rails.   99
8. 1946-1962. The Train of the Cold War.   105
9. 1962-1977. The End of a Myth.   123
10. Since 1977. Nostalgia on Rails.   133
    Appendices.   145

220. *The authors Jean-Paul Caracalla and Jean des Cars at the window of a sleeping car mock-up shown at the Belgian Cultural Centre in Paris during "The Crazy Years of the railway" exhibition, in 1981.*

BY THE SAME AUTHORS

Le Transsibérien, Denoël, Paris, 1986. (Uniform with this volume)

JEAN DES CARS

Louis II de Bavière ou le roi foudroyé. Librairie académique Perrin, Paris, 1975. Republished by J'ai lu and France-Loisirs. Japanese and Spanish translations. Academie Francaise prize.
Les Chateaux fous de Louis II de Bavière. Librairie académique Perrin, Paris, 1986. Photographs by Jérôme da Cunha.
Sleeping Story, la fabuleuse épopée des wagons-lits (with the collaboration of Roger Commault, preface by Paul Morand), Julliard, Paris, 1976. Republished by J'ai lu. German and Japanese translations. Prix Chatrian prize. (French text).
Haussmann, la gloire du Second Empire, Librairie académique Perrin, Paris, 1978. Republished by J'ai lu and Édito Service ("Les Hommes illustres" collection, Geneva). Grand prix Historia prize.
L'Aventure des chemins de fer, 1832-1914, Éditions André Barret, Paris, 1978.
Elizabeth d'Autriche ou la fatalité. Librairie académique Perrin, Paris, 1983. Republished by Grand Livre du mois, France-Loisirs, Club du Livre R.T.L. and J'ai lu. Japanese and Spanish translations. Ambassadeurs prize.

JEAN-PAUL CARACALLA

Voyages, Olivier Orban, Paris 1981. Anthology articles published in *La Revue des Voyages* from 1950 to 1970 and assembled under the direction of Jean-Paul Caracalla.
Haut de Gamme, Flammarion, Paris, 1985. In collaboration.
Paris rive droite, rive gauche, Éditions Jean-Paul Mangès, Paris, 1987.

PHOTOGRAPHIC CREDITS

The photographs have been put at our disposition by the C.I.W.L., except those mentioned below whose figures refer to the numbers of the illustrations.
Intraflug collection: Nos. 183-187. A. Dumage: title pages. Editions du Masque No. 169. Nadar, Hachette photo library: No. 23. La Vie du Rail: Nos. 65, 66, 98. R. Commault: No.s 130, 131, 134, 141-147, 162, 168, 171-174. Paris-Match No. 175. Rank Films No. 170. Roger-Viollet Nos. 22, 41, 43, 64, 73, 88, 102, 153, 154. Sea Containers Library Nos. 80, 181, 182. Sygma illustration Nos. 100, 103. Warner Bros. No. 179, 180.

First published in English November 1987.

All English language rights (worldwide) reserved by the English publishers and may not be reproduced in any form without written permission.
English translation typeset by Multiplex medway ltd, Walderslade, Kent ME5 8XT.
Printed and bound in Italy by Pizzi of Milan.